CCNA Cyber Ops SECOPS – Certification Guide 210-255

Learn the skills to pass the 210-255 certification exam and become a competent SECOPS associate

Andrew Chu

BIRMINGHAM - MUMBAI

CCNA Cyber Ops SECOPS – Certification Guide 210-255

Commissioning Editor: Karan Sadawna
Acquisition Editor: Shrilekha Inani
Content Development Editor: Ronn Kurien
Senior Editor: Rahul Dsouza
Technical Editor: Mohd Riyan Khan
Copy Editor: Safis Editing
Project Coordinator: Jagdish Prabhu
Proofreader: Safis Editing
Indexer: Pratik Shirodkar
Production Designer: Alishon Mendonsa

First published: July 2019

Production reference: 1030719

Published by Packt Publishing Ltd.
Livery Place
35 Livery Street
Birmingham
B3 2PB, UK.

ISBN 978-1-83855-986-1

www.packtpub.com

Packt.com

Subscribe to our online digital library for full access to over 7,000 books and videos, as well as industry leading tools to help you plan your personal development and advance your career. For more information, please visit our website.

Why subscribe?

- Spend less time learning and more time coding with practical eBooks and Videos from over 4,000 industry professionals

- Improve your learning with Skill Plans built especially for you

- Get a free eBook or video every month

- Fully searchable for easy access to vital information

- Copy and paste, print, and bookmark content

Did you know that Packt offers eBook versions of every book published, with PDF and ePub files available? You can upgrade to the eBook version at www.packt.com and as a print book customer, you are entitled to a discount on the eBook copy. Get in touch with us at customercare@packtpub.com for more details.

At www.packt.com, you can also read a collection of free technical articles, sign up for a range of free newsletters, and receive exclusive discounts and offers on Packt books and eBooks.

Contributors

About the author

Andrew Chu is a networking and cybersecurity lecturer at London Metropolitan University (LMU). LMU is a Cisco Academy, Academy Support Center, and Instructor Training Center.

He has a postgraduate certificate in computer science education, and teaches CCNA routing and switching, as well as CCNA Cyber Ops, through LMU. A former military engineer, he enjoys testing systems to destruction, and learning from this and sharing the results.

He has over 10 years' experience of working in physical and electronic systems security, including advising on and authoring security policies and risk assessments. This includes creating a community-owned ISP; working in government service; and training industry professionals, career changers, and new students.

I would like to thank the many people who helped bring this project to fruition; specifically, Shrilekha Inani, who first brought the idea to me, and Amy Leigh, for persuading me to take it on and for keeping me motivated throughout the process.

Thanks also to the people at a variety of institutions (LMU, HMPPS, and others) over the years – your training, inspiration, and stories have given the book flavor. I would also like to thank Chetan and Martin, and the rest of the team at Packt, for their guidance.

About the reviewers

Rishalin Pillay has over 12 years' cybersecurity experience, and has acquired a vast number of skills consulting for Fortune 500 companies while taking part in projects performing tasks in network security design, implementation, and vulnerability analysis. He has reviewed several books, and has authored the book *Learn Penetration Testing*. He holds many certifications that demonstrate his knowledge and expertise in the cybersecurity field from vendors such as (ISC)^2, Cisco, Juniper, Checkpoint, Microsoft, and CompTIA. Rishalin currently works at a large software company as a senior cybersecurity engineer.

Darragh Merrick is a sergeant in the Irish Defense Forces. In 2005, he joined the Communications and Information Services (CIS) Corps. He graduated in 2008 from IT Carlow with a BEng in electronic engineering and military communications systems. He worked in a network operations center (NOC) until 2013, when he graduated from University College Dublin with an MSc in forensic computing and cybercrime investigation. He has worked as a network security engineer in computer forensics and investigations in a security operations center (SOC). During his time with the army, he served with the United Nations on missions in Lebanon, Liberia, Kosovo, and Syria. Darragh has also completed the following programs: Certified Ethical Hacker – CEH V9, Associate Android Developer, CCNA Cyber Ops – 210-250 SECFND, and 210-255 SECOPS exams.

Packt is searching for authors like you

If you're interested in becoming an author for Packt, please visit `authors.packtpub.com` and apply today. We have worked with thousands of developers and tech professionals, just like you, to help them share their insight with the global tech community. You can make a general application, apply for a specific hot topic that we are recruiting an author for, or submit your own idea.

Table of Contents

Preface

Since the emergence of computer networks (for example, the internet) about 50 years ago, it is estimated that 50 billion devices will be connected to the internet by 2020.

Businesses now, more often than not, are run as online services; host sensitive databases; have several different office locations; and share large quantities of sensitive data. Cyber attacks, in several forms, are increasing in frequency, complexity, and impact. Cyber incidents (for example, cybercrime, IT failure, and data breaches) are considered the second biggest global risk to business. The world is currently short of 3 million cybersecurity experts.

The CCNA Cybersecurity Operations certification demonstrates candidates' knowledge and abilities. This book equips readers with the skills required to succeed at the SECOPS 210-255 exam, and, for those resitting, to understand their score report and quickly identify the appropriate sections to concentrate on.

The book will step readers through threat analysis and forensics in computers, the fundamentals of intrusion analysis, and various approaches to incident response. These skills underpin operations in cybersecurity, and will allow readers to showcase their skills at interview, as well as through the mock tests (with answers) at the end of each chapter.

By reading this book and applying the knowledge it provides, readers should go forward to the SECOPS 210-255 exam with confidence in their knowledge to recall and apply real-world cybersecurity skills, including threat analysis, event correlation, and malicious activity identification.

Who this book is for

This book is designed for everyone who wants to prepare for the Cisco 210-255 (CCNA Cyber Ops – SECOPS) certification exam. You may have noticed the cybersecurity market as an opportunity to change careers; you may have already completed cybersecurity training as part of formal education, or you may already work in cyber operations and just require a new certification; or you may even just have a general interest in all things digital.

This book looks at cyber operations from the ground up, consolidating concepts you may or may not have heard about before, to help you become the operator you are capable of becoming.

What this book covers

Chapter 1, *Classifying Threats*, looks at the Common Vulnerability Scoring System (CVSS v3.0) to introduce common terminology, as well as split the substantial topic of cyber threat into three areas of impact, and five areas of vulnerability. You must be able to define the common terminology for the purpose of the exam.

Chapter 2, *Operating System Families*, does a side by side comparison of these factors, which differs from the CISCO approach. Terms of reference between Linux and Windows operating systems are easy marks in the 210-255 exam. Again, they only require definitions and memory. A knowledge of these factors is necessary for the next chapter.

Chapter 3, *Computer Forensics and Evidence Handling*, covers the standards of investigation required for catching criminals and bringing about prosecutions. Evidence – properly collected – also enables organizations to attribute blame, which can be important in maintaining compliance with government requirements, as well as maintaining customer confidence.

Chapter 4, *Identifying Rogue Data from a Dataset*, teaches regular expressions (Regex), which always appears as at least one of the questions in the 210-255 exam. Regex is a sequence of characters that define a search expression. Regex enables security professionals to quickly sift through large datasets, grouping data entries, highlighting signs of rogue data, and identifying patterns in it.

Chapter 5, *Warning Signs from Network Data*, teaches you how to differentiate normal header content from abnormal and rogue content to conduct an initial analysis of network intrusions.

Chapter 6, *Network Security Data Analysis*, looks at different network security files and identifies different bits of information. This is always a question in the 210-255 exam and an important part of the job of an SOC.

Chapter 7, *Roles and Responsibilities During an Incident*, teaches you to identify individual and team responsibilities during an incident response, in accordance with NIST guidelines. This section makes up 8-10% of the questions in 210-255, but applying a similar model based on your own national guidelines is the principal job of the operations center and, hence, of a cybersecurity professional.

Chapter 8, *Network and Server Profiling*, teaches you about network and server profiling, which is used to establish the 'normal' traffic on a network and server. Profiling allows administrators to identify any potential vulnerabilities, such as a lack of redundancy, or bottlenecks in the system, and deal with them ahead of time, and to detect abnormal behaviors that might indicate an incident in progress.

Chapter 9, *Compliance Frameworks*, teaches you about the requirements of three of the principal pieces of legislation and the industry requirements that affect IT and cybersecurity professionals. Each organization will be covered by one compliance framework or another and, frequently, many overlapping pieces of guidance. It is the fundamental role of a cybersecurity professional to ensure organizational compliance.

Chapter 10, *Data Normalization and Exploitation*, covers the process of collecting and organizing data from multiple different sources. You will also look at some of the fields that are useful for correlating incidents, including timestamps and the IP 5-tuple.

Chapter 11, *Drawing Conclusions from the Data*, explains the different forms of data analysis, and some of the more detailed aims of this process. This will feed into how users can prioritize certain signs, and use Cisco products to generate alerts according to these priorities.

Chapter 12, *The Cyber Kill Chain Model*, teaches you about the adapted Cyber Kill Chain model. In this model, an attack is laid out in chronological sequence, which helps cybersecurity professionals to appreciate the maturity of an attack in progress. This model also helps to structure the response, guiding the security operations center (SOC) as to what actions are likely to have already occurred, and the ones that may be about to emerge.

Chapter 13, *Incident Handling Activities*, covers three guidance frameworks that guide incident handling. You will learn about the terminology used, the non-technical activities involved, and the forensic guidance for conducting incident handling. The questions for this chapter will draw heavily from all the previous chapters.

Chapter 14, *Mock Exam 1*, allows you to practice and analyze the style of Cisco exam questions and test your ability to apply the correct areas of your learning to answer them.

Chapter 15, *Mock Exam 2*, allows you to further practice and analyze the style of Cisco exam questions and test your ability to apply the correct areas of your learning to answer them.

To get the most out of this book

Before starting this book, you should be familiar with computers and networks from the point of view of a user. This should include knowledge of the home setup, as well as computer networks in a commercial setting. Familiarity with the technologies used to administer and maintain a network, particularly Cisco products, is helpful, but not essential. Knowing that switches, routers, and servers exist – and how they differ – is a requirement.

This book follows on from the 210-250 (SECFND) syllabus, so support materials for those courses may be a useful start, and could be used as reference material if you feel that you are struggling with any of the topics found here. You will have to pass both the 210-250 and 210-255 certification exams for CCNA Cybersecurity Operations anyway, so the 210-250 certification book is a good investment regardless.

To get the most out of the course, you should try to engage with the teaching methods used. The content is broadly separated into three 3 elements – theory, formative questions (with reasoned answers), and testing questions. The theory sections contain a distilled version of the knowledge required – there is a direct correlation between the theory sections and the syllabus. Formative questions are included at the end of each chapter, and are designed to test your ability to recall information from the chapter, analyze a scenario, and apply the theory in practice. The back of the book includes the answers and, most importantly, the rationale. Finally, there are two mock exam papers. These will test your ability to apply the theory in practice, and to help prepare you for the certification exam. The answers, but not the rationale, are provided for these questions. If you are making mistakes, a good activity would be to try to reanalyze the question with the correct answer, and see whether you can generate the rationale retrospectively.

Conventions used

There are a number of text conventions used throughout this book.

`CodeInText`: Indicates code words in text, database table names, folder names, filenames, file extensions, pathnames, dummy URLs, user input, and Twitter handles. Here is an example: "The only method of differentiation is that the legitimate `csrss.exe` process is run from the `C:\Windows\System32` folder."

Any command-line input or output is written as follows:

```
$ tcpdump -ns 0 -eX -r dns.pcap
```

Bold: Indicates a new term, an important word, or words that you see on screen. For example, words in menus or dialog boxes appear in the text like this. Here is an example: "Select **System info** from the **Administration** panel."

Warnings or important notes appear like this.

Tips and tricks appear like this.

Get in touch

Feedback from our readers is always welcome.

General feedback: If you have questions about any aspect of this book, mention the book title in the subject of your message and email us at customercare@packtpub.com.

Errata: Although we have taken every care to ensure the accuracy of our content, mistakes do happen. If you have found a mistake in this book, we would be grateful if you would report this to us. Please visit www.packt.com/submit-errata, selecting your book, clicking on the Errata Submission Form link, and entering the details.

Piracy: If you come across any illegal copies of our works in any form on the internet, we would be grateful if you would provide us with the location address or website name. Please contact us at copyright@packt.com with a link to the material.

If you are interested in becoming an author: If there is a topic that you have expertise in, and you are interested in either writing or contributing to a book, please visit authors.packtpub.com.

Reviews

Please leave a review. Once you have read and used this book, why not leave a review on the site that you purchased it from? Potential readers can then see and use your unbiased opinion to make purchase decisions, we at Packt can understand what you think about our products, and our authors can see your feedback on their book. Thank you!

For more information about Packt, please visit packt.com.

Section 1: Endpoint Threat Analysis and Forensics

In this section, readers will learn how a single machine can be compromised and how to investigate it. In this section, which comprises 15% of the 210-255 exam, readers will learn how to categorize and communicate threats and vulnerabilities, understand how and why different vulnerabilities can affect different operating systems more or less severely, and explain the principles of computer forensics, evidence handling, and how to use that information.

This section builds heavily on prior knowledge, particularly from the 210-250 (SECFNDS) course, but will underpin the actions of cyber security operators as they carry out routine tasks, as well as responsive tasks. Evidence may be required from before the threat is identified.

The following chapters are included in this section:

- Chapter 1, *Classifying Threats*
- Chapter 2, *Operating System Families*
- Chapter 3, *Computer Forensics and Evidence Handling*

1
Classifying Threats

This chapter looks at the **Common Vulnerability Scoring System v3.0 (CVSS v3.0)** in order to introduce common terminology, as well as to split the large topic of *cyber-threat* into three areas of impact, and five areas of vulnerability. Candidates for 210-255 must be able to define these terms.

CVSS 3.0 terms and definitions are 5% of the 210-255 certification exam, and they are marks which only require memory; no analysis is required. This will ease you into the book and provides a baseline that you can work from. CVSS 3.0 is also important because part of your future role in a SOC may involve briefing non-technical staff about CVSS reports.

The following topics will be covered in this chapter:

- Categorizing and communicating threats
- Exploitability metrics
- Impact metrics
- Scope

Categorizing and communicating threats

One of the primary roles of technical staff is to communicate threat severity to non-technical members of staff. This technical judgment informs operational decision-making, so it is important to have standard measurements and vocabulary. In this section, you will learn about the need for a common framework to describe threats; specifically, we will look at two important analysis tools to identify differences between their outputs.

All information systems carry inherent risks. Even paper-based systems have vulnerabilities (how is paper stored? What happens if there's a fire or flood? Can the records be lost?). In cybersecurity, endpoint threat analysis covers all threats that affect a computer system that a user interacts with. Whilst this seems self-explanatory, it is important to dig down into the terms. **Endpoint** is specified as distinct from network elements; **threat** refers to potential, as well as known risks (that is, malware or known incidents); **analysis** covers both known and hypothetical effects.

Two malware analysis tools are Cisco's **Advanced Malware Protection** (**AMP**) Threat Grid and Cuckoo Sandbox. In CISCO 210-255, candidates are required to interpret output reports from these systems.

AMP Threat Grid

Cisco Threat Grid is a tool that provides AMP for networks and endpoints. It is powered by Cisco's threat intelligence research group (**Cisco TALOS**), which uses data from around the World to produce reports and signatures for different threats. Cisco AMP is integrated into a number of Cisco products so that it can take preventative action and perform sandboxing and retrospective alerting (after an attack). Preventative action can be taken at the firewall or anti-malware package level. This is where a file matches a known threat signature.

Sandboxing allows an unknown file to be checked for dangerous behavior. This is run through AMP Cloud, but takes time to run and analyze. Reports from this process can be used to determine whether something is a threat or not. Retrospective alerting comes after sandboxing is complete. With the updated knowledge about the file, Cisco AMP can inform the organization or security operations center that a suspect file was able to enter the system, and where it has spread to.

AMP Cloud allows you to do submissions via manual file uploads, or through an OpenAPI. These files are then executed in a virtual machine on the cloud (the option to run locally is available, but the cloud is the quickest option). There are two modes of operation for Threat Grid: a **black-box**, which provides an overview of the analysis, and in-depth information regarding the file, with additional functionality to explore the activity further. Both modes (or a combination of both) are accessible through the same interface. For the exam, you will only be required to get the results and a very basic interpretation.

AMP Threat Grid provides a virtual machine environment to execute the submitted file. It provides the functionality to view a video feed of the environment running the file in order to further analyze the threat, although this is not examined in CCNA cybersecurity operations. The results are given as a threat score (out of 100) which combines severity and confidence measures (each out of 100) against over 500 other metrics regarding the file's behaviors (for example, what kinds of file are modified, what URLs it tries to communicate with, are there registry changes, and so on?).

A threat score of 95-100 is known malware, 75-90 is very dangerous, and 56 - 70 is suspicious. Obviously, there are gaps in-between these levels, and these should be considered alongside organizational priorities. The AMP Threat Grid analysis report for a given file lists the file name, type, date of analysis, and the score, which is given in the top line, which would be the *headline* if the report were analyzing multiple files. In the expanded view, which is shown in the following screenshot, details such as how often the threat signature has been seen and the behavioral indicators that have contributed to the score are shown. The following screenshot shows an analysis report for the file named setup.exe:

> 🔒 setup.exe	exe 10/21/16 9:31 am		
First Seen 2016-10-21T1...	Behavioral Indicators		
Last Seen 2016-10-21T1...	**Name**	**Severity**	**Confidence**
Times Seen 1			
Q SHA-256 ad6e115ce09...	modified-file-in-user-dir	70	80
Q SHA-1 4a15e9a3fc1b...	pe-tls-callback	40	60
Q MD5 45d5fe26ae1...	hook-installed	35	40
	pe-certificate	10	100
Network Streams 5	imports-	20	20
Registry Actions 147	IsDebuggerPresent		

An analysis report for the file named setup.exe

The file type is given in the middle of the top line (exe, as expected). The threat is rated as 56, which is *suspicious*. The file modified the files in the user directories, and also checked **IsDebuggerPresent** (a sign that it might be checking whether it is running in a virtual machine). This threat should be passed up for further investigation.

Network File Trajectory is an analysis tool which shows the path of a file through the system. This is shown by host IP addresses and timestamps. The following screenshot shows the **Network File Trajectory** output from Cisco AMP Threat Grid in Cisco's Firepower Management Console; this screen can be found by going to **Analysis | Files | Network File Trajectory**. It shows an unknown file entering the system at 10:57 on the 10.4.10.183 host. It spreads to three additional hosts before 18:10, where it is identified as Malware. At 18:14, it is quarantined by 10.5.11.8, and the original is blocked.

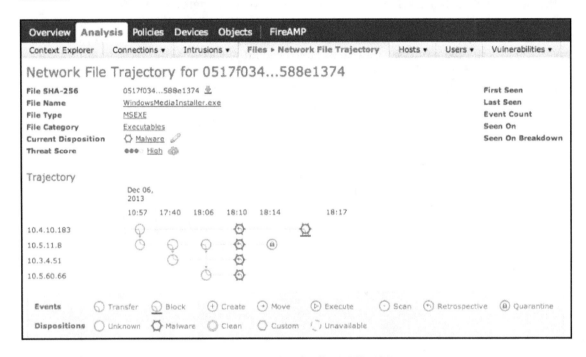

Network File Trajectory Output from Cisco AMP Threat Grid

This type of activity log is particularly useful to cybersecurity researchers because it maps the path of the file through the system. This allows the operations team to verify that all instances of the file have been contained/quarantined/removed. Grouping events by file, in this case, allows the security operations center to better prioritize its workload so that people aren't concurrently working on the same problem.

Cuckoo Sandbox

Cuckoo Sandbox is an open source automated malware analysis tool. Unlike Cisco AMP Cloud, it is designed to be run locally. This means that any files to be uploaded are totally secure, but means that users don't benefit from signatures that are discovered by other users. It also means that virtualization software, with any licensing, must be run on the host system. This means that there can be speed and performance variations compared to the AMP Cloud virtual machine.

Cuckoo Sandbox analysis reports include details such as **file hashes**, **Yara**, and **VirusTotal** details for any threatening behaviors that are detected. It also has a maliciousness score out of 10, which can assist organizations in making decisions about what to do with the file.

The following screenshot shows a Cuckoo Sandbox report for a PDF file. This PDF file has some suspicious features, specifically an embedded Windows 32 executable, and the ability to detect whether it is running in a virtual machine. Although the executable file has not specifically matched any **PEiD** threat signatures, the **Yara** field lists the suspicious features for future analysis. The specific file is from a known threat, so the signature list might not be up to date:

File name	CVE-2009-4324 PDF 2009-11-30 note200911.pdf
File size	400918 bytes
File type	PDF document, version 1.6
CRC32	11638A9B
MD5	61baabd6fc12e01ff73ceacc07c84f9a
SHA1	0805d0ae62f5358b9a3f4c1868d552f5c3561b17
SHA256	27cced58a0fcbb0bbe3894f74d3014611039fefdf3bd2b0ba7ad85b18194c
SHA512	5a43bc7eef279b209e2590432cc3e2eb480d0f78004e265f00b98b4afdc9a
Ssdeep	1536:p0AAH2KthGBjcdBj8VETeePxsT65ZZ3pdx/ves/QR/875+:prahGV6B
PEiD	None matched
Yara	• embedded_pe (Contains an embedded PE32 file) • embedded_win_api (A non-Windows executable contains win32 API) • vmdetect (Possibly employs anti-virtualization techniques)
VirusTotal	Permalink VirusTotal Scan Date: 2013-12-27 06:51:52 Detection Rate: 32/46 (collapse)

Cuckoo Sandbox report for a PDF file

Analysis tools are not 100% effective, so the **PEiD** has not matched the signature, but **Yara** analysis did. There were 14 systems that didn't detect the file as a virus, which could be a concern. This output underlines the importance of defense in depth, where a number of different systems and technologies are all employed with the aim of discovering and eradicating threats; if one system lets it through, the next might find it, or the one after that. This may well throw up high volumes of positive results – some of which will be false or hoaxes – but this is generally better than having threats fall through the gaps.

Requirements for CVSS

The difficulty with risk is the ability to communicate how severe it is on an objective scale. Consider the difference between a perfect score in gymnastics (10.0) to a perfect score in figure skating (6.0) or a perfect GPA (4.0). Without knowing which scale was used, and the calculations to get to it, it is difficult to compare one score against another. Here, we have an AMP Threat Grid with a score out of 100, and a Cuckoo Sandbox with a score out of 10. Add in all the other analysis systems with their different scoring systems, and it becomes increasingly difficult to know which things to prioritize during the cybersecurity incident response.

To fix this, FIRST and the CVSS **Special Interest Group (SIG)** created the **Common Vulnerability Scoring System (CVSS)**, which is now on version 3.0. CVSS is an open standard which captures the main characteristics of a vulnerability as a numerical score reflecting its severity, as well as a description and breakdown of that score.

Organizations can translate numerical scores into qualitative representations (for example, low, medium, high, and critical) if this helps them prioritize vulnerability management. If they have particular concerns, they could even look at individual metric scores to drive their vulnerability management policy.

CVSS is composed of three metric groups:

- Base
- Temporal
- Environmental

Base metrics refer to characteristics of a vulnerability that are consistent for all users at all times. There are two sets of metrics:

- Exploitability metrics (attack vector, attack complexity, privileges required, user interaction)
- Impact metrics (confidentiality, integrity, and availability)

There's also **scope**, which is a new scaling factor. Each of these is discussed in detail later in this chapter.

CVSS v3.0 base scores can be expressed as a numerical base score (up to 10); a **National Vulnerability Database** (**NVD**) Vulnerability Severity Rating (*0 = None, 0.2-3.9 = Low, 4.0-6.9 = Medium, 7.0-8.9 = High, 9.0-10.0 = Critical*); or the score can be written out in full for transparency in the following format:

CVSS:3.0/AV:X/AC:X/PR:X/UI:X/S:X/C:X/I:X/A:X

Here, *X* is the score for each metric in the form of a single letter.

Temporal and environmental groups cover the characteristics that might change over time (temporal), or which differ between different user settings (environmental). These metric groups are beyond the scope of this certification, and are not mandatory under CVSS v3.0 – they are only calculated and listed if they are considered specifically relevant (normally post-incident).

Exploitability metrics

Exploitability is a series of metrics in CVSS 3.0 that describe how difficult it would be for an attacker to exploit a vulnerability. In this section, you will learn how to define the four areas of vulnerability and how these relate to the ease of exploitation of the threat.

To understand the importance of exploitability, consider an example from the retail world. A generally acknowledged principle in retail is that shrinkage (or shoplifting) increases if it is easier to do. For most people, the value that's gained from an attack is rarely worth the effort or risk of being caught. In the same way, the easier it is to exploit a vulnerability and conduct an attack, the more likely it is to happen, and therefore the more dangerous the vulnerability is.

Attack vector

An **attack vector** (**AV**) refers to the logical and physical path through which a vulnerability can be exploited. The metric value increases with distance (or **remoteness**) because there are fewer potential attackers who have the means to be close to the target. There are four potential values (Physical, Local, Adjacent, or Network).

Physical (P) is defined as follows:

> *"CVSS 3.0 Definition: A vulnerability exploitable with Physical access requires the attacker to physically touch or manipulate the vulnerable component. Physical interaction may be brief or persistent. An example of such an attack is a cold boot attack, which allows an attacker to access to disk encryption keys after gaining physical access to the system, or peripheral attacks such as Firewire/USB Direct Memory Access attacks."*

It is sometimes worth looking at information security in terms of a more physical example. When considering an attack vector, let's consider a company payroll. The HR team commands a vast budget, and makes payments to the workers based on a list given to them by management. If an attacker wanted to invent a fake persona to gain an extra paycheck, they would have to have physical access to the team or the payroll system.

Local (L) is defined as follows:

> *"CVSS 3.0 Definition: A vulnerability exploitable with Local access means that the vulnerable component is not bound to the network stack, and the attacker's path is via read/write/execute capabilities. In some cases, the attacker may be logged in locally in order to exploit the vulnerability; otherwise, they may rely on User Interaction to execute a malicious file."*

As the company is growing rapidly, it becomes the norm that if new recruits have come on board too late to get on the management list, middle managers make direct requests to the HR team to add a new employee. In this system, the attacker would no longer need to make the payment themselves. They could just ask the payroll department to make the payment on their behalf. This would count as a local vulnerability.

Adjacent (A) is defined as follows:

> "*CVSS 3.0 Definition: A vulnerability exploitable with adjacent network access means the vulnerable component is bound to the network stack, however the attack is limited to the same shared physical (for example, Bluetooth, IEEE 802.11), or logical (for example, local IP subnet) network, and cannot be performed across an OSI layer 3 boundary (for example, a router). An example of an Adjacent attack would be an ARP (IPv4) or neighbor discovery (IPv6) flood leading to a denial of service on the local LAN segment. See also CVE 2013 6014.*"

The company has continued to grow so much that payroll is on a different floor from everyone else. Rather than go upstairs to payroll themselves, middle managers have begun to send runners with new-starter details on pieces of paper to the HR team for processing and payment. An attacker would now only need to be able to intercept the runner and add their own details. This kind of attack vector would be adjacent as the attacker would still need to be in the building to intercept the runner.

Network (N) is defined as follows:

> "*CVSS 3.0 Definition: A vulnerability exploitable with network access means the vulnerable component is bound to the network stack and the attacker's path is through OSI layer 3 (the network layer). Such a vulnerability is often termed "remotely exploitable" and can be thought of as an attack being exploitable one or more network hops away (for example, across layer 3 boundaries from routers). An example of a network attack is an attacker causing a denial of service (DoS) by sending a specially crafted TCP packet from across the public Internet (for example, CVE 2004 0230).*"

As the company grows further, they decide to contract out the payroll. Now, the pieces of paper are replaced with a telephone conversation with the payroll company. An attacker could now ring up from anywhere and instruct the payroll to add their non-existent employee. The attacker has gone from needing to be physically on the payroll machine to conducting the attack from his or her own home:

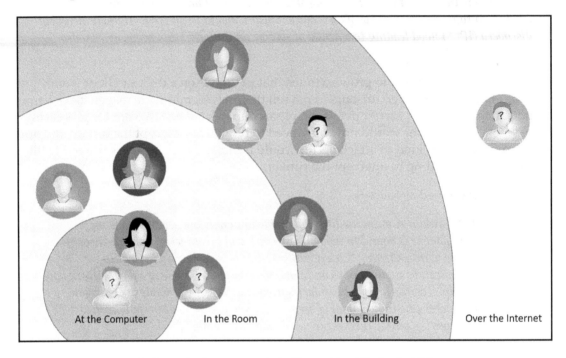

Attack vector – how far away can an attacker be while successfully exploiting the vulnerability?

Access control is the principal method for increasing the proximity that's required by an attacker (hence reducing the risk to the company). Vetting employees further reduces this risk.

Attack complexity

Attack complexity refers to the conditions which must exist in order to exploit a vulnerability successfully. These conditions are beyond the attacker's control, so may require the attacker to conduct research on specific targets. The lower the attack complexity, the more dangerous the vulnerability.

High (H) is defined as follows:

> *"CVSS 3.0 Definition: A successful attack depends on conditions beyond the attacker's control. That is, a successful attack cannot be accomplished at will, but requires the attacker to invest in some measurable amount of effort in preparation or execution against the vulnerable component before a successful attack can be expected.*
>
> *For example, a successful attack may depend on an attacker overcoming any of the following conditions:*
> *The attacker must conduct target-specific reconnaissance. For example, on target configuration settings, sequence numbers, shared secrets, etc.*
> *The attacker must prepare the target environment to improve exploit reliability. For example, repeated exploitation to win a race condition, or overcoming advanced exploit mitigation techniques.*
> *The attacker must inject herself into the logical network path between the target and the resource requested by the victim in order to read and/or modify network communications (for example, a man-in-the-middle attack)."*

An attack with high complexity relies on a number of other factors to be right in order to succeed. This measure takes into account both the number of things that must be correct, and the rarity of those events. Imagine that you are beginning a new job, and you are looking for the best way to get to work. You check online, and it takes one hour to get from one stop to the next by taking a series of trains. If the trains only come once an hour, and the timing between getting off one and getting on the next is small, there is a high level of complexity. If one train is slightly delayed, the whole plan fails.

Low (L) is defined as follows:

> *"CVSS 3.0 Definition: Specialized access conditions or extenuating circumstances do not exist. An attacker can expect repeatable success against the vulnerable component."*

Instead, you can walk to work. Although it might take you longer to get there, you can expect repeated success since you are not relying on the trains being on time, or on any other factors.

The following diagram shows the attack complexity. The green route is more dangerous because it has fewer actions in the path. At each point (**B-G**), the attack could slow down or even be halted. The green route bypasses all these checks and balances:

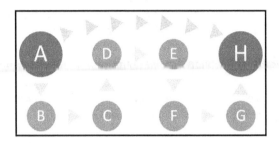

Attack complexity – how many different things need to happen to set the conditions for a successful attack?

Designing for increased complexity is double-edged. On the one hand, requiring an attacker to exploit a very complex vulnerability is useful for information security. However, this complexity is experienced by legitimate users every day. If the system becomes so complex that legitimate users are put off using it, the system/systems administrators have effectively attacked their own availability!

Privileges required

This metric describes the level of privileges an attacker must possess before successfully exploiting the vulnerability.

The metric has possible values of high, low, and none, with the most serious vulnerabilities being those that require the fewest privileges to be successful. It is important to note that this metric measures the privileges required to begin the attack. It is possible that an attacker could change their privileges during the attack, and this will be covered further in a later metric.

High (H) is defined as follows:

> *"CVSS 3.0 Definition: The attacker is authorized with (that is, requires) privileges that provide significant (for example, administrative) control over the vulnerable component that could affect component-wide settings and files."*

One of the best ways to think about this metric is to consider access to the CEO's office desk drawers. A vulnerability that leaves a desk drawer open would rank as high, as you still need to get into the office to exploit the system. Why is this the lowest exploitability situation? To exploit this vulnerability, an attacker would have to be either the CEO or his/her assistant!

Low (L) is defined as follows:

> *"CVSS 3.0 Definition: The attacker is authorized with (that is, requires) privileges that provide basic user capabilities that could normally affect only settings and files owned by a user. Alternatively, an attacker with Low privileges may have the ability to cause an impact only to non-sensitive resources."*

If the company were open-plan, or the CEO had an open door policy, the vulnerability would require only enough privileges to get into the building. An attacker could be anybody with access to the office. This is a much larger number of potential attackers, and is, therefore, more serious.

None (N) is defined as follows:

> *"CVSS 3.0 Definition: The attacker is unauthorized prior to attack, and therefore does not require any access to settings or files to carry out an attack."*

The most serious rating in this metric would be if the CEO's office were directly accessible to the public. An attacker in this instance could be any member of the public, at any time.

The following diagram presents the hierarchy of a company. **Privileges required** describes the level of access and privilege an attacker needs in order to exploit the vulnerability. If the attacker could access the system by pretending to be a store team member, but can subsequently elevate their profile so they appear to be an executive, the privileges that are required still come up as none since the attack really begins when they first start to access the system:

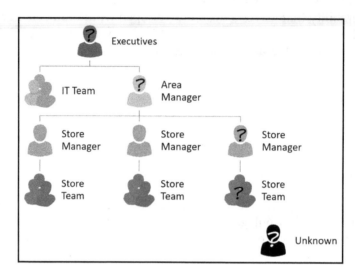

Privileges required – how trusted does the attacker need to appear?

A classic defense against this kind of vulnerability is to layer defense systems. Having a series of locked doors which verify an individual's privilege levels limits exposure. A related technique is ensuring that other staff members are vigilant enough to question why someone they didn't know was trying to access the CEO's desk. Network monitoring and access control systems would provide this functionality in a digital system.

User interaction

User interaction refers to whether another user (other than the attacker) is required to participate in a successful attack. The metric has possible values of required or none.

Required (R) is defined as follows:

> "CVSS 3.0 Definition: Successful exploitation of this vulnerability requires a user to take some action before the vulnerability can be exploited. For example, a successful exploit may only be possible during the installation of an application by a system administrator."

Imagine that a vulnerability exists which allows an attacker to print their own ID card so that they can pretend to be from the local utilities company. The attacker shows up at a victim's door and asks for access. The victim is required to open the door in order for the attacker to gain access.

None (N) is defined as follows:

> *"CVSS 3.0 Definition: The vulnerable system can be exploited without interaction from any user."*

If the system had automatic ID card recognition, an attacker could walk straight in.

The following diagram demonstrates the difference between complete automation and human interaction. A computerized (even AI) system allows choices based on rules rather than with any context or ability to question actions:

User interaction – fully automated or personal touch?

Two-factor authentication is the classic method of demanding user interaction in a security system. The person attempting to gain access has to provide a code for different means. From a home access point of view, the homeowner could ring the utility firm directly and ensure that they had sent someone with those credentials before opening the door, hence defeating the attack.

Impact metrics

The most common model that's used to understand a threat's impact on information security is the **confidentiality, integrity, availability** (**CIA**) triad. In this section, you will learn how to explain these three types of consequence that result from a threat. The CIA triad is very common across the whole industry.

In CVSS v3.0, these three components are referred to collectively as impact metrics. Each is scored independently as either high, low, or none to give the user an overview of how severe the effects of the threat would be if they were realized. If multiple components are vulnerable to the threat, the scores are taken from the component which suffers the most severe consequences.

Confidentiality

Confidentiality is often thought of in terms of privacy. In an ideal scenario, access to information should be granted to authorized users, and denied to unauthorized ones. Of course, access to some information is more important than others, and the metrics reflect this.

For confidentiality, imagine the security threat posed to a bank. For each of the examples given, imagine that a bank robber is able to gain access to the bank through some vulnerability.

None (N) is defined as follows:

> *"CVSS v3.0 Definition: There is no loss of confidentiality within the impacted component."*

So, in the bank robber analogy, imagine that the bank robber has gained access to the bank overnight, and has access only to the lobby. All the bank tellers have gone home, and the cash registers are empty. The robber steals all that they can, making off with a number of information leaflets and a pen. The bank hasn't really suffered any loss here.

Low (L) is defined as follows:

> *"CVSS v3.0 Definition: There is some loss of confidentiality. Access to some restricted information is obtained, but the attacker does not have control over what information is obtained, or the amount or kind of loss is constrained. The information disclosure does not cause a direct, serious loss to the impacted component."*

Returning to the bank example, if the robber enters the vault and a safety deposit box is open, this is a risk to the money that is currently in that single box. Although this is a problem, the metric would be rated as low; the robber has no control over what items are in the box, and the loss is limited to that single box.

High (H) is defined as follows:

> *"CVSS v3.0 Definition: There is total loss of confidentiality, resulting in all resources within the impacted component being divulged to the attacker. Alternatively, access to only some restricted information is obtained, but the disclosed information presents a direct, serious impact. For example, an attacker steals the administrator's password, or private encryption keys of a web server."*

With the final vulnerability, the attacker enters the vault to find that all the boxes are open; this would result in a high rating. There is a total loss of access control, and all the items held by the bank are accessible. Similarly, if the attacker enters the vault and finds all the safety deposit box keys on a hook on the wall, this would be a high rating. The items that the robber has access to have a direct, serious impact: with those items, they could access all the other items.

A slightly different analogy which is often used is the idea of defending a castle. The classic castle design has layers of protection. Getting into the outer gate doesn't confer many opportunities, but the closer the attacker can get to the center, the more treasure can be looted. Worst of all is having the key to the castle gates and doors; the attacker would be able to access everything repeatedly:

Confidentiality – when the attacker gets in, how much can they do?

A layered system of defense would help limit exposure on confidentiality. Just like the bank example, a series of different locks are used to prevent the loss of one key, thus leading to the entire system being compromised. In information security terms, having different logon details for different levels of privilege could be a suitable strategy, as could a password protecting particularly confidential documents and folders.

Integrity

Integrity refers to how trustworthy information is after an attack. Has the attacker been given access to financial data, with the result that customers are going to be charged incorrectly at the end of the month? Is the attacker able to edit data, and what effect could these edits have? There is some overlap between confidentiality and integrity when we examine a case where the attacker has limited access to files, and this will be examined with a physical example so that we have some context.

None (N) is defined as follows:

> *"CVSS 3.0 Definition: There is no loss of integrity within the impacted component."*

For integrity, imagine there was a vulnerability which allowed an attacker to access student records in the school office. The attacker is able to view everyone's records, but has no ability to change anything. They now know who is performing well in class, but they could have got this information by asking the teacher!

Low (L) is defined as follows:

> *"CVSS 3.0 Definition: Modification of data is possible, but the attacker does not have control over the consequence of a modification, or the amount of modification is constrained. The data modification does not have a direct, serious impact on the impacted component."*

Returning to the school example, imagine if the vulnerability allowed the attacker to modify a pupil's timetable; this would have limited consequences. In general, pupils and teachers know where they are going, so it would be pretty obvious that a change had been made, and people would still be in the right place at the right time. The rating for the integrity metric would be low in this case.

High (H) is defined as follows:

> *"CVSS 3.0 Definition: There is a total loss of integrity, or a complete loss of protection. For example, the attacker is able to modify any/all files protected by the impacted component. Alternatively, only some files can be modified, but malicious modification would present a direct, serious consequence to the impacted component."*

For our final scenario, the student records were only written in pencil. Now, the attacker could change everybody's grades, which might have an impact on their futures. This vulnerability would score high for integrity, as the attacker can access, edit, and modify all the records/data, which could have serious consequences for somebody:

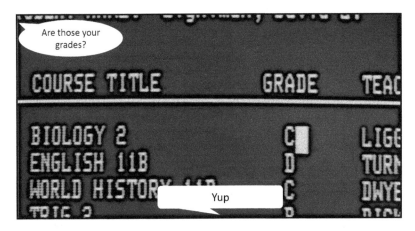

Integrity – how trusted does the attacker need to appear?

A system with suitable backups and other checks (for example, check digits or hashes) would help to identify when data had been modified, and by whom. Backups can also help to reduce exposure to the highest impact threats.

Availability

While confidentiality and integrity refer to the information inside or used by an impacted component, the availability metric refers to the loss of availability of the component itself. This could be because of bandwidth issues, processor cycles, or hard disk space.

None (N) is defined as follows:

> *"CVSS 3.0 Definition: There is no impact to availability within the impacted component."*

Imagine a private library. There are plenty of library books, and these are very useful. An attacker could reduce the availability of the library in a number of different ways. Imagine that an attacker has managed to gain access to the library, and has been able to photocopy all the pages of a book. While there might be confidentiality issues, the book is still available to be read by legitimate users. There is no impact on availability.

Low (L) is defined as follows:

> *"CVSS 3.0 Definition: There is reduced performance or interruptions in resource availability. Even if repeated exploitation of the vulnerability is possible, the attacker does not have the ability to completely deny service to legitimate users. The resources in the impacted component are either partially available all of the time, or fully available only some of the time, but overall there is no direct, serious consequence to the impacted component."*

If there was a vulnerability which gave an attacker a library card, they could borrow a book, making it unavailable to legitimate users. This would be a low-impact score, because they are only limiting the availability of this single book, and a legitimate user could always come back in a couple of weeks' time when the attacker has to return it.

High (H) is defined as follows:

> *"CVSS 3.0 Definition: There is total loss of availability, resulting in the attacker being able to fully deny access to resources in the impacted component; this loss is either sustained (while the attacker continues to deliver the attack) or persistent (the condition persists even after the attack has completed). Alternatively, the attacker has the ability to deny some availability, but the loss of availability presents a direct, serious consequence to the impacted component (for example, the attacker cannot disrupt existing connections, but can prevent new connections; the attacker can repeatedly exploit a vulnerability that, in each instance of a successful attack, leaks a only small amount of memory, but after repeated exploitation causes a service to become completely unavailable)."*

If an attacker were to use a vulnerability which allowed their library card to borrow unlimited books, the attacker could, in theory, borrow all the books, and hence this would be a high-impact vulnerability. Another high impact vulnerability would be to close and lock the doors of the library. The books have not been improperly accessed, nor changed, so the confidentiality and integrity scores don't change, but the books wouldn't be accessible to legitimate users.

The attack itself may not directly result in a denial of legitimate service. This may even happen as part of the security response. Imagine an attacker trying to steal data over the network. One of the responses might just be to shut down the outgoing connection, but this might have consequences, such as the following screen appearing for all users:

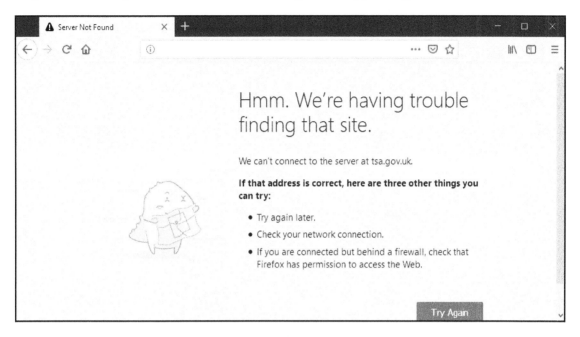

Availability – will the attack affect a legitimate user's access?

A system with multiple means of access can help to reduce exposure against the highest-impact threats. Using the library example, if the attacker has barricaded one door, it is important that there is another. Alternatively, the ability to go to another library would also mitigate against the threat. In information security terms, having two different network routes to the affected component, or holding backups at a separate site, could be used.

Scope

CVSS v3.0 incorporated a new measure which reflects the ability for a vulnerability in one component to impact other resources and components. In this section, you will come to understand that a threat can sometimes have impacts beyond its individual capacity, and this must be captured in CVSS v3.0 under the scope metric.

The **authorization scope** or **scope metric** refers to the privileges associated with a computing authority (for example, process, application, operating system, or sandbox environment) when granting access to computing resources (for example, files, processing, RAM, permanent storage, and so on). If a vulnerability is able to gain more (or different) access to resources than the original (normal working) authority is able to assign. The base score is greater when a scope change has occurred.

A clear example of scope change is a vulnerability escaping a sandbox and deleting files on the host OS, or even in another VM. In this example, there are privileges associated with the virtual machine, and these are separate from the privileges associated with the host system and its users.

Scope changes get more complex when you think about the following specific example from the CVSS v3.0 specification documentation:

> *"A scope change would not occur, for example, with a vulnerability in Microsoft Word that allows an attacker to compromise all system files of the host OS, because the same authority enforces privileges of the user's instance of Word, and the host's system files."*

If a similar vulnerability were to exist in Microsoft Word Online (run through a browser), a scope change would occur because the infected component is in the web application, and the affected component is on the host system.

Unchanged (U) is defined as follows:

> *"CVSS 3.0 Definition: An exploited vulnerability can only affect resources managed by the same authority. In this case, the vulnerable component and the impacted component are the same."*

Imagine that you are at your family home and a sibling borrows some of your things from your room without telling you. While this is a vulnerability, and there is a confidentiality issue, there is no scope change because access to both rooms is under the same authority (that is, the house).

Changed (C) is defined as follows:

> *"CVSS 3.0 Definition: An exploited vulnerability can affect resources beyond the authorization privileges intended by the vulnerable component. In this case, the vulnerable component and the impacted component are different."*

Alternatively, if your sibling were to borrow things from your next-door neighbor's home, there is a scope change. The authority to be in one house does not carry over to the house next door.

The following diagram represents how a vulnerability in one area could affect others. *One bad apple spoils the bunch* is a classic English language proverb, but what if the bad apple could spoil the oranges and plums too?

Scope – which is the affected component? Is it controlled by the same authority as the vulnerability is?

Defending against scope changes is difficult by definition. The computing authority which controls a system operating in normal conditions defines the scope of that system, so a scope change indicates that the authority's design is compromised in itself. If you think back to the house example, a defense against scope change is the use of door locks. This could be extended to lock each individual room to prevent unauthorized access. The problem with this is that some legitimate application will need to leave the room. Putting ever increasing numbers of workarounds and holes in the doors will eventually mean that the locked doors have no effect.

Summary

Threats are classified using a number of different applications and methods, including AMP Threat Grid and Cuckoo Sandbox. Each threat prevention/detection/reparation tool works slightly differently, and their scores are not always transparent. The CVSS v3.0 system is open source and transparent, giving comparable results across the board. How exploitable vulnerability is depends on how far away an attacker can be from the target (attack vector), how difficult the exploit is (attack complexity), how trusted an attacker would have to become to be successful (privileges required), and whether anyone else is involved (user interaction). The impact of a vulnerability is measured against the (C)onfidentiality (I)ntegrity (A)vailability triad.

In the next chapter, we will be looking at the fundamental differences between the Windows and Linux operating systems.

Questions

 In Cisco exams, you are not permitted to go back and review or change previous answers.

 Questions in the exam increase in complexity and difficulty, and later questions may assist you with earlier ones. Test yourself under Cisco exam conditions as you get more confident!

1. Which metric relates to "the context by which vulnerability exploitation is possible"?
   1. Attack Vector
   2. Attack Complexity
   3. Attack Pathway
   4. Attack Vulnerability

2. Which metric relates to "conditions beyond the attacker's control that are required in order to successfully exploit a vulnerability"?
   1. Privileges Required
   2. Attack Complexity
   3. Attack Prerequisites
   4. Attack Vector

3. An attacker is able to place a call and listen to a victim's microphone without the victim accepting the call. Which CVSS 3.0 metric will rate the highest?
   1. Availability
   2. Confidentiality
   3. Integrity
   4. Scope

4. An attacker is able to change the contents of a file on a networked computer. Which metric will rate the highest?
    1. Availability
    2. Integrity
    3. Attack Vector
    4. Attack Complexity

5. Which of the following is an example of an attack whose scope has been potentially changed?
    1. A denial-of-service attack
    2. An attack against a web server which compromises web browsers which connect to it
    3. An attacker editing the contents of a file on a networked computer
    4. A script in an Excel file which modifies a file in the user's documents

6. Which CVSS impact scores might represent a threat against a gaming server which leaves it completely offline?
    1. CVSS:3.0/{Portion Removed}/C:H/I:L/A:N
    2. CVSS:3.0/{Portion Removed}/C:H/I:L/A:N
    3. CVSS:3.0/{Portion Removed}/C:N/I:N/A:H
    4. CVSS:3.0/{Portion Removed}/C:N/I:N/A:N

7. Which CVSS exploitability scores might represent an exploit which requires an attacker to construct a URL to a vulnerable `phpMyAdmin` web server that injects malicious code? The URL must be clicked for the malicious code to execute in the victim's web browser. This code is limited to the website running the vulnerable `phpMyAdmin` software:
    1. CVSS:3.0/AV:P/AC:L/PR:N/UI:R/S:U/C:N/I:L/A:N
    2. CVSS:3.0/AV:N/AC:L/PR:N/UI:R/S:U/C:N/I:L/A:N
    3. CVSS:3.0/AV:L/AC:L/PR:N/UI:N/S:U/C:N/I:L/A:N
    4. CVSS:3.0/AV:N/AC:L/PR:N/UI:N/S:U/C:N/I:L/A:N

The following screenshot refers to an item that's been uploaded to AMP Threat Grid. The following three questions are related to this screenshot:

| > 🔒 ee911438c31e5f820a70de27... | zip | 10/21/16 7:30 pm | 100 |

First Seen	2016-10-21T...		Behavioral Indicators		
Last Seen	2016-10-21T...		Name	Severity	Confidence
Times Seen	1				
Q SHA-256	6d02561fb2a...		malware-ransomware-	100	100
Q SHA-1	7d20a64f3f7...		bandarchor		
Q MD5	4a25fa76ff6d...		antivirus-service-	100	95
			flagged-artifact		
Network Streams	20		modified-file-in-system-	90	100
Registry Actions	177		dir		
			registry-autorun-key-	90	100
			data-dir		
Artifacts					
Memory	18		modified-file-in-	80	90
Disk	392		program-dir		

Screenshot from AMP Threat Grid

8. What type of file was uploaded?
    1. An image file
    2. A portable executable file
    3. A portable document file
    4. A compressed (archive) file

9. What actions should a tier 1 analyst take?
    1. Immediately quarantine and block access to the file
    2. Refer the report to a tier 2 analyst
    3. Remove the file from quarantine
    4. Log a report about a suspicious file with a tier 3 analyst

10. What kind of malware has been detected?
    1. Virus
    2. Worm
    3. Ransomware
    4. Spyware

Further reading

- A user guide to CVSS v3.0 can be found at `https://www.first.org/cvss/cvss-v30-user_guide_v1.6.pdf`.
- Cisco also uses CVSS. A guide to CVSS usage within Cisco can be found at `https://tools.cisco.com/security/center/resources/cvss.html`.

Operating System Families

2

There are fundamental differences between the Windows and Linux operating systems. These have an impact on the types of vulnerability that exist, as well as the ability of a vulnerability to spread from one system to another. This chapter does a side-by-side comparison of these factors to help you understand the differences between the operating systems, and the impact of these differences on cybersecurity.

Defining the terms of reference between the Linux and Windows operating systems only requires definitions and memory; there is minimal interpretation or ambiguity with these Cisco questions. Knowledge of these factors impacts on the chapters that follow.

The following topics will be covered in this chapter:

- Starting the operating system
- Filesystems
- Making, finding, accessing, and editing data

Starting the operating system

An **operating system** (**OS**) is a software system that manages computer hardware and software resources and provides common services for computer programs. An operating system is responsible for controlling access to, and the efficient management of, system resources (for example, memory allocation, input and output devices, and processing time). This is done by acting as an intermediary between programs and computer hardware.

In this section, you will learn about the way the operating system is stored in the main memory, as well as how it is located and booted differently by Linux and Windows systems.

The two major groups of operating systems are Unix-like systems (for example, Linux and macOS) and Microsoft Windows. Linux is open source, which means that all the source programming files are available for download for viewing and modification, and therefore Linux can be tailor-made for a given set of hardware and software requirements rather than building hardware and software to comply, as would have to be the case in a Windows environment. Linux-based systems are the dominant operating system of choice in security operations centers.

When a computer is started, it must find, load, and run the operating system. If you think about the time taken to search an entire **hard disk drive** (**HDD**) for a single file, you can see that this process would take far too long. Instead, computers use a smaller system – originating within the ROM – to establish whether operating systems are present, where they are, and which one to load if there is more than one.

Power-on is linked with a self-test, which allows the computer to discover what hardware is connected, and if and how it can interact with the user. There is then a choice of whether to use the **Basic Input Output System** (**BIOS**) or **Unified Extensible Firmware Interface** (**UEFI**) to load the operating system.

Basic Input Output System

The BIOS is the firmware that performs hardware initialization during the booting process (power-on startup). It is preinstalled on a motherboard, and is held in ROM or another non-volatile medium (such as flash memory). It is the first software to run when powered on, and is responsible for detecting, starting up, and testing hardware and loading the boot loader, which will then initialize the operating system. The classic blue CMOS setup/BIOS screen is shown in the following screenshot, and can be used to apply settings (such as system times) before the operating system is even initiated. This can be password-protected to help protect the system, but is often easily overridden by a CMOS battery pull (to clear memory) or via a jumper on the board:

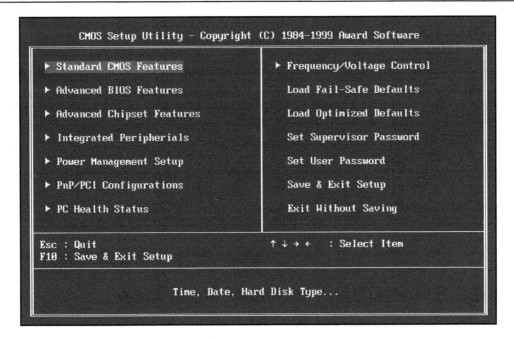

BIOS basic system settings

In the MS-DOS (and therefore also the early Windows systems), the BIOS provided the control layer for the keyboard, display, and other devices, providing a standardized interface for the operating system and application programs, regardless of any differences in the physical hardware. This platform is now provided by the operating system, so the BIOS is only really required to find and load the operating system, initialize the hardware, and then hand over control.

When booting, the BIOS looks to the **Master Boot Record** (**MBR**) to point it to the location of any operating systems that are present. The BIOS is an often overlooked security vulnerability, perhaps due to its historical position in ROM (and therefore uneditable). The Mebromi rootkit changed this. Discovered in 2011, it set out to plant itself inside the BIOS in order to corrupt the system's MBR and make the target system inoperable.

Master Boot Record

MBR is a type of boot sector at the very beginning (normally the first 512 bytes) of partitioned computer mass storage devices (for example, hard disk drives or removable drives). MBR holds information about how logical partitions are organized on the drive. The way that MBR describes addressable partitions involves having 32 bits for the first sector of the partition and 32 bits for the size (number of sectors) in the partition. This sets a size limit of $(2^{32} - 1)$ *sectors* $\times$ *512 bytes/sector*, or 2 TB.

The MBR also contains executable code which points to and begins the operating system loading process. The last 66 bytes are reserved for partitions and other information, so the MBR boot sector program must be small enough to fit within 446 bytes of memory. This is why the boot sector program typically only contains enough information to point to another, larger resource.

Unified Extensible Firmware Interface

UEFI, like the BIOS, is the first software that is run when a computer is turned on. UEFI is programmable, so **original equipment manufacturer (OEM)** developers can add applications and drivers, allowing UEFI to function as a lightweight operating system. UEFI doesn't need to sit in ROM. Instead, it can sit in any non-volatile memory: in NAND on the motherboard, on a hard drive, or on a network share. It can sit alongside, on top of, or instead of the BIOS.

UEFI is able to control drivers and runtime services, and also supports a more capable GUI, including pointing device support, as shown in the following diagram:

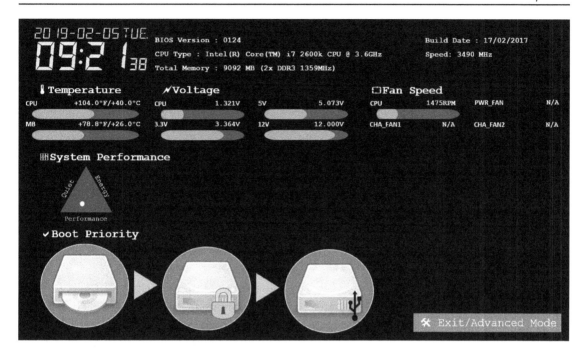

Unified Extensible Firmware Interface

UEFI allows for an extended user interface during boot. This includes pointing device (mouse) support and more capable configuration tools, including secure boot.

In terms of security, the most significant upgrade in terms of UEFI is secure boot. Secure boot, which was enabled from Windows 8 onward, allows UEFI to check the security credentials of the OS loader, and can therefore detect any rootkit or malware loader and prevent it from running.

While there are many benefits to UEFI, the **National Institute of Standards and Technology** (**NIST**) guidance reflects the additional threat to the pre-OS environment. With a totally programmable boot system, UEFI must be considered and protected like any other system component, must stay up to date with patches and updates, and ensure any add-on applications are also compliant.

GUID Partition Table

The **GUID Partition Table** (**GPT**) is part of the UEFI standard, and was designed to address the limitations of MBR. The 2 TB limit has been extended by creating larger partition entries (64 bits rather than 32 bits). This has extended the drive size limit to 8 ZB (~8 billion TB), assuming there are 512-byte sectors.

GPT also overcomes the issue of corrupted MBR (for example, the Mebromi rootkit) by storing a copy of the partition data, as well as storing **cyclic redundancy check** (**CRC**) values to verify that the drive is intact and whether the stored copy might need to be restored. GPT is compatible with most operating systems, although for Windows only UEFI-based computers can utilize GPT.

Booting Windows and Linux

In Windows, a program called `bootmgr.exe` begins the loading process. This file is contained in the root directory of the active partition (either called system reserved or existing without a drive letter). If it is starting from fresh, `winload.exe` will conduct kernel-mode code signing, which verifies the kernel image to be loaded and passes it to `ntoskrnl.exe`, which will initiate the **hardware abstraction layer** (**HAL**) and **Session Manager Subsystem** (**SMSS**) to complete the preparation for a user to log in. If the system is waking from hibernation, `winload.exe` is not required, and `winresume.exe` executes the required processes to resume the system detailed in `hiberfil.sys`. This data allows the user to log in to the previous session.

In Linux, the boot process is controlled by the **Grand Unified Bootloader** (**GRUB**). This is loaded in three parts due to the size constraints of the Master Boot Record. Stage 1 loads just enough information to correctly verify the first 30 Kb of the HDD, which contains Stage 1.5. Stage 2 is also held on the HDD, but is not fixed to the first 30 Kb. The kernel is initiated from `/sbin/init`, which contains the root process in Linux; all other processes branch from `init`. A session is created, referencing the `/etc/inittab` file. This file dictates the run levels (resources and services) that are available and any processes that should be run prior to subsequent user login.

The following diagram shows a side-by-side comparison of the Linux and Windows boot sequences:

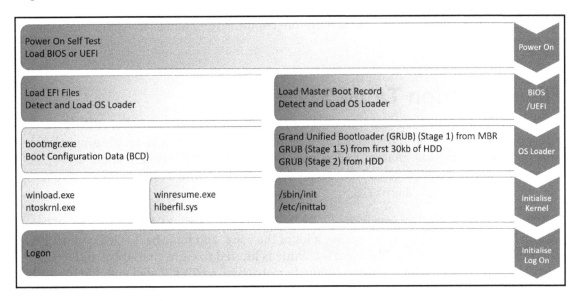

Boot process for Windows (Orange) and Linux (Green) systems. Blue processes are common to both systems

Booting the operating system is multistage in order to support increasing volumes of storage. Typical operating systems now run to over 10 GB, which would be particularly expensive in terms of ROM!

Filesystems

The filesystem is a way of organizing objects on a drive. It specifies how data is stored, including where data may be stored on the drive, how items are named, size limits, and how data can be retrieved, and by whom.

In this section, you will learn about the different methods of memory formatting that are used by Linux and Windows operating systems, and how the chosen filesystem affects security.

Modern versions of Windows utilize the **New Technology Filesystem** (**NTFS**) by default for the system drive, where as Linux tends to use **Extended Filesystem 4 (Ext4)**. **File Allocation Table 32** (**FAT32**) is a much older filesystem, although it does offer better compatibility between systems, and is therefore common for smaller, transferable media (for example, USB flash drives).

File Allocation Table 32

FAT32 is a filesystem which was introduced in Windows 95 as an extension of the FAT family of filesystems, which date from the late 70s. FAT32 utilizes a 32-bit file allocation table (from which the designation FAT comes), which, like MBR, brought about a maximum volume size of 2 TB (2^{32} sectors at 512 bytes each), and a maximum file size of 2^{32} - 1 bytes, or 1 byte less than 4 GB.

FAT32 still uses the 8.3 filename format, which was used in earlier FAT systems (that is, FAT8, 12, and 16). This allows it to reuse a lot of the code, and have backward compatibility with these formats. In the 8.3 filename, the name is limited to eight characters, plus a file extension of three characters. This is obviously restrictive, so FAT32 also uses the **long file name** (**LFN**) extension, which stores both the 8.3 filename (for compatibility) and the full filename. This is limited to a 260-byte path (including the file extension), although the convention is for a file path to be no greater than 80 characters in order to fit on a single line of a **command-line interface** (**CLI**). FAT32 sets a maximum directory depth of 60 levels, which is fine for most common home usage, but can be a problem in server-based systems.

FAT32 is a very common standard filesystem format for compatibility. FAT32 is supported by Windows, macOS, and Linux, as well as many other devices such as TVs, games consoles, and digital cameras. The bulk of USB flash drives are shipped formatted as FAT32 in order to work straight out of the packet.

New Technology Filesystem

NTFS has been the default partition type for the Windows system drive since Windows XP. NTFS was designed with file size and partition size limits that are very large, thus overcoming some of the limits of FAT32. For example, an .iso copy of a Windows operating system installation straddles the 4 GB file size limit, which poses problems when you want to download a new operating system to a FAT32 drive.

NTFS has a number of additional features that are not available to FAT32, including native support for encryption, hard links, and file permissions – all of these things make the filesystem more secure.

Despite the many advantages it has, NTFS has struggled for compatibility beyond Windows, with macOS X and most Linux distributions supporting access to the drive in read-only mode, if at all. Even the Microsoft Xbox 360 was unable to read NTFS drives.

Extended Filesystem 4

Ext4 was released in the early 2000s, roughly when NTFS was arriving on the scene for Microsoft. Ext4 is an extension of the extended filesystem, which was released in the early 90s. The extended filesystem has been specifically designed for Linux, although extensions to the operating system are available for macOS X and Windows, but these don't guarantee full functionality.

Ext4 maintained the journaling ability from Ext3, while also supporting very large file, partition size, and subdirectory limits (16 TB file, 1 EB (~1 million terabytes) volume size, and unlimited subdirectories) and introducing extents that reduce the fragmentation of large files.

Making, finding, accessing, and editing data

One of the primary uses of computing is the ability to work with files. These files might be used by the operating system itself, or other applications and programs.

In this section, you will learn how to explain the concept of virtual memory, and how this can cause long-term residuals of activity. We will look at how both the Linux and Windows operating systems manage virtual memory, and how journaling, alternative data streams, and metadata are produced and managed differently by Linux and Windows.

While we have already considered some of the restrictions that result from the filesystem format, operating systems also utilize resources differently, meaning that system files are created, read, updated, and destroyed in different ways. Operating systems also implement different methods of making, finding, and editing user files. This information can be particularly useful for cybersecurity researchers.

Creating files

In both Windows and Linux, files can be created by the operating system, the user, or applications. In Linux, all configuration files are text files, so an administrator can make configuration changes via the command line, including over a remote shell connection (Telnet or SSH). In Windows systems, configuration changes rely much more heavily on the GUI:

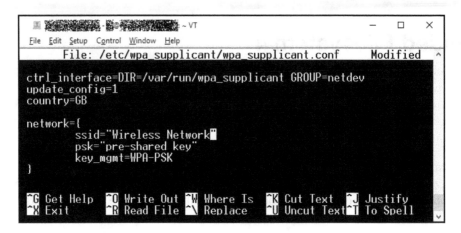

Adding wireless settings using nano over SSH (through Tera Term)

Linux operating systems are often used in server setups. An associate in a SOC may, therefore, be required to review some of the logs. There are four types of log – application, event, service, and system – and these are recorded by default. The following table lists some common log files and their locations:

Log	Purpose
/var/log/messages	Used to store non-critical system messages
/var/log/auth.log	Authentication-related events
/var/log/secure	Used by RedHat and CentOS and tracks sudo (enhanced privilege) logins and SSH (secure remote access) logins
/var/log/boot.log	Boot-related messages during startup
/var/log/dmesg	Kernel ring buffer messages
/var/log/kern.log	Kernel log information
/var/log/cron	Schedule of automated tasks
/var/log/mysqld.log or /var/log/mysql.log	MySQL database server log files

Notice that they are all in the `/var/` folder. This folder stores all the data that varies through the normal operation of the system. Logging files, printer spool directories, and transient and temporary files are all held in this folder.

Locating files

Files are often stored sequentially, or wherever a suitably sized gap on the drive is found. This leads to fragmentation issues, but more importantly, means that the files on disk are not necessarily organized logically. To organize the files, the different filesystem formats operate slightly differently. On top of this, Windows and Linux organize their file structures differently.

In FAT32, a table is used, which contains the name and an index for the start position of each file. To view a file, FAT32 must check the record for the file and then begin retrieving the chain of sectors. This two-stage process can become very inefficient.

NTFS uses a structure called the **master file table** (**MFT**), which contains more information per record. While this makes MFT much larger than FAT, it has some distinct advantages, particularly when it comes to processing small files or directory trees (fewer than 512 bytes) as the contents can be stored directly in the MFT.

Ext4 uses a similar system to NTFS, although it uses a hash of the filename rather than the filename itself. This allows for constant size entries, which assists in the speed of searching, but can create problems due to hash collisions (where two filenames result in the same hash value).

In NTFS and Ext4, there is support for searching or sorting by factors other than the filename. This could be, for example, the date of creation or the date of last modification. This data is called metadata and includes timestamps on a filesystem, and sometimes details about ownership and permissions.

Reading files

Files are accessed by a user through either the command line or the GUI. If the file is not an executable (a program/application), another piece of software is required to open it. In Chapter 1, *Classifying Threats*, confidentiality was discussed. In order to maintain confidentiality, it is important for the operating system to control who has permission to access each file.

For single user files, this can be done by having user areas. In order to access a different user's area, the user would have to log out and log in as the other user. This makes collaboration very difficult, and therefore business – and increasingly home – settings need a different system of control.

In Windows Server environments, **Management of Access Control in the Enterprise** (**MACE**) is used to classify files and control access. MACE combines data collection with data visualization so that an administrator gets a representation of who has access to what over the network. The data collection element discovers the server's effective permissions on folders, shared drives, and **File Classification Infrastructure** (**FCI**) files, as well as group and user information from Active Directory. This allows MACE to understand which users have access to which files and folders.

Windows uses a series of **Access Control Lists** (**ACL**), which grant or limit access based on the individual user ID, groups, and roles. The CEO's personal assistant, for example, would sit in the admin's group, but would still require access to exec documents. It doesn't make sense to allow him/her to be an exec, nor to allow all the admin group access to exec documents. The ACL may, therefore, be broadly group/role-based, and then a specific exception can be made for the user. The following screenshot shows the MACE visualization of the users and groups who have access to the `TestResearchServer1\Areas\Resources` folder. Notice that access control is at the group-based and user-based access levels:

MACE visualization

In Linux, ACLs may also be used. However, most systems don't operate ACLs, and instead use traditional Unix permissions. This is often referred to as *owner-group-world* and is not as granular as ACLs. Each file specifies what users can do (read, write, or execute) depending on what group they belong to (owner, group, or world). When listed with the `ls` command, as in the following table, the symbolic notation has an additional character (and the numeric notation has an additional number) which relates to the file type –this is not related to permissions. In symbolic notation, there are three values (`rwx`) which are given to owner, group, and world in turn. In numeric notation, there is a file type number, and then a single number each for owner, group, and world. A read bit adds 4 to the total, the write bit adds 2, and the execute bit adds 1. The digit is therefore limited to values between 0 and 7:

Symbolic notation	Numeric notation	English
`----------`	0000	No permission
`-rwx------`	0700	The file owner can read, write, and execute; no one else has any permission
`-rwxrwx---`	0770	The file owner and group can read, write, and execute; others have no permission
`-rwxrwxrwx`	0777	Anyone can read, write, and execute
`---x--x--x`	0111	Anybody can execute
`--w--w--w-`	0222	Anybody can write
`--wx-wx-wx`	0333	Anybody can write and execute
`-r--r--r--`	0444	Anyone can read
`-r-xr-xr-x`	0555	Anyone can read and execute
`-rw-rw-rw-`	0666	Anyone can read and write
`-rwxr-----`	0740	The owner can read, write, and execute; the group can only read; others have no permissions

The following screenshot shows the output from the Linux `ls` command. The `-a` argument denotes all, including hidden files, while the `-l` argument denotes long list format, which shows things such as file size and permissions. When multiple option arguments (for example, `-a` and `-l`) are used on the same process, they can be written with a single hyphen (–) sign, as shown (that is, `-al` specifies both `-a` and `-l`). Notice the symbolic notation associated with each file; `mm.sh` is executable by anybody, whereas `raspberry.sh` is only executable by the owner. Notice that all of the folders (denoted by the d on the left-hand side) are 4,096 bytes in length, reflecting a 4 k-sector instead of a 512-byte sector:

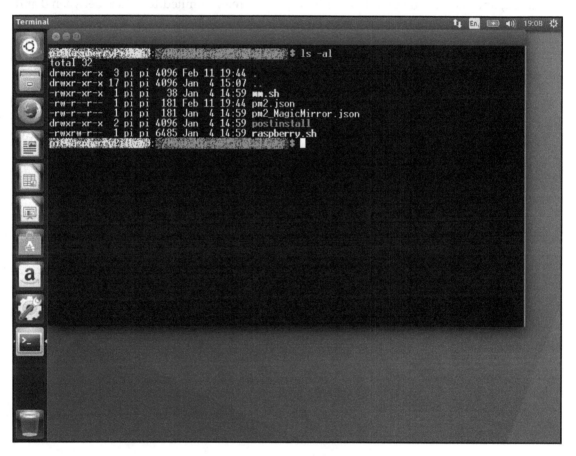

The results of the ls command in Linux

Once a user's credentials have been verified, the relevant application or process allocates the file to memory. As programs and files increase in size, they become too large to be held in RAM. Operating systems can use mass storage (for example, HDD/SSD) space to extend RAM capacity. In Windows, this memory is called virtual memory and in Linux it is called swap. This can either be a swap partition (a completely separate disk space which is only used for swap), or a (series of) swap file(s). Swap files are created on the same partition as other system and user files, and so they can be allocated and extended by the user, rather than our having to create or extend a disk partition.

Windows has a number of different methods for generating and allocating virtual memory, as described in the following table:

Memory allocation function	Description and usage
`VirtualAlloc`	• Allocation of virtual memory via reserved blocks of memory • Utilizes a full page, which can result in higher memory usage
`HeapAlloc`	• Dynamic allocation of virtual memory • Can allocate any size, as demanded by the application • Cannot be moved; must be freed after use
`LocalAlloc`	• Specialized wrapper to HeapAlloc (has all HeapAlloc features) • Allows memory to be moved by reallocation without changing the handle value
`CoTaskMemAlloc`	• The only way to share memory (for example, for COM-based applications)

Each memory allocation method has advantages and disadvantages, so the choice of which to use is dependent on the application and what functionality is required of the page file/virtual memory allocation.

Changes to files and properties

To save a file back to the storage device, the file must be moved from RAM or virtual memory onto the disk. If there is a power failure during the writing process, it is difficult to know which bits of the file are correct and which aren't. This is a particular problem because RAM is volatile, and therefore the changes that were made will have been lost in the power failure. In order to prevent this problem, filesystems can conduct an additional step, which involves storing the changes in a journal on non-volatile memory (normally the storage device) before the original file location is overwritten. The journal should not be confused with logs. The journal is not typically accessed by anything other than the operating system, where as logs are designed for human readability.

Both NTFS and Ext4 are able to keep a journal of data about what changes are due before a commit, so this can be compared to the actual result. Although NTFS is technically only able to keep a journal of metadata changes and not the data itself, the actual way this is implemented means that it is very reliable. Ext4 is able to journal both data and metadata, although by default it only maintains the metadata journal.

Using a metadata journal allows for much quicker consistency checking than in the days of WindowsXP/FAT32 checks, as shown in the following screenshot:

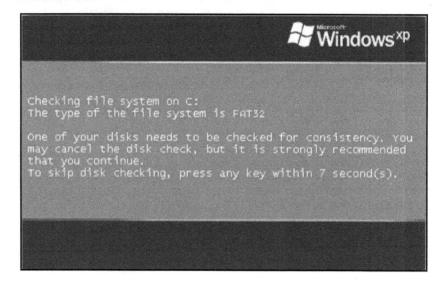

Windows XP conducting consistency checks before the use of NTFS and journaling

In addition to normal file content (data), there is a range of other information that's held about the file. This includes metadata that is mandated by the filesystem (for example, date stamps or user permission data), but also includes additional data. In NTFS and Windows, files are able to maintain this data as an **additional data stream** (**ADS**). These streams can contain a variety of information, including the source of a file (that is, internet files, local intranet zones, and trusted or restricted sites zones). However, this can also be hijacked by malware and disguised as a stream from a legitimate program. Microsoft allows users and administrators to view and manipulate ADS using `streams.exe` and, with effect from Windows 8.0 and Server 2012, has rolled this functionality and more into PowerShell.

In Linux, four timestamps are held per file. Accessed (`atime, stat %x`) is the time the file was last opened. Modified (`mtime, stat %y`) relates to the time the contents were last edited. Changed (`ctime, stat %z`) is the time the metadata was last changed (for example, the permissions were edited). Create (`crtime`) in Ext4 replaces the birth time from older systems. The following screenshot shows the timestamps associated with the `mm.sh` file. The file was created elsewhere and imported using `curl`, so there is no `Birth` time. The file was then edited in nano, made executable using `chmod` 3 days later, and then accessed later that day (probably to execute it):

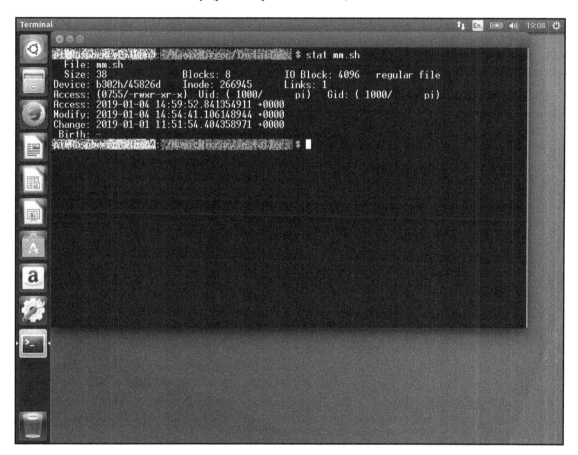

Different values for the timestamps are created by differing actions

NTFS holds two timestamps for all of the files that are created and modified, although other programs (for example, Microsoft Word) add further metadata to the file (using ADS). Note that the timestamps in the following screenshot don't appear to be correct; for the `New PNG Image` file (second in the list), the Date modified is over a month earlier before the date that it was created. Why do you think this is?

Name	Type	Date created	Date modified	Size	Authors	Title
New Microsoft Po...	Microsoft PowerP...	07/02/2019 13:23	07/02/2019 13:23	32 KB	Chu	PowerPoint
New PNG Image	PNG File	07/02/2019 13:24	31/12/2018 10:45	5 KB		
New Text Document	Text Document	07/02/2019 13:23	07/02/2019 13:24	1 KB		
Old PNG Image	PNG File	31/12/2018 11:07	31/12/2018 11:07	3 KB		

Some of the metadata which is available through NTFS

This pictured instance of `New PNG Image` was copied in from another folder. The original file would have a much older created date, but this copy was created at the point of moving it. The copy has only existed since February 2019. `Old PNG Image` (fourth in the list) was moved from another folder; it is the original file and, most importantly, is just updating the original entry in the MFT. This file keeps the original creation date and modification time.

Deleting files

When deleting files, the actual physical blocks in which the files were held are not necessarily written over. Instead, the MFT or GPT marks the block as available for writing, and the links from block to block are removed. When a new file is allocated one of these blocks, the new data is written to the block. It is only at this point that the data is removed. Even formatting the disk usually just marks blocks as available rather than truly randomizing the elements and returning the block to its factory condition. This speeds up the deletion process, but leaves remnants of deleted files in unallocated space.

Deleting files in Windows doesn't actually overwrite the blocks. Applications such as Recuva can be used to scan the blocks, rather than simply the file table (NTFS, MFT, or FAT). The deleted file is not seen in the Windows Explorer window, but is visible to Recuva. As a small file, the entire file is in a single cluster, so it can be previewed in its entirety with no fragmentation. The following screenshot shows Recuva finding the deleted text file, even though it does not appear in File Explorer. The file has been deleted from the MFT and not hidden (you can see the hidden file in File Explorer with the icon partially grayed out):

Finding deleted files using Recuva

This functionality in the MFT means that there are times where files can still be recovered and recreated from empty drives and unallocated space. This can be useful for recovering from legitimate mistakes, but also for files which have been purposefully deleted to hide activity.

Summary

There are two major families of operating systems in general usage. Unix-like systems include Linux, which is used extensively in servers. Windows systems also have servers, although they are mainly used as end-user devices. There are several areas in which Linux and Windows systems are similar, for example, support for UEFI and the older-style BIOS. The differences come from the preference for NTFS (Windows) or Ext4 (Linux) filesystems, which have different approaches to metadata and journaling.

At the operating system level, the way that virtual memory is allocated and used varies. In Linux, a separate partition, or a pre-designated file called swap, is used. In Windows, there is some reserved space that's used by `VirtualAlloc`; otherwise, free disk space is allocated as required using `HeapAlloc`.

Access to files is managed both by the filesystem and the operating system. Linux and Windows both support Access Control Lists, although Windows is used more often. Linux systems tend to revert to the UNIX-style user-group-world permissions system.

Questions

1. Which type of virtual memory allocation allocates memory based on what is dynamically requested in Windows?
    1. HeapAlloc
    2. VirtualAlloc
    3. Swap
    4. CoTaskMemAlloc
2. Which type of virtual memory allocation in Windows has reserved blocks of memory?
    1. HeapAlloc
    2. VirtualAlloc
    3. LocalAlloc
    4. Pages

3. Which of the following systems are used by Linux to provide extra memory on permanent storage devices (more than one may be required)?
   1. A swap partition
   2. Swap files
   3. Dynamic allocation using the virtual memory allocation function
   4. NVRAM

4. What is Journaling?
   1. A system which maintains a record of changes that aren't yet committed to the filesystem
   2. A filesystem format
   3. A log of all system actions that have been conducted since power on
   4. A record of all system actions that have been conducted since the last file commit

5. In which directory would the print spool be held?
   1. In the `/var/log/` folder as a separate file
   2. In the `/var/` folder within a folder called spool
   3. In the `/etc/` folder within a folder called spool
   4. In the `/var/log/` folder within a folder called messages

6. Which command would be issued to change the permissions of `setup.sh` so that the owner can read, write, and execute the script, and everyone else can only execute it?
   1. `chmod 770 setup.sh`
   2. `chmod 711 setup.sh`
   3. `chmod 733 setup.sh`
   4. `chmod 777 setup.sh`

7. What date options are available in Windows 8 running on NTFS?
   1. Created and modified
   2. Created and accessed
   3. Created and last saved
   4. Accessed and modified

The following three questions are related to the following screenshot:

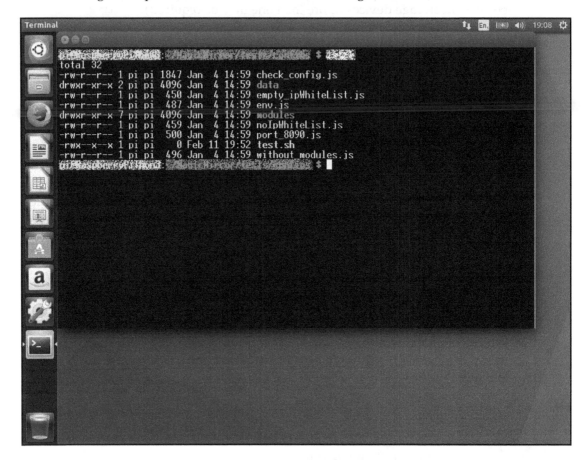

Screenshot from the Linux Terminal

8. What does the d mean against data and modules?
    1. This is a data file
    2. This is a directory
    3. This is a hidden (dark) file
    4. This is a dangerous file

9. Which of the following commands yield this result?
    1. `ls -l`
    2. `ls -a`
    3. `ls`
    4. `ls -al`

10. Who can execute `test.sh`?
    1. The `pi` user only
    2. The `pi` group only
    3. External users only
    4. Everybody

Further reading

- The NIST BIOS Protection Guidelines can be accessed at `https://nvlpubs.nist.gov/nistpubs/Legacy/SP/nistspecialpublication800-147.pdf`. This document is beyond the scope of this course, but it should be noted that when they refer to BIOS, they are also including UEFI.
- For more information on timestamps, Tony Knutson for SANS has written an excellent white paper, which can be accessed at `https://www.sans.org/reading-room/whitepapers/forensics/paper/36842`.
- LINUX.ORG has a number of good forums. The Linux Original Content forum can only be posted to by LINUX.ORG staff, so it is a well-informed, non-authoritative resource. It can be found at `https://www.linux.org/forums/linux-security.179/`.

3
Computer Forensics and Evidence Handling

Computer forensics is a subject that covers how to collect and maintain evidence, and how to use it for attribution. In your future career, you will use this attribution to establish what happened and how to fix it, alongside whose fault it was.

This subject comprises about 5% of the 210-255 exam, and is a requirement for catching criminals and bringing about prosecutions. It also allows organizations to attribute blame, which can be important in maintaining compliance with government requirements, as well as maintaining customer confidence.

The following topics will be covered in this chapter:

- Types of evidence
- Maintaining evidential value
- Attribution

Types of evidence

There are a variety of different reasons to conduct an investigation, each with different requirements as to the standard of evidence. In addition to the standard, there is also a burden on the investigator to present the evidence in different ways for each environment.

In this section, you will learn how to differentiate between best, corroborative, and indirect evidence. You will be able to describe why these are, and are not, useful to the investigator.

In general society, forensics relates to the preparation of criminal proceedings. Indeed, public investigations – resolved in a court of law – is also an important category of digital forensic work. Public investigations do not necessarily have to be *in the public domain*; this term refers to the idea of independent judgment.

Investigations can also be held privately – normally regarding a single person of interest – either on behalf of another, or on behalf of a corporation. These investigations are most often judged between the parties, rather than an outside organization.

Finally, an individual may investigate for their own curiosity. There is normally minimal judgment made, or a resultant consequence.

Digital forensics versus cybersecurity forensics

At this point, it is worth noting that digital forensic work is not always the same as cybersecurity forensics, although a lot of the principles are still relevant. Digital forensics relates to any investigation related to any felony, misdemeanor, or infraction where evidence may be found on a digital device. Cybersecurity forensics relates to a subset of these investigations which have specific security implications **for the affected party**. The following diagram shows that incidents that require cybersecurity forensics include those that require digital forensics, but not all cases that require digital forensics will require cybersecurity forensic investigation:

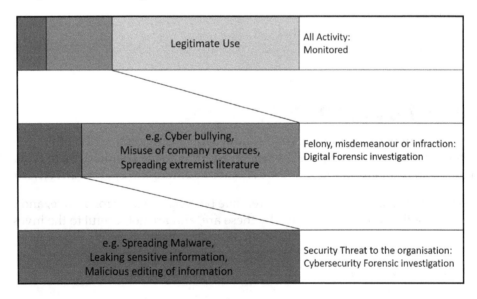

Cybersecurity terminology, and how digital forensics is a broader term than cybersecurity forensics

For example, digital forensic investigations may be required if an individual was found to be planning acts of violence or drug-related crime on their computer. However, these incidents don't actually impact on the security of their host computer, so it would not be a cybersecurity investigation. A case involving an individual planning conventional terrorism through their computer is a more extreme case of this; while there are clearly security implications, these do not affect the cyber domain. Conversely, if an individual was to send internal network diagrams to a criminal associate, this would be both a crime (stealing company data) and a potential cybersecurity threat.

Regardless of the crime, civil action, or whether it is or isn't a cybersecurity concern, digital forensic techniques should be employed wherever possible. In fact, many local and national regulations are in place to compel practitioners to ensure that their own tactics, techniques, and procedures are compliant with, and support law enforcement.

Best evidence

The idea of best evidence relates to a legal principle derived from 18th century British case law, at a time where copies were made by hand and therefore could be unreliable. The rule holds that if an original exists and can be produced, the original is superior to any copies. The US Federal Rules of Evidence further specify that, if a copy is to be used, it is the responsibility of the party relying on that copy to explain why the original either doesn't exist or cannot be produced.

The best evidence principle is used when there is dispute over the contents, analysis, or conclusions drawn from the copy; if a defendant questions the evidence, and there is no good reason why the original cannot be produced, the evidence is inadmissible. Loss or damage to the original may, therefore, undermine an entire case.

An exact (block by block) copy of a mass storage device (for example, HDD/SSD/flash drive) may be possible, but this can be complicated when it comes to files on cloud storage, data in RAM/swap files which are volatile, or transient information like network transmissions. In general, a properly created system image and some copies of files can be used in court, although the methods to collect these images may be challenged over time, and it is, therefore, important to keep up to date with statutory guidelines.

The best evidence principle also specifies that the original document/storage/item should be in its original form. This means that issues might arise through the analysis process. It is therefore typical to take a copy of the original to analyze, and to secure the original elsewhere.

Direct versus indirect evidence

Distinguishing between direct and indirect (also called **circumstantial**) evidence is a tricky subject, even in the established legal field, with a number of different instructions given to juries across America and other legal systems. Heeter (Heeter, E.M., 2012. *Chance of Rain: Rethinking Circumstantial Evidence Jury Instructions*, Hastings LJ, 64, p.527.) is one of many who describe the use of the *ubiquitous rain example* to distinguish between the two:

> *"Suppose a man comes inside the building you are in and says to you, "I just saw that it is raining outside." This is direct evidence of the fact that it was raining when the man was outside. Now suppose that the man comes in and is holding a wet umbrella, and has water droplets on his clothes. This is circumstantial evidence that it was raining when the man was outside. It requires you to make an inference from the facts (the wet umbrella and the water on his coat) that it was raining."*

Direct evidence is evidence which seeks to prove or disprove a fact. Eye-witness accounts tend to be the accepted standard of direct evidence, although documentation is increasingly used too. Direct evidence can be false, but still direct; an eye-witness might not be telling the truth, but their statement still relates to the matter at hand (whether or not it is raining).

Indirect, or circumstantial evidence, does not seek to prove or disprove a fact, but a series of other related points. There must be a judgment as to whether – given all the related points – the original fact is more or less likely. The evidence may well prove all of the related points (the man has water on his clothes, therefore he has recently gotten wet), but this doesn't mean that the original fact is proven. (The man could have gotten wet through rain, but was maybe caught under someone watering plants on a balcony above.)

In cybersecurity terms, it is often very difficult to gain direct evidence in its truest sense; a users' actions are carried out through the operating system and are therefore indirect by definition. However, there are instances where direct evidence could still be gained. An example might be found in investigating a ransomware attack. The attack is successful and the victim wires the money to the specified account. When someone comes to collect the cash, this directly links this individual to the original crime.

Instead, suppose the cash gets collected by some co-conspirators and delivered to the attacker. The presence of the money in his/her house would only be indirect evidence that they committed the attack. The burden is still on the investigator to prove that the money did, in fact, originate from this crime.

Corroborative evidence

Corroborative evidence is evidence which supports a theory that was deduced from initial evidence (either direct or indirect, best, or a copy). This evidence is used to confirm the proposition, or as a backup plan if the initial evidence is challenged. Corroborative evidence in the case of the rain example would be a second person coming in wet, or the local weather forecaster saying that rain is currently falling.

These bits of evidence support the direct evidence given by the man (the man's statement) and the indirect evidence given by the clothing and umbrella. The following diagram demonstrates an extended rain example, complete with corroboration, direct, and indirect evidence examples. The TV weather forecast is indirect, because the forecast is generically about the area, rather than the localized, specifically-outside-your-office weather. This would be different if it was an outside broadcast and the reporter happened to be outside your office:

Extended version of the rain example

Corroborative evidence in a ransomware attack might be that the attacker was seen meeting the co-conspirators and receiving cash, along with communications discussing the attack and subsequent money collection. Neither the meeting, nor the communications, are direct evidence – it can be easily argued that the discussions were hypothetical and that the cash was unrelated – but both events do support the other evidence, thus linking the attack to the money and the attackers.

Maintaining evidential value

Creating an image of a device allows the original to be preserved, thus protecting information from damage and specifically protecting it during analysis.

In this section, you will learn to explain what altered and unaltered disk images are, and how these can be used in evidence.

An image in which block by block copying is possible, sometimes referred to as a **physical copy**, image retains every block, regardless of whether they are free, unallocated space, or if they contain a file. As discussed in the previous chapter, mass storage devices rarely have truly blank space from the time they have left the factory. Virtual memory pages/swap files, previously deleted files, metadata, and auto recovery information all leave a trace among the free space. A physical copy may, therefore, yield information that a **logical copy** (a copy of all the files) might not.

A generally accepted practice is to take two images at every stage of the investigation; one to analyze, and one as a reference copy. This should allow investigators to demonstrate that their analyses are repeatable, and therefore that their copy is *as good as* the best evidence original.

Altered disk image

Any form of investigation on digital evidence can result in the contamination of or damage to the original data. With Ext4, for example, simply opening the data will change the **accessed** timestamp. Creating a logical copy of a file in NTFS will make a new **create** timestamp, even though the **last modified** date will not change. With any of these changes, the evidence would no longer be in the original form, and therefore could not be called best evidence.

In the following screenshot, the router checks the compressed image checksum to check that it's as expected and realizes that changes have been made. This is a much shorter hash than MD5 (this one is CRC-32, so 32 bits, rather than the 128 bits for MD5), so it has more collisions. This is suitable for checking basic identity, but is combined in Cisco iOS with other methods for verifying the image's integrity. The operating system image is rejected on this basis:

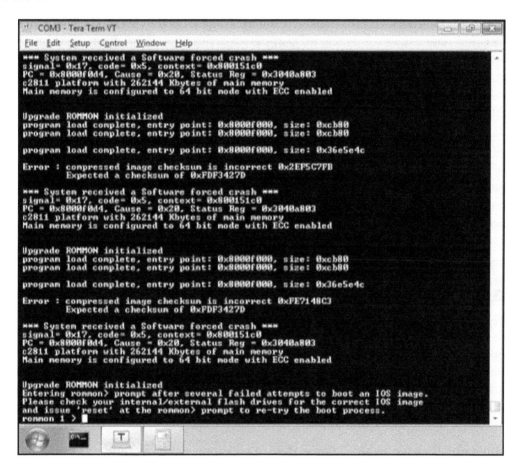

Attempting to load a modified image onto a Cisco 2811 Router.

Despite not being best evidence, an altered disk image is not of zero value. An investigator may have to alter the information on an image as part of the process. An example of this might be opening a file in a hex editor to review its contents, or intentionally running a piece of malware in a sandbox to observe the process. These actions would change the data on the disk, but it would still be an important piece of evidence.

Unaltered disk image

While making a block by block image is definitely a step toward best evidence, there is clearly still a case that a copy – even a good physical copy – is not the original article. This means that there must be a mechanism to verify the integrity of the copy. The most common method of verifying data in computing is the checksum.

The most common checksum that's used is the **Message Digest 5** (**MD5**) checksum, which was specified under IETF RFC 1321. MD5 applies a series of mathematical algorithms on the image file and its contents in order to generate a 128-bit hash value. A 128-bit value has almost 3.4×10^{38} different combinations, which means that the chances of a collision (two files generating the same hash value) are exceedingly low; if a single hash was attempted per second, and each hash value was stored, it would take longer than the universe has existed to have a 50% chance of a repeat. Comparing just 128 bits is obviously much easier to compare than going through the actual image itself block by block to verify that the image has not been compromised.

If copies of disks/disk images have corresponding MD5 hashes, this is a fair indication that the image has not been contaminated. However, if the case was to progress to court, the original best evidence may still be requested. Practitioners must be aware of the limitations of hashes, as well as the confidence levels associated with them.

Chain of custody

Having created and maintained high-quality disk images, it is important to preserve the evidence and be able to prove that nothing has been added, amended, or removed. The technical solution to this is the creation of the MD5, or another hash, but, generally, courts still require an unbroken chain of custody which follows the device through from its point of seizure to the court case. After all, the suspect could always claim that the images are indeed a copy of the best evidence drive you have in the evidence locker, but that this device was not theirs in the first place.

At a minimum, the investigator's name, date of creation, case name, and number should be included with any image. In addition, the method and time of collection, transportation, tracking, storage, and access should all be clearly documented. After the case, the records and methods of disposal should also be maintained. At a minimum, information on who did what, when from the point of capture (evidence gathering), all the way through to the final use in the court case/disciplinary hearing/investigation should be recorded. The more steps in the process, the greater the risk that the evidence will be degraded:

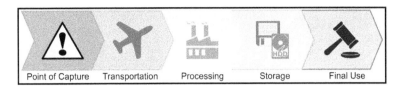

Chain of custody

NIST has additional guidance on the procedures that are required prior to reuse of media that's used for digital forensics so that artifacts from one case do not affect the integrity of the next.

At all times, steps to prevent damage to evidence is very important. **Electrostatic discharge (ESD)** is a specific threat to stored information, but other environmental factors (for example, humidity and temperature of the storage center) must also be considered.

Attribution

A digital forensic investigation will normally attempt to discover how and why an incident has occurred, but is also focused on identifying and holding individuals or groups accountable for their actions. The process and ability to identify and hold accountable is called attribution, and is one of the greatest challenges in the cybersecurity field.

In this section, you will learn how to describe the role of attribution of assets and threat actors in an investigation.

Attribution is important because it leads to a reduction of attack incidence. This reduction is driven from two independent directions. Firstly, attribution allows a wrongdoer to face justice and reduces their ability to carry out subsequent attacks (through incarceration or restrictions on computer/network access). Secondly, attribution and the threat of justice has a deterrent effect.

Difficulties in attribution – and the resultant availability of anonymity – leads to a system where users act with impunity. This is seen in real life, from playground bullying through to state on state espionage.

Asset attribution

Asset attribution describes the act of establishing ownership of a physical or digital asset. Physical assets might include endpoints devices, network devices, or even smaller items like removable media or transmission devices. A digital asset might include books, code, programs, or other intellectual property.

The easiest cases of attribution are where one or both parties volunteer information about the asset which may not be public knowledge. This could be information that's hidden within a file, for example, comments in non-functional lines of code, unique fonts tags within a document, hidden codes within music tracks, or watermarks on printed works.

Assets can also be attributed without any potential owner coming forward, although this can be more difficult. Asset attribution can be done by examining the asset itself for potential identifying features – commenting styles that can be compared to other works, digital signatures or remnants of digital signatures, or even names and email accounts associated with the asset. This method of attribution can be complicated by the deliberate implication of others, or obfuscation (hidden, contradictory, or confusing information) by the real owner.

The following diagram shows some of the parallel methods of asset and actor attribution that are used digitally and in the non-digital space. Digital rights management became prevalent around 2005, at the peak of peer-to-peer file sharing; it was the digital equivalent of a receipt, but placed significant restrictions on legitimate users (remember the availability principle?). In retaliation, SharpMusique worked to remove DRM from Apple iTunes.

Attribution can be self-certified, for example, using a digital signature, which is similar to signing for credit/debit card transactions, or signing a contract. This system relies on trust; that is, the signature on the back of the card is only used by the legitimate user.

Government-issued IDs like a driving license allow vendors to be more confident of the signature. This idea has started to migrate online, with the use of central identity authorities like Facebook, Google, and Apple, which might alleviate cross-platform copyright claims:

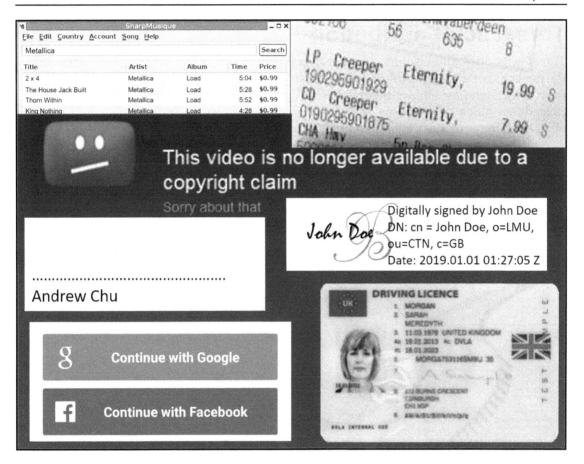

Forms of digital asset and identity checking

Another method of asset attribution works on a similar premise to chain of custody. If an unbroken chain of transactions can be established, this would tie an asset to individuals through time, and could be used to identify the originator. This ledger concept – combined with a system for storing, sharing, and synchronizing – forms the basis for a distributed ledger, with blockchain being one implementation of this technology.

Threat actor attribution

Threat actor attribution is important because it helps to prevent further attacks. Knowing the person(s) or group(s) behind an attack can assist cybersecurity professionals and help them understand the aims of the threat actor, predict the tactics, techniques, and procedures which might follow, search for the point of entry (including attack vector and other enabling activities), and strengthen defenses.

Digital devices often betray information like user, device type, and location, but these can also be faked to *muddy the water* or deliberately implicate somebody else. It is the role of the security investigator to work out what is going on! The following diagram shows a person intending to post anonymously, but the metadata in their image actually reveals their GPS location, which can be mapped using open source mapping:

How anonymous are digital actions?

All of these benefits are additional to the ability to prosecute; many corporations and institutions may not want to seek prosecution for reputational, financial, or security reasons. Attribution is still important to affected corporations and institutions for the preceding reasons.

The investigation of the WannaCry ransomware attack provides a few good examples of direct, indirect, and corroborative evidence toward threat actor attribution. Upon analyzing the WannaCry malware, a number of pieces of circumstantial evidence became apparent. Direct evidence found by the FBI linked a series of email accounts to the attack, each associated with an individual with alleged links to North Korea. The use of a font tag for Hangul (the Korean alphabet) was found, which indirectly corroborated this attribution.

Code samples, including the style of commenting and pseudorandom sequences for domains that are used, also suggested that the keyboard layouts and linguistic structures were likely to be of a non-native English speaker – further circumstantial corroboration.

Complexity, in this case, was the reuse of code that was used in other attacks, and the apparent **modular** nature of the malware. This, added to the use of Tor exit nodes, can be seen as steps being taken to introduce doubts into the attribution.

Summary

Investigating a cyber attack, or even just maintaining IT assets, may uncover evidence against an individual or group. Gathering this evidence can contribute toward criminal charges, and/or dismissal or further investigation. In order to maintain the value of the evidence, investigators must be careful to gather, process, and store evidence appropriately.

The best evidence is the original copy, closely followed by a physical copy which has an identical hash to the best evidence. In the absence of these, logical copies may still be useful.

Evidence that relates directly to the incident can be supported by other evidence. This evidence might demonstrate a threat actor's capabilities or motive, or that tools or assets were owned by them. This can all help attribute an incident with that individual.

Questions

1. Which definition best describes corroborative evidence from the point of view of a cybersecurity investigator?
    1. Evidence which stands alone and would be admissible, in the current format, in court
    2. Evidence which supports the conclusions made from a primary piece of evidence
    3. Evidence which directly contradicts the primary evidence
    4. Evidence which requires an explanation from "expert" testimony
2. An investigator discovers evidence of a crime on a client's hard drive. They copy the files from the client's drive to removable storage, creating the required documentation, and pass this on to the police. Which statement about the quality of the evidence is most suitable?
    1. The evidence is not "best" evidence as it doesn't attribute the files to the identified client
    2. The evidence has been contaminated by being copied and therefore won't be admissible in court
    3. The evidence is a "logical" copy, which will have degraded value compared to the original drive
    4. The evidence is the best evidence and can be submitted directly to court
3. In the situation in *Question 2*, what could the investigator have done to improve the chances of prosecution?
    1. Produced a physical copy of the drive using block-by-block copying
    2. Produced two copies of the removable storage using a hashing algorithm to check that both sets of removable storage were identical
    3. Used software (for example, Recuva) to undelete any other files on the drive before copying them
    4. Installed spyware on the client's drive to monitor the crime and collect more evidence
4. Which of the following pieces of information should accompany data through the chain of custody?
    1. MAC addresses and serial numbers
    2. The case number
    3. Who the evidence is about
    4. When the evidence was collected, moved, or accessed

5. After making which type of copy can the original device be returned to the owner without having to be examined repeatedly?
    1. A physical, verified copy of the drive, including free and unallocated blocks.
    2. A logical copy of the drive's files.
    3. A copy of the drive – including hidden files – made on an identical, but brand-new hard drive.
    4. You can never return the device to the owner if it might be needed later in court.

6. What are the benefits of creating a hash of any disk image?
    1. Comparing hashes is a quick method of verifying that two images are identical and therefore that one has not been changed.
    2. Creating hashes is a good way of encrypting data.
    3. Creating hashes is a method of signing data as an investigator.
    4. Comparing hashes is a way of proving that the image has been created correctly from the physical drive.

7. Why is it important to attribute an incident to a threat actor?
    1. To catch criminals
    2. To deter future attacks
    3. To understand tactics, techniques, and procedures
    4. All of the above

8. Which of the following best describes the benefits of a physical disk copy?
    1. A physical disk copy allows for multiple tests to be carried out without risking damage to the original drive.
    2. A physical disk copy allows the drive's contents to be compressed
    3. A physical disk copy allows the drive's contents to be preserved, even if the original drive is destroyed
    4. A physical disk copy allows the files to be available in court

9. Which of the following is most likely to be considered the "best" primary evidence?
    1. A logical copy of the USB drive which was the point of entry for malware onto the network
    2. A network log detailing the spread of malware on the network
    3. The original USB drive which was the point of entry for malware onto the network
    4. A physical copy of the USB drive which was the point of entry for malware onto the network

10. Which of the following would be a suitable course of action while maintaining chain of custody?
    1. Emailing a file from one investigator to another
    2. Uploading a file to a shared drive
    3. Physically transporting a mass storage device containing the file from one investigator to another
    4. Physically transporting a mass storage device containing the file, plus the MD5 hash, from one investigator to another

Further reading

- A report on the WannaCry ransomware attack can be read at the website of CISCO's threat intelligence arm (TALOS). This can be found at `https://blog.talosintelligence.com/2017/05/wannacry.html`.
- A copy of the FBI affidavit in United States of America vs PARK JIN HYOK, primarily regarding the Sony Pictures hack 2014, but including references to the WannaCry attack, can be read at `https://www.justice.gov/opa/press-release/file/1092091/download`.

Section 2: Intrusion Analysis

Collecting evidence and using this in an internal investigation (disciplinary hearing) or in an external investigation (criminal proceedings) is dependent on actually identifying that an intrusion has occurred.

By the end of this section, readers should be able to analyze data from a range of security platforms and identify an intrusion. This includes filtering and grouping information from network logs, and a range of security software packages, to identify patterns indicating an anomaly, and to use these in combination to specify the key threat and/or vulnerability that these could indicate.

The following chapters are included in this section:

- Chapter 4, *Identifying Rogue Data from a Dataset*
- Chapter 5, *Warning Signs from Network Data*
- Chapter 6, *Network Security Data Analysis*

4
Identifying Rogue Data from a Dataset

A **regular expression** (**regex**) is a sequence of characters that defines a search expression. A regex enables security professionals to quickly sift through large datasets, grouping data entries, highlighting signs of rogue data, and identifying patterns within it.

This short chapter teaches you about regexes, which are specifically referenced in *section 2.1* in the 210-255 specification, and always makes an appearance as one of the questions in the exam.

The following topics will be covered in this chapter:

- Using regexes to find normal characters
- Using regexes to find characters in a set
- Using regexes to extract groups of characters
- Using regex logical operators

The techniques shown (specifically the regex strings used) have been created for demonstrating the concepts. They are not the most efficient way of performing some of these searches, although they will work.

Using regexes to find normal characters

In this section, you will learn how to create regex statements that check for the letter, number, and optional formatting characters and character combinations.

Matching specific strings of letters and/or numbers works in exactly the same way as in a standard *Ctrl + F* style search, except that it is case-sensitive by default; the search string abc would match the words *crabcake*, *drabcloth*, and *labcoat*, but would not match the channel ABC or the taxi firm CabCo.

The search string 123 would match any number containing those three digits in that sequence. Log files (and other things that contain autogenerated dates) should be labeled in ISO 8601-compliant format (YYYYMMDD), so 123 would also match any log file from December 30 or 31 each year.

ISO 8601 only specifies the order of the year, month, and date (plus hours, minutes, seconds, and so on), but does not specify any additional formatting (for example, 1999/12/31 is as acceptable as 1999-12-31 as 19991231). Thankfully, standard searching is also able to search for most keyboard accessible characters too (including Unicode characters for international users).

The characters ("?$^*()+|.[]\ ) cannot be searched for directly, as they have a special meaning in regexes. To search for one of these characters, you must use the escape character (\) before the character. In order to search for the date 1999.12.31, you would enter the search string 1999\.12\.31. If searching for the escape character itself, this method still works, so, for 1999\12\31, you would enter the search string 1999\\12\\31.

The escape character, which changes special characters to work as normal characters, can also be used to make normal characters special. This opens up a number of **wildcard** characters.

In some search systems (for example, SQL), wildcards are available that match multiple (including zero) characters or single characters (SQL uses % and _, where Microsoft uses * and ?); a regex allows for more granular control over what type of characters are available. A regex can differentiate between digits (\d) and non-digits(\D), alphanumeric (\w) and non-alphanumeric (\W), whitespace (for example, spaces, tabs, or line breaks) (\s) and non white-space (\S), or just any character (.). For each of these types of character (or indeed specific characters), a regex also uses quantifiers, which specify multiple (including zero) characters (*), multiple (not including zero) characters (+), zero or one characters (?), or a specified quantity range of characters ({m,n}).

To match a sequence a number of times, parentheses (( )) can be used, followed by the quantifier.

In the following two diagrams, a regex is used to match all events occurring in the first minute of January 13th of any year this millennium. Compare the use of the quantifiers in \d{3} for exactly 3 digits, \d{0,2} for zero, 1, or 2 digits, and (00:?){2} for the literal string 00:00::

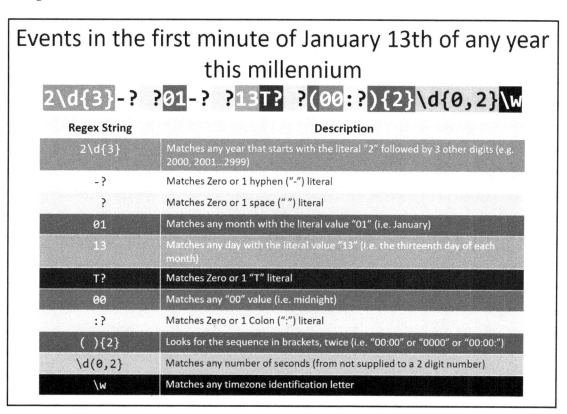

Regex matches examples with wildcards and quantifiers

This regex is used in the following command to filter one large log file into another, filtered file. The *greater than* sign (>) is used to output the results of the left operation into the right file instead of back to the command line. The –E command is used to enforce an *extended* regex, which allows for the {m, n} quantifiers. Notice how the regex string is enclosed in double quote marks ("). This is to circumvent any characters that might be special characters in the command line (for example, the parentheses):

```
[user@Vubuntu~]# grep -E "2\d{3}-? ?01-? ?13T? ?(00:?){2}\d{0,2}\w" largelog.txt > filteredlog.txt
[user@Vubuntu~]#
```

Passing the results of grep to another file

Being able to search through a file is very useful, but the key benefit of this work in the command line is the ability to output each line that is found, into a second file for either reference or evidential/archive purposes. This means that Linux can use its log files much more like a database than a straightforward, flat, serial file.

Using regexes to find characters in a set

In this section, we extend character checking to be more specific regarding the characters that we are checking for. You should ensure that you understand this in both directions—so you can create your own regex statements, and so you can interpret premade statements and which things they will match.

There are times when you might want to be more specific than just digit/non-digit or alphanumeric/non-alphanumeric.

One example might be checking a Cisco router message log based on severity (where the levels range from emergencies 0 through to debugging 7). While an **8** would match the \d search string, this would not be a valid severity level. Equally, if the logs were made from **Simple Network Management Protocol** (**SNMP**), the levels instead range from emergencies being 1 through to debugging at 8.

Alternatively, we might examine a file access log for files with specific security classification identifiers (for example, **U** for **unclassified**, **C** for **confidential**, and **S** for **secret**). A letter **D** would not be a valid security level, even though it would match the alphanumeric criteria.

To select characters from a set, you can enclose the set within square brackets [ ]. This string will then match any single character from the list or within the range. The search string [abcd] will match any of the individual letters—a, b, c, or d—but not the letter e. The same matches could also be made using the search string [a-d], which represents the range a to d. This notation has obvious benefits for long, continuous sequences.

When it comes to using the hyphen to denote sequential letters/numbers, it is worth noting that this requires continuous ASCII sequences. A breakdown of this is in the preceding diagram, but, of particular note, is the fact that the numbers run from 0-9 (rather than 1 to 9, and then 0), and then there are a few punctuation characters before the capital letters; the lowercase letters run from 97-122, separated from the capital letters by further punctuation characters. This means that a sequence like [0-F], which you might expect to filter only characters from a valid hexadecimal representation, would actually also match the **question mark (?)**, **colon (:)**, and the **ampersand (&)** or **at (@)** symbols.

To only match valid hexadecimal characters, the string [0-9A-F] would be used; separating the two ranges with a comma is not recommended, as this will also match the , symbol.

In the following two diagrams, a regex statement is constructed for matching MAC addresses in the Linux format. Notice how the hexadecimal characters are matched to allow for capital letters (standard notation) or lowercase (cisco ios preferred formatting), although the Cisco format will not match, as the separators are in different places in the Cisco format (aaaa.bbbb.cccc instead of aa:bb:cc:dd:ee:dd):

MAC Addresses (Colon Separated)	
([0-9A-Fa-f]{2}:){5}[0-9A-Fa-f]{2}	
Regex String	**Description**
[0-9A-Fa-f]	Matches hexadecimal characters, including lowercase (which is Cisco's default)
{2}	Applies the set for 4 characters
:	Matches the literal colon character (":")
( ){5}	Repeats the enclosed pattern 5 times

Matches:
☑12:34:56:78:90:AB
☑12:34:56:78:90:ab

No Matches:
☒1234567890AB (no colons)
☒123:4:56:7:89:AB (colons in the wrong place)

Regex statement to match MAC addresses in the Linux format

This statement is used to extract the MAC addresses for all networking interfaces on the host as follows. The `ifconfig` command returns the interface information, which is then passed to the `grep` function using the pipe (|) character. Only the matched section is matched, as we have issued the option, `-o`, in addition to the option `E` (extended regex).

```
user@Vubuntu~]# ifconfig | grep -oE "([0-9A-Fa-f]{2}:){5}[0-9A-Fa-f]{2}"
38:DD:D6:CE:AA:DD
```

Using grep to filter the output of other system functions

Being able to use grep on system functions as well as on existing log files is very important. A server might have multiple network interfaces, so this would be a legitimate method of documenting the available equipment. If we were to put another pipe in the command line, we could pass the results of `grep` into a log file for later reference.

Using regexes to extract groups of characters

In this section, you will learn to extract data using regex statements. This functionality allows greater specificity than a standard find and replace, particularly assisting the cybersecurity investigator to filter logs and cybersecurity data.

Grouping and subgrouping regex operators captures sections of the matched text for later use. These groups and subgroups can be referenced using a number. Group 0 is the match for the entire matched sequence; group 1 refers to the first set of parentheses found, and each subsequent set is 2, 3, 4, and so on.

The ability to group and subgroup might be an attempt to capture the source and destination IP addresses from a `tcpdump` output. In each line of packet capture, there are two IP addresses (source and destination). They always follow one another, separated by a > character, as in the following diagram. A search string of `\d{1,3}\.\d{1,3}\.\d{1,3}\.\d{1,3}` would match both of the IP addresses individually. To capture just the destination one, you could instead match the string including both addresses, and use parentheses to extract the addresses separately.

In the following example, notice the three different groups. Because the first and third capturing groups `(\d{1,3}\.){4}` are captured before the quantifier, it actually only captures the last matched octet in the IP address. The second group is the red group, because the parenthesis opens second, even though it is closed after the third group is:

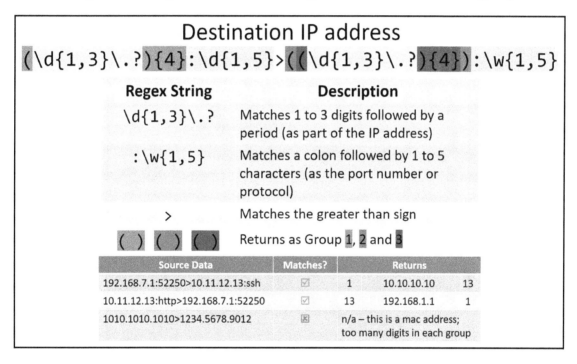

Extracting the destination IP address from a (simplified) tcpdump stream

Notice that, on the following command line, `grep` does not capture the groups enclosed in parentheses. To do this on the command line, the Perl functional `pcregrep` command can be used instead. The option `-E` is used to allow for extended regexes again, but the option `-o2` is added now, which saves the second captured group and outputs this to `DestIPLog.txt`:

```
[user@Vubuntu~]# pcregrep -Eo2 "(\d{1,3}\.?){4}:\d{1,5})((\d{1,3}\.?){4}):\w{1,5}" CommsLog.txt > DestIPLog.txt
[user@Vubuntu~]#
```

The Perl capable pcgrep on the command line

Another example may involve capturing the filenames (less extensions) of files of a certain extension from a list (for example, JPG files from a list of image files). This script extracts all the filenames of `.png` files:

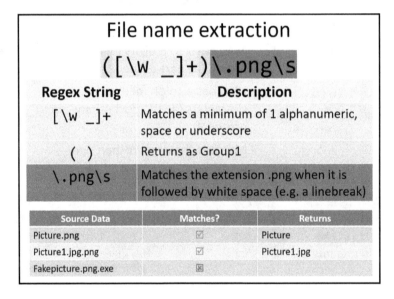

Extracting filenames of all .png files from a list

This can be applied to the output of the Linux command, `ls`, by piping `ls` to `pcregrep`, shown as follows:

Extracting the filenames of all .png files from the ls command

Because operating systems can be set up to hide known extensions within the file explorer, the `Fakepicture.png.exe` file may appear to the user as `Fakepicture.png`. This regex could partially protect the user accidentally opening this file in their search for a picture. Again, `pcregrep` is used, this time with the option `-o1` (to save the first captured group). Because there is no further pipe on the right-hand side, the output is passed to `STDOUT` (and, hence, displayed in the command line).

Using regex logical operators

In this section, you will learn to use logical operators to combine regex strings. This can be used to tailor search terms to be more specific about what variance is permitted.

Logical operators can be used to extend the usability of the match types already specified. Take, for example, the situation with security classifiers from the *Using regexes to find characters in a set* section of this chapter. In addition to U, C, and S, there is the designation *TS* for top secret. If specifying this using the set construct (square brackets []), this could be fixed by matching `[UCST]{1,2}`, but this would also match the invalid TU, TC, and TT combinations.

Instead, the logical OR character (|), (also known as pipe) can be used to separate out a group of options. For the security classifiers, something like (U|C|S|TS) would work.

The logical OR can also be used to combine different sections of a regex string, or to combine two complete strings.

An example would be for examining MAC addresses on a network. In the following diagrams, the regex statement matched MAC addresses in the conventional notation (six pairs of hexadecimal characters separated by the colon (:) character). The Cisco format, however, has three quartets of hexadecimal characters separated by a period. Either of these constructions is fine, but there must be consistency; it would not be possible to have a mix of colons and periods, or four pairs and a quartet. To match MAC addresses in a log file, you could construct two independent regex strings and search twice. Alternatively, separating them using the logical OR would give all matches for either format:

MAC Addresses (Generic)

```
( ([0-9A-Fa-f]{2}\:){5}[0-9A-Fa-f]{2} |
  ([0-9A-Fa-f]{4}\.){2}[0-9A-Fa-f]{4} )
```

Regex String	Description
`[0-9A-Fa-f]`	Matches hexadecimal characters, including lowercase (which is Cisco's default)
`{2}` or `{4}`	Applies the set for 2 or 4 characters
`:` or `\.`	Matches the Colon or literal period sign,
`( ){6}` or `( ){3}`	To make 6 pairs, or 3 quartets
`(	)`	To force format to be either the 6 pairs or the 4 quartets, but not a mix of both.

```
Matches:                        No Matches:
☑1234.5678.90AB                 ☒1234567890AB
☑1234.5678.90ab                 ☒123.4567.89AB
☑12:34:56:78:90:AB              ☒12:34:56:78.90ab
☑12:34:56:78:90:ab              ☒12.34.56.78.90.ab
```

MAC address matching for either six colon separated, or three period separated, sets of hex characters, but not a combination of both

On the following command line, notice that the pipe command allows for either format to be returned. Because this regex string has started to get very long, we have saved the search string as a variable, Regex, and used the identifier $Regex to recall the variable in the grep command:

```
[user@Vubuntu~]# regex="(([0-9A-Fa-f]{2}\:){5}[0-9A-Fa-f]{2}|([0-9A-Fa-f]{4}\.){2}[0-9A-Fa-f]{4})"
[user@Vubuntu~]# ifconfig | grep -o $regex
```

MAC address filtering ifconfig using grep

A regex uses the caret sign (^) for a logical NOT, although only within square brackets, []. Outside of square brackets, the caret sign (^) signifies the start of a line, and can be combined with the dollar sign ($) that signifies the end of the line.

This negated set will match any character that is not specified within the set.

Summary

The cybersecurity investigator is often confronted by huge amounts of data. To make sense of it, searching techniques must be employed to filter and/or find data. Regexes specifically when using the (g)lobal search with the (r)egular (e)xpression and (p)rinting all matching lines function (grep), is a powerful tool for matching and manipulating files by name and by content (in combination with, for example, cat).

We have learned that regexes are capable of character matches, such as a standard word processor style search, but also of using wildcards (including \w, \d, and \s) with a range of precision, sets of characters ([ ]) for user-specified options, quantifiers ({m,n}) to create powerful, but shortened, strings for easier entry and readability, and logical operators (| or ^).

Regexes are further able to extract, using numbered groups, denoted by parentheses. Parentheses can also be used alongside quantifiers to repeat a requirement multiple times.

Questions

1. If one of the devices in the network has an address of 10.114.115.55/24, which regex string would represent any address in the network?
    1. 10.114.115.55
    2. 10\.114\.115\.\d{0,3}
    3. 10\.114\.d{0.3}\.\d{0,3}
    4. 10.\D{0,3}\.D{0.3}\.\D{0,3}

The following three questions are related to the scenario and the following screenshot.

`syslog` in Linux (`/var/log/syslog`) captures information about a range of different activities. The following edited log has extracted some of the events between 22:52 and 22:59 on February 2nd:

```
Feb  2 22:52:31 VUbuntu rsyslogd: [origin software="rsyslogd" swVersion="8.16.0" x-pid="797" x-
info="http://www.rsyslog.com"] rsyslogd was HUPed
Feb  2 22:53:52 VUbuntu systemd-tmpfiles[2370]: [/usr/lib/tmpfiles.d/var.conf:14] Duplicate line for path
"/var/log", ignoring.
Feb  2 22:53:52 VUbuntu systemd[1]: Started Cleanup of Temporary Directories.
Feb  2 22:54:48 VUbuntu dhclient[1374]: DHCPDISCOVER on wlp5s0 to 255.255.255.255 port 67 interval 8
(xid=0xc634fb3f)
Feb  2 22:54:49 VUbuntu dhclient[1374]: DHCPREQUEST of 192.168.1.172 on wlp5s0 to 255.255.255.255 port 67
(xid=0x3ffb34c6)
Feb  2 22:54:49 VUbuntu dhclient[1374]: DHCPOFFER of 192.168.1.172 from 192.168.1.254
Feb  2 22:54:50 VUbuntu dhclient[1374]: DHCPACK of 192.168.1.172 from 192.168.1.254
Feb  2 22:55:16 VUbuntu systemd[1]: Starting Disk Manager...
Feb  2 22:55:16 VUbuntu udisksd[1971]: udisks daemon version 2.1.7 starting
Feb  2 22:55:16 VUbuntu dbus[808]: [system] Successfully activated service 'org.freedesktop.UDisks2'
Feb  2 22:55:16 VUbuntu systemd[1]: Started Disk Manager.
Feb  2 22:55:16 VUbuntu udisksd[1971]: Acquired the name org.freedesktop.UDisks2 on the system message bus
Feb  2 22:55:28 VUbuntu anacron[850]: Job 'cron.monthly' started
Feb  2 22:55:28 VUbuntu anacron[850]: Job 'cron.monthly' terminated
Feb  2 22:55:28 VUbuntu anacron[850]: Normal exit (3 jobs run)
Feb  2 22:55:51 VUbuntu crontab[2395]: (ac) AUTH (crontab command not allowed)
Feb  2 22:56:41 VUbuntu crontab[2410]: (root) BEGIN EDIT (root)
Feb  2 22:57:15 VUbuntu crontab[2410]: (root) REPLACE (root)
Feb  2 22:57:15 VUbuntu crontab[2410]: (root) END EDIT (root)
Feb  2 22:59:43 VUbuntu anacron[754]: Can't find sendmail at /usr/sbin/sendmail, not mailing output
Feb  2 22:59:43 VUbuntu anacron[754]: anacron: Can't find sendmail at /usr/sbin/sendmail, not mailing output
```

2. An analyst suspects that a piece of malware has amended `cron`—the Linux task scheduler—in order to run itself. How could the analyst filter `syslog` for only logs related to `cron`?
   1. CRON
   2. cron
   3. [cron]*
   4. [CRONcron]

3. The investigator creates a separate file for CRON, by combining the cron daily, weekly, and monthly files into a file called `analyseme.txt` in the home directory. How could the investigator search this file for all tasks running `nastyfile.exe`?
   1. `grep -i nastyfile\.exe ~/analyseme.txt`
   2. `grep -i nastyfile.\exe ~/analyseme.txt`

   3. `grep -i nastyfile\.\exe ~/analyseme.txt`

   4. `grep -i nastyfile\.exe ~analyseme.txt`

4. The preceding search string did not yield any results. The investigator believes that perhaps the malware renamed itself and edited an existing `cron` task to hide itself. What `grep` command could be used to find events where the `cron` job was either `edited` or `replaced`?

   1. `grep -i[^editreplace] ~analyseme.txt`

   2. `grep -i "(edit or replace)" ~/analyseme.txt`

   3. `grep -i "(edit|replace)" ~/analyseme.txt`

   4. `grep -i [edit|replace] ~/analyseme.txt`

The following three questions are related to the scenario and the following screenshot.

An investigator suspects that suspicious activity on one host is caused by a user who has got round the access controls, and is executing commands as root.

The following screenshot shows a segment of the auth log (`/var/log/auth.log`):

```
Feb  2 15:57:38 VUbuntu sudo:       ac : TTY=pts/4 ; PWD=/home/ac ; USER=root ; COMMAND=/bin/chmod +x alarm.sh
Feb  2 15:57:38 VUbuntu sudo: pam_unix(sudo:session): session opened for user root by (uid=0)
Feb  2 15:57:38 VUbuntu sudo: pam_unix(sudo:session): session closed for user root
Feb  2 15:58:41 VUbuntu sudo:       ac : TTY=pts/4 ; PWD=/home/ac ; USER=root ; COMMAND=/usr/bin/crontab -e
Feb  2 15:58:41 VUbuntu sudo: pam_unix(sudo:session): session opened for user root by (uid=0)
Feb  2 15:59:15 VUbuntu sudo: pam_unix(sudo:session): session closed for user root
Feb  2 16:00:58 VUbuntu pkexec: pam_unix(polkit-1:session): session opened for user root by (uid=1000)
Feb  2 16:00:58 VUbuntu pkexec: pam_systemd(polkit-1:session): Cannot create session: Already running in a session
Feb  2 16:00:58 VUbuntu pkexec[3241]: ac: Executing command [USER=root] [TTY=unknown] [CWD=/home/ac]
[COMMAND=/usr/lib/update-notifier/package-system-locked]
Feb  2 16:03:17 VUbuntu pkexec[3371]: ac: Executing command [USER=root] [TTY=unknown] [CWD=/home/ac]
[COMMAND=/usr/lib/update-notifier/package-system-locked]
Feb  2 16:07:01 VUbuntu CRON[3392]: pam_unix(cron:session): session opened for user root by (uid=0)
Feb  2 16:07:01 VUbuntu CRON[3392]: pam_unix(cron:session): session closed for user root
Feb  2 16:09:38 VUbuntu polkitd(authority=local): Registered Authentication Agent for unix-session:c2 (system bus
name :1.74 [/usr/lib/policykit-1-gnome/polkit-gnome-authentication-agent-1], object path
/org/gnome/PolicyKit1/AuthenticationAgent, locale en_GB.UTF-8)
Feb  2 16:10:16 VUbuntu pkexec: pam_unix(polkit-1:session): session opened for user root by (uid=1000)
Feb  2 16:10:16 VUbuntu pkexec: pam_systemd(polkit-1:session): Cannot create session: Already running in a session
Feb  2 16:12:01 VUbuntu CRON[4855]: pam_unix(cron:session): session opened for user root by (uid=0)
Feb  2 16:12:01 VUbuntu CRON[4855]: pam_unix(cron:session): session closed for user root
Feb  2 16:14:17 VUbuntu polkitd(authority=local): Unregistered Authentication Agent for unix-session:c2 (system bus
name :1.74, object path /org/gnome/PolicyKit1/AuthenticationAgent, locale en_GB.UTF-8) (disconnected from bus)
```

5. Which command prints to screen all lines regarding `sudo` sessions being opened?

    1. `grep -o sudo\.*open /var/log/auth.log`

    2. `grep -o sudo.*open /var/log/auth.log`

    3. `grep sudo\.*open /var/log/auth.log`

    4. `grep sudo.*open /var/log/auth.log`

6. How would the investigator create a file with the times that sessions were opened?

    1. `pcregrep -o0 "(([0-9A-Za-z :]){15})sudo.*session opened" | newfile.txt`

    2. `pcregrep -o1 "(([0-9A-Za-z :]){15})sudo.*session opened" | newfile.txt`

    3. `pcregrep -o0 "(([0-9A-Za-z :]){15})sudo.*session opened" > newfile.txt`

    4. `pcregrep -o1 "(([0-9A-Za-z :]){15})sudo.*session opened" > newfile.txt`

7. Which command would output commands issued with `sudo`?

    1. `pcregrep -o1 "sudo\.*COMMAND=(\.*)]?"`

    2. `pcregrep -o1 "sudo.*COMMAND=(.*)"`

    3. `pcregrep -o1 "sudo\.*COMMAND=(\.*)"`

    4. `pcregrep -o1 "sudo.*COMMAND=(.*)]?"`

The following three questions are related to the scenario and the following screenshot.

A log file, `log.txt`, has been created in Linux. This file is human readable using `cat` or `nano`, and contains a timestamp followed by an activity log. Regexes (`grep`) can be piped to the `cat` command to only show the matching lines of text:

```
[user@Vubuntu~]# cat log.txt | grep
07:05:59.551728 IP 192.168.16.20:ssh > 192.168.10.100:59657 : [ACK] SEQ=5
07:06:45.972341 IP 192.168.10.107:16354 > 192.168.78.8:http : [SYN] SEQ=0
07:06:58.065872 IP 192.168.78.8:http > 192.168.10.107:16354 : [SYN, ACK]
07:17:06.165521 IP 192.168.10.107:13549 > 192.168.22.13:ssh : [FIN] SEQ=1
07:17:07.064221 IP 192.168.10.107:16354 > 192.168.78.8:http : [ACK] SEQ=1
07:17:17.230351 IP 192.168.10.107:16354 > 192.168.78.8:http : GET / HTTP/
```

8. An analyst is looking to output all the transactions that occurred at 6 minutes past 7 in the morning (lines 3 and 4 of the file). What regex string could be used for this?

   1. `07:06:[0-59]`
   2. `07:06:[0-5][0-9]`
   3. `^07:06*$`
   4. `$07:06:[00-59]^`

9. What is a potential problem associated with achieving this with the `cat log.txt | grep 07\W16\W\d{2}.*` command?

   1. The non escaped period sign (.) instead of (\.) matches any character, and, therefore, also matches the IP:port combinations in lines 5 and 6.
   2. The statement matches minutes and seconds, as well as hours and minutes (line 4), because the colons are not specified, instead using the non-alphanumeric wildcard.
   3. The 07:06 section of the timestamp refers to June 2007, and not Hours and Minutes.
   4. The statement should be preceded by a dollar sign($) to denote the fact that the matched sequence is at the start of the line.

10. Which of the following regex statements would extract to group 1 the IP addresses of all devices that supported an incoming SSH connection (for example, `192.168.22.13`)?

    1. `(\d{1,3}\.\d{1,3}\.\d{1,3}\.\d{1,3}:ssh)`
    2. `(\d{1,3}\.\d{1,3}\.\d{1,3}\.\d{1,3}):ssh`
    3. `(\d{1,3}\.?){4}:ssh`
    4. `(\d{1,3}\.){4}:ssh`

Further reading

- This link isn't really for further reading, but there are many regex emulators online that allow you to create regexes, enter test strings, and see the output, along with an explanation. One very accessible site can be found at `https://regex101.com/`.

Warning Signs from Network Data

5

By now, you have learned about the main networking protocols in SECFND or other courses. In this chapter, we will learn how to differentiate normal header content from abnormal and rogue content to conduct an initial analysis of network intrusions.

Protocol headers contain a lot of information, so rapid identification of abnormalities is key to avoiding confusion in the workplace and in the exam. A lot of time can be lost on the exam if candidates cannot exclude normal data rapidly.

The following topics will be covered in this chapter:

- Physical and data link layer (Ethernet) frame headers
- Network layer (IPv4, IPv6, and ICMP) packet headers
- Transport layer (TCP and UDP) segment and datagram headers
- Application layer (HTTP) headers

Physical and data link layer (Ethernet) frame headers

Ethernet (IEEE 802.3) is the most common protocol, operating at layers 1 (physical) and 2 (data link) of the OSI network model. In the TCP/IP model, these layers are combined into a single layer called **network access**.

In this section, we will learn how to describe the fields in the Ethernet frame and how they could betray an intrusion.

The Ethernet (layer 2) frame manages connections between two directly connected devices, regardless of whether this is between a host and another host, a host and a networking device, or two networking devices. The two devices must be connected directly through a single medium (that is, a cable or wireless signal).

The basic structure of the IEEE 802.3 Ethernet frame is shown in the following diagram. The frame itself has two portions; the *red* section occurs at layer 1, and aims to coordinate data transmission. The orange section comes from layer 2. This section coordinates where the data is sent, and also contains information that checks that the data arrived correctly. There are a few other flavors of Ethernet, with Ethernet II (DIX 2.0, or Ethernet version 2) being the most commonly used as it is often used directly by the Internet Protocol. Layers 1 and 2 add data at both the start and the end of the **protocol data unit** (**PDU**). The frame adds 42 bytes of overhead to every packet; the packet is a minimum of 46 (although bytes can be borrowed for the optional VLAN tags), and a maximum of 1,500 bytes in size, so the system could be as bad as 63% efficient, but could be as good as 97% efficient:

1	2	3	4	5	6	7	8	1	2	3	4	5	6
Preamble							SFD	Destination MAC					
7	8	9	10	11	12	13	14	15	16	17	18	19	...
Source MAC						(VLAN Tag)				Type/ Length		Payload	
Minimum size (46 - Length of VLAN fields); Max size 1500												-4	-3
Payload												CRC	
-2	-1	-12	-11	-10	-9	-8	-7	-6	-5	-4	-3	-2	-1
CRC		Inter Frame Separation											

Layers of headers applied to a network transmission

The Ethernet frame has some features that are particularly useful for cybersecurity operations. In the following sections, each field will be discussed, particularly where there is specific relevance to cybersecurity.

Layer 1

The Ethernet layer 1 frame contains information that coordinates data transmission over the physical medium. This medium may be a copper cable, for example, a Cat5/Cat5e/Cat6 twisted pair or coaxial, fiber optic, or wireless. The physical layer is where data is most susceptible to faults and problems. Signals are exposed to electromagnetic interference, physical damage/degradation (for example, signal strength loss or cable breaks), and network device errors.

Preamble

The preamble and **start frame delimiter** (**SFD**) are used to coordinate the transmission of data over the physical medium (fiber optic/copper/wireless). The preamble consists of alternating 1s and 0s, which assist in establishing the speed at which data is transferred.

Imagine that a very important person is visiting. They have an escort of 64 police motorbikes. Imagine somebody reviewing CCTV of their arrival. It is hard for the operator to know which police bike in one image corresponds with one from the next? Have they counted a single motorbike moving slowly, or have they missed several bikes moving quickly?

By having alternating black then white bikes, the CCTV operator can see that the bike has changed position, and therefore that they are looking at a different one. To check that this wasn't a fluke, they can repeat the timings to get better precision. In the Ethernet preamble, the first 7 bytes (56 bits) alternate, which allows the receiving device to improve its timing 56 times to ensure that the bits alternate each time.

Start frame delimiter

SFD is the 8th byte in the Ethernet frame. This byte reads 10101011. Essentially, it changes the final bit to a 1. Therefore, after 62 alternating bits, there are 2 1s in a row. This helps to signal that the preamble is over, and that the frame is about to begin in case any bits were missed (for example, at the start of the transmission).

While the CCTV operator was figuring out the timing, they may or may not have missed some bikes passing by. To help identify which is the vehicle carrying the important guest, they might use something out of the ordinary, like a police horse. Now, instead of counting 64 motorbikes go by, the operator uses the motorbikes to ascertain timing, and then looks for the horse to identify the important visitor.

Interframe separation

Interframe separation was enforced in the original specification in order to give the signal time to pass through all the network device electronics, and then for the network device to cycle (reset) its resources, ready for the next bit of information to arrive. This was originally specified as 96 bits (12 bytes) in order to give a 9.6-microsecond gap between frames (based on a 10 Mbps transmission). Some network devices have reduced their requirements for an interframe gap, but the 96 bits are as specified in the Ethernet protocol standards.

Layer 2

Layer 2 in the OSI model (data link layer) is responsible for establishing a connection between the (correct) two ends of the physical connection. It is responsible for working out which physical interface to send a message out of, and where it will be received. In order to do this, each physical interface has a burned-in address that identifies it (also known as a physical or MAC address). Once the correct interface has been identified, layer 2 is also involved in determining whether the data has arrived correctly using a **Frame Check Sequence (FCS)** in combination with a predetermined algorithm. In the Ethernet protocol, this algorithm is the **cyclic redundancy check (CRC)**.

Addressing

At layer 2, Ethernet identifies devices using the burned-in address. These are 6 bytes (48 bits) of unique identifiers made up of two halves: the **Organizational Unique Identifier (OUI)**, which denotes the manufacturer of the device, and a vendor-assigned address. This arrangement should ensure that each device is uniquely identified. However, some hardware MAC addresses are programmable, which means that uniqueness is not globally guaranteed.

Layer 2 addressing is only used within a logical (layer 3) network. This means that the lack of globally guaranteed uniqueness isn't normally a problem. The network administrators only need to ensure that there are no duplicates *within* the network.

One cybersecurity issue exists when data needs to leave the logical (layer 3) network. When this happens, devices need to identify the location of the default gateway. All data exiting the network passes through this device, and this is identified by its MAC address. Because some devices have programmable MAC addresses, an attacker could change its MAC address (spoofing) to that of the default gateway interface so that all outgoing traffic is directed to the attacker's device instead of to the gateway. This could be used to gain unauthorized access to information (affecting confidentiality), or could be used to deny access to other networks (affecting availability).

MAC address spoofing to impersonate existing devices is particularly problematic in wireless environments, where no physical access to the network is required. Wireless devices tend to make decisions based on signal strength, and will, therefore, associate with the nearest device that appears to have legitimate credentials.

The other key issue with MAC addresses is that layer 2 network devices (that is, switches) must maintain a list of which MAC addresses are where. MAC addresses – being burned in at the point of manufacture – are not linked to the position in the network, and therefore cannot be guessed. Imagine trying to figure out the cell phone number of your neighbor. There is no relationship between their geographic location and their cell phone number. In order to be able to contact them, you would need to keep a list (address book). Network devices do the same kind of thing. Devices are asked to identify themselves using **address resolution protocol** (**ARP**) broadcasts, and the results are stored in the MAC address table.

MAC address spoofing of non-existent devices could be used to pollute the MAC address table. If the MAC address table gets too large, processing time is affected, and *in extremis*, the MAC address table could be so large as to deny service to legitimate users.

VLAN tagging

Virtual LANs are used to reduce the size of layer 2 broadcast domains. This assists in keeping the MAC address table small. VLAN tags can be used to distinguish which virtual LAN the frame belongs to, and hence informs the switch which ports are part of the same broadcast domain.

Changing VLAN tags can be advantageous for an attacker because it gives them access to a virtual LAN that they shouldn't have access to. This can be done by pretending to be a switch trunk port (switch spoofing) and therefore being able to access data from every VLAN, or by double tagging. In double tagging, a device that's connected to a trunk enabled port (on the native VLAN) transmits two VLAN tags in each frame. The first VLAN tag belongs to the VLAN they should have access to, and the second is the VLAN that they are targeting. As the VLAN tags get stripped when they get to trunk ports, the second VLAN tag is then exposed to subsequent switches, and a message hops between the two VLANs.

The presence of two VLAN tags can be a potential sign of VLAN hopping, but there are other instances where this is possible, particularly **internet service providers (ISPs)** using the 802.1ad standards.

Type/Length fields

There are two different forms of Ethernet in common usage. The key difference is in the **Type/Length** fields. Ethernet II is the most common type in use today. It is used directly by the Internet Protocol. In Ethernet II, the two octets (bytes) immediately before the **Payload** indicates the EtherType. This field refers to the protocol used in the layer above so that the data link layer at the receiving end knows which protocol to hand the payload over to.

In the 802.3 standard Ethernet, the 2-byte field immediately before the **Payload** denotes the length of the payload. In 802.3 standard Ethernet, the maximum length is 1,500, so EtherType field values must be greater than 1,536 (0x0600) so that there is no confusion.

Because of this distinction, the value in the **EtherType/Length** field can be used as an indication of which Ethernet standard is being used.

Jumbo frames are frames with a payload length exceeding 1,500 bytes – commonly up to 9,000 bytes. Several vendors, including Cisco, are able to support jumbo frames, which allows for more efficient processing of larger transmissions. In these cases, the EtherType is used instead of a length, and the end of the frame is signaled by the inter-frame gap or managed by the higher layer protocol.

Edits made to this field could cause problems if the receiving device is anticipating an 802.3 frame but receives a jumbo frame instead. This would be interpreted as a collision incident and the device would then drop the packet.

Cyclic redundancy checking

Cyclic redundancy checking (**CRC**) is the algorithm of choice for Ethernet. When the packet is encapsulated at layer 2 (Ethernet), the payload is passed through the CRC algorithm, and a 4-byte check value is produced and attached as a trailer. When the Ethernet frame arrives, the payload is passed through the same algorithm, and the check value is compared to the trailer value. If they match, the likelihood is that both the payload and the check value have been transmitted and received correctly.

A CRC collision is not to be confused with the collision of two frames on the wire. A CRC collision describes a situation where two different payloads generate the same CRC hash value. With a payload of 1,500 bytes, there is about a 1% chance of two payloads generating the same hash value. Therefore, a random/accidental change to the payload will be detected 99% of the time. As the payload size increases (for example, with Ethernet II rather than 802.3 Ethernet), the likelihood of a CRC collision increases.

Network layer (IPv4, IPv6, and ICMP) packet headers

The network layer (layer 3) is the layer that coordinates the transmission of data to other networks (that is, outside of the user's own network). This is particularly important to the cybersecurity analyst because it is this network that informs you whether the threat is internal or external, and therefore allows the operations center to focus its attention on preventing access or segmenting the network.

In this section, we will learn how to describe the fields in network layer packet headers and how they can betray an intrusion. Ensure that you know the difference between the addresses at layer 2 and the addresses at layer 3.

The network layer contains routing information – the addresses identify the device requesting the information, and the resource on which it is held. Where the MAC addresses at layer 2 describe how to get from one device to the next in the line, the IP addresses at layer 3 contain information for the original device and its ultimate target.

IPv4 is the dominant addressing scheme in use. It uses a 4-byte (32-bit) address, which is normally represented in **dotted decimal** format. The 4 byte address contains both the network identifier and the host address. These can be differentiated using the subnet mask. IPv4 has a limit of 4,294,967,296 unique addresses, although many of these are reserved for special purposes, including broadcasts, multicasts, test environments, and loopbacks. The anticipated 45 trillion networked sensors by 2040 can clearly not be supported by this alone (even with the use of private addresses, networks, and port address translation).

IPv6 uses a 16-byte (128- bit) address that allows for several orders of magnitude more (approximately 3 followed by 38 zeros) addresses.

Internet Control Message Protocol (ICMP) is used for network testing, and sits between the network layer and the transport layer. It is dependent on IPv4 or IPv6 for addressing, and must be encapsulated in an IP packet (as if it were a higher-level protocol). ICMP and IP are co-dependent; when IP is implemented, ICMP is implemented alongside it by design.

Internet Protocol (IPv4 and IPv6)

The outline of an IPv4 header is shown in the following diagram. The labels are in terms of whole bytes, in order to maintain consistency between all the diagrams in this chapter. If we search for the IPv4 header elsewhere, it is commonly labeled in terms of bits, so the numbering is 32 bits per line. The IPv4 header precedes the payload – there is no data being added as a trailer like there is in Ethernet. The header is 24 bytes long, which comes off the 1,518 byte payload allowance set by Ethernet layer 1/2:

1		2	3	4
Version	Header Length	Type of Service	Total Length	
5		**6**	**7**	**8**
Identifier			Flags	Fragment Offset
9		**10**	**11**	**12**
Time to Live		Protocol	Header Checksum	
13		**14**	**15**	**16**
Source Address				
17		**18**	**19**	**20**
Destination Address				
21		**22**	**23**	**24**
Options			Padding	

The IPv4 header

The IPv6 header is shown in the following diagram. It contains fewer fields than the IPv4 header, although the header itself is longer (caused by 128 bits per address instead of 32). Again, the numbering is in terms of full bytes, but in this diagram, the two address fields have been shortened to fit better. If the same scale were to be used, the **Source Address** and **Destination Address** fields would have four lines each, which also precede the payload. Notice how the first half a byte (4 bits) is the version – the same as in IPv4. This allows the IP protocol family to determine what kind of packet header it should be expecting (IPv4 or IPv6) and therefore where the address information is going to be held:

1		2	3	4
Version	Traffic Class		Flow Label	
5		**6**	**7**	**8**
Payload Length			Next Header	Hop Limit
9		...		**24**
Source Address				
25		...		**40**
Destination Address				

The IPv6 header

Many of the IPv6 fields overlap with the IPv4 fields, so discussions about fields will be carried out in parallel, and we will highlight both similarities and differences.

Version

The first 4 bits in both headers is the **Version**. For IPv4, the field contains 0100 (binary 4), and for IPv6, the field contains 0110 (binary 6). This version field is what allows the layer 2 (Ethernet II) frame to populate its **Type** field. A version field that doesn't contain 4 (0100) or 6 (0110) could indicate a problem.

IPv4: Internet Header Length, options, and padding

The **Internet Header Length** (**IHL**) is used only in IPv4. The IHL counts the number of 32-bit words that make up the header. The minimum for this is 5 (no options or padding used). The maximum header length is *15 x 32 bits = 60* bytes since the IHL field can only hold 4 bits, which is a maximum value of 1111 (binary 15).

Options is a rarely used field, and has a number of different purposes. These include methods for dealing with fragmentation, the methods to be used during source routing, as well as a number of experimental features.

The different values for **Options** may not fill a 32-bit word, so padding bits are added in order to fill the word up. This allows the IHL field to indicate the start of the payload data.

In IPv6, the header length is fixed at 40 bytes (as in *The IPv6 header* diagram).

IPv4 – Type of Service and IPv6 – Traffic Class

The **Type of Service** field (also known as **Differentiated Services**) in IPv4 records the different priorities of IP traffic. Certain services need to be prioritized to enable efficient network utilization. Services such as voice services (for example, IP telephones) need to be relatively real-time, where web browsing might be allowed on a bigger delay. The **Type of Service** field allows each type of service to identify itself, and therefore routing decisions can take this into account (for example, when load balancing).

In IPv6, the **Traffic Class** field performs the same function.

IPv4 – Total Length and IPv6 – Payload Length

The **Total Length** field in IPv4 is a 16-bit field that defines the entire packet size (header and payload) in bytes. The minimum is 20 bytes, which would be the minimum size header (with no options) and no data. The maximum size is 65,535 (2^{16}-1) bytes.

In IPv6, a similar 16-bit field is used, although the value does not include the IPv6 header length. If the payload is greater than 65,535 bytes long, the field is set to 0 and it's specified as a jumbo payload.

IPv4 – Time-to-Live and IPv6 – Hop Limit

The **Time-to-Live** (**TTL**), or **Hop Limit**, specifies how long a packet can exist on the internet. The idea is to ensure that packets don't get caught in a cycle, and to remove any packets that do. In IPv4, TTL is related to time, although for transfers (or hops) that take less than a second, this is rounded up to 1. With the increased speeds now available, the likelihood is that each hop takes less than a second; if we consider that an average ping to google.com replies within 27 ms, the **time** element is now irrelevant, and this field operates as a hop counter.

In IPv6, the time component is completely removed, and the field is explicitly a hop counter. With each hop, the field is reduced by one. When a router receives a packet with a TTL/Hop Limit of 1, it will reduce the value to 0 and then discard the packet.

The default value for TTL or hop count is 64, although it can be up to 255, given that it is an 8-bit field.

IPv4 – Protocol and IPv6 – Next Header

The **Protocol** field is used to identify the protocol that's used in the data portion of the IP datagram. This is often the protocol that's used at layer 4. The protocol numbers are defined by the **Internet Assigned Numbers Authority** (**IANA**), so they are consistent across all vendors and implementations. Typically, the values are 0x06 for TCP and 0x11 for UDP, although other important routing protocols also utilize IP, so **Enhanced Interior Gateway Routing Protocol** (**EIGRP**, 0x58) and **Open Shortest Path First** (**OSPF** 0x59) might also show up in the **Protocol** field.

IPv6 adds complexity to this system. IPv6 can sometimes be carried inside an IPv4 packet – a process known as **tunneling**. In this case, the IPv6 header would be a part of the data segment of the IPv4 packet, and the protocol would be 0x29 to denote IPv6 encapsulation.

In the IPv6 header, the **Next Header** field performs a similar role to the IPv4 **Protocol** field. However, IPv6 also implements IPv6 extension headers, which act similarly to the **Options** field in IPv4. In this case, the Basic IPv6 header will reference **Next Header** code 0, or hop-by-hop options, and then each specific set of options after that. The payload follows after all the necessary extension headers have been applied.

IPv4 – identification and flags

When a packet is larger than the path **maximum transmission unit** (**MTU**) (for example, 1,500 bytes for Ethernet II), the packet must be split into fragments by the sending node. In IPv4, each fragment is tagged with a unique identification field to assist with reassembly at the receiving end.

In addition to the identification field, flags are used to control how fragmentation occurs. If a packet is marked **Don't Fragment** (**DF**), but the packet is too large to send without doing so, the packet is dropped. If the **More Fragments** (**MF**) flag is present, but no more follow, the field will eventually time out without being sent on.

In IPv6, extension headers are used to control fragmentation.

Source and destination addresses

Source and destination addresses in IP remain consistent from the source to the destination hosts, with individual hops being coordinated at layer 2. One instance where this is important is if changes are made to these addresses during transmission, or if the source address doesn't appear to be from the right address. For example, source addresses might be changed to subvert access control lists, or to direct traffic incorrectly. This could be to allow information to leave the system (for example, by sending a request from a legitimate host, but having the return address outside the corporation), or as a means of hiding the originator's identity.

ICMP

The ICMP header is a 32-bit extension to an IP carrying protocol number 1 (0x01). Each ICMP datagram varies in structure, depending on the type of ICMP message it is. The first two bytes are the ICMP type and code, the next two are the checksum, and the following four bytes are type-specific. The payload is then a variable length field of up to 576 bytes.

The most commonly seen messages are the echo request (for ping; type 8, code 0) and echo reply (for ping; type 0, code 0), although messages such as destination unreachable (type 3, codes 0-15) perhaps include more helpful information for network analysts.

Transport layer (TCP and UDP) segment and datagram headers

The transport layer is responsible for providing connectivity support to applications. Services that are provided include establishing connections, providing reliable delivery (delivery confirmation and error detection), and data segmentation, sequencing, and reassembly.

In this section, we will learn how to describe the fields in TCP segment and UDP datagram headers, and how they can betray an intrusion.

The transport layer in particular can be identified by its use of ports. These are used as identifiers for each higher-layer application protocol (for example, web services have different ports to file hosting services). In the TCP/IP model, the transport layer also includes ways of tracking which instance of an application each connection is for (for example, which of the multiple open web browser tabs to display the page in). In the OSI model, this functionality is attributed to the session layer (layer 5).

TCP

The TCP header is shown in the following diagram. Ports are the most distinctive features of the transport layer, and are at the front of the TCP and the UDP headers. TCP controls data segmentation and reassembly, whereas UDP doesn't. There are therefore more fields in the TCP header than the UDP header. The TCP header is 24-bytes long. It contains information that tracks the protocols being used, information that establishes connections, and information that verifies the data that has been transmitted:

1	2	3	4
Source Port		Destination Port	
5	6	7	8
Sequence Number			
9	10	11	12
Acknowledgement Number			
13	14	15	16
Hlen / Reserved / URG ACK PSH RST SYN FIN		Window	
17	18	19	20
Checksum		Urgent Pointer	
21	22	23	24
Options			

The TCP header

The increased TCP header size is one of the reasons why some protocols use UDP over TCP; it reduces overhead and therefore allows for more efficient network utilization.

Source and destination ports

The **source port** and **destination port** are used to track the applications using the data stream. These ports allow connected data to flow through to the right program, and to the right instance of it. Tracking multiple instances of the same protocol (for example, which room is streaming which TV shows) is technically managed at the session layer (layer 5), although it can be managed in TCP and UDP.

There are a number of well-known ports (ports 0 to 1023) that are reserved for specific services and applications (see the following table). Ports 1024 to 49151 are registered ports, which are assigned to requesting entities by IANA for specific processes or applications.

Ports 49151 to 65535 are dynamic, or private ports. These are assigned by the client's OS at the start of communication, and used to identify the specific instance of the client application.

During communication, the IP address, along with the port number, is referred to as a socket. Sockets are typically written as the IP address, followed by the port, separated by a colon. To prevent confusion, in IPv6, the IP address is enclosed in square brackets (for example, port 80 on a server could be written as sockets 192.168.0.1:80 or [2001::1]:80):

Port number	Application	Acronym
20	File Transfer Protocol (Data)	FTP
21	File Transport Protocol (Control)	FTP
22	Secure Shell	SSH
23	Telnet	--
25	Simple Mail Transfer Protocol	SMTP
53	Domain Name Service	DNS
80	Hypertext Transfer Protocol	HTTP
110	Post Office Protocol version 3	POP3
143	Internet Message Access Protocol	IMAP
443	Hypertext Transfer Protocol Secure/Secure Socket Layer	HTTPS or SSL

Table 5.1: Well-known port numbers in the TCP protocol. These are the default ports for these applications, although some servers might use registered ports, or even non-standard ports, depending on their security posture.

In general, requests are initiated from the client rather than the server, so having well-known and registered port numbers allows the client to direct their segment to the correct port number, without having to discover the server's details (like you would using DNS to find the IP address, or ARP to find the MAC address).

Sequence and acknowledgment numbers

Sequence and acknowledgment numbers are used in segmentation and data reassembly. When data is segmented, the segment number relates to which byte will follow. For example, if packet 1 had the first 100 bytes, the next sequence number would be 101. The sequence numbers that are most commonly seen are actually *relative* sequence numbers. The first sequence number is selected at random – any number between 0 and 2^{32}-1 (~4 bn). Such large numbers can be hard to track, so most packet capture software will deduct the starting value from each sequence or acknowledgment number (so as to start at sequence 0).

The acknowledgment number follows a similar pattern, and is effectively a receipt of each segment.

Header length

The header length can vary since the options may or may not be used. The header length field is used to track this in a similar way to how header length fields are used in IPv4.

Flags

Flags, or control bits, are used to denote the purpose and function of the TCP segment. These are used to initiate the three-way handshake that establishes a TCP session, and are also used in acknowledgment reply messages. The control bits are vital to the functioning of TCP. Without the **ACK (acknowledgment)** flag, the sender would continuously send data (subject to application layer timeouts), which can adversely affect network performance. Alternatively, without **SYN (synchronize)**, no sessions would ever be initiated, and there would be an effect on availability.

Flags are particularly important to cybersecurity due to their use in the SYN flood attack and in connection hijacking. In the SYN flood attack, the attacker sends a number of SYN and ACK packets, which forces the server to consume resources to keep track of the connections. As the volume of connections increases, this can result in a denial-of-service attack.

In connection hijacking, an attacker predicts the next sequence number from a live connection and forges a segment to look like the next segment. When this is received and accepted, synchronization is lost – subsequent packets that arrive have incorrect/unexpected sequence numbers. This attack allows the attacker to send erroneous or dangerous information that will be automatically accepted in order to disrupt the data stream and result in a denial-of-service attack.

Window

The window refers to the amount of data that can be received without loss. When data is received, it gets passed to a buffer while it is being processed. If the buffer is filling faster than it can be processed, the window size will be reduced in the following acknowledgment messages to inform the sender to slow down transmissions so that the receiving host can catch up and process its buffer.

Checksum

The checksum is used for the error checking of the segment. The checksum ensures that the header, payload, and other data has arrived as expected. Remembering that there are checksums at other layers too, it is very unlikely that an accidentally modified data stream will present a valid collision at all the layers simultaneously.

Urgent pointer

TCP is centered around the data stream, and each connection (socket pair) can only deal with one thing at a time under normal circumstances.

The urgent pointer is used to send data out of sync with this normal data stream. This could be because the current data stream is erroneous (imagine recalling an email before people have taken the time to read it), or because there is more important data that must be processed first (imagine an important email languishing at the bottom of the pile while you filter through the cat pictures in your emails). The urgent pointer is only used if the corresponding URG flag is also set.

UDP

UDP has a considerably smaller header than TCP. UDP doesn't keep track of segmentation as TCP does, so packets are received and processed on a first come, first served basis. This is acceptable to some applications but not to others, and it comes with the benefit of much-reduced overheads, as well as quicker processing. There is no requirement for UDP to wait for a data stream to be completed before sending the next message, and so there is no need for the many flags to control traffic flow. The UDP datagram header is just 8 bytes long, compared to the 24 byte TCP header. This makes for very efficient data transfer (maximizing the amount of useful data being transmitted per datagram). This comes at the cost of data verification, guarantees of delivery, or datagram sequencing:

1	2	3	4
Source Port		Destination Port	
5	6	7	8
Length		Checksum	

The UDP header

The UDP header contains only the **Source Port** and **Destination Port**, **Length**, and **Checksum**, which makes for a header less than half the size of TCP.

Source and destination port

The source and destination ports in UDP fulfill a very similar role as they do in TCP. The UDP protocols and their associated ports are as follows:

Port number	Application	Acronym
53	Domain Name Service	DNS
67	Dynamic Host Configuration Protocol (Server)	DHCP
68	Dynamic Host Configuration Protocol (Client)	DHCP
69	Trivial File Transfer Protocol	TFTP
161	Simple Network Management Protocol	SNMP

Table 5.2: Well-known port numbers in the UDP protocol. These are the default ports for these applications, although some servers might use registered ports, or even non-standard ports, depending on their security posture.

Again, the ports are specific to the protocol, so UDP datagrams can be directed to the correct place just by the port number.

Length

The **Length** field denotes the size of the UDP header and the UDP data section. As a 16-bit field, it can be anything from 8 bytes (the header size) to 65,535 bytes. However, because the IPv4 header also contains a 16-bit size limit, the maximum UDP size carried by the Internet Protocol is actually 65,507 bytes (65,535 – 8 byte UDP header – 20 byte minimum IPv4 header size). If there are IPv6 headers and/or extension headers, this size limit is reduced further.

When the size limit would otherwise be exceeded (for example, IPv6 jumbo packets), the length field can be set to 0 at the UDP side, with the length being dealt with at another layer instead.

Checksum

Like TCP, UDP has a **Checksum** field to ensure that the packet header and its contents have arrived as expected.

Application layer (HTTP) headers

In this section, we will learn how to describe the fields and their functions within the HTTP header. Note that protocols are fields that appear repeatedly across cybersecurity and networking, so you need be clear about how to identify an HTTP header as being HTTP.

HTTP is an important protocol to know about because it is one of the most common uses of networked devices. HTTP is therefore enabled by most network security policies in some form or another, and is often seen as a *partially open door* by attackers. HTTP requests are used in a variety of different ways during attacks, from checking for sandbox environments, to command and control signals, to communicating data outside of the intended domain.

It is important at this stage to reiterate that HTTP, although primarily used for hypertext (web pages), is a generic protocol that can be used for other tasks, such as name servers and distributed object management systems by manipulating the methods, error codes, and headers, and how they are interpreted by the host applications on either side of the transmission.

The client and server communicate with each other using request and response messages. These consist of a message header and an optional message, separated by a blank line.

Request header

HTTP requests are sent from the host to the server. These are of particular concern for cybersecurity, as they generally flow outwards from the network.

The structure of an HTTP request header is shown in the following diagram. In general, the header is split into a **Request Line** and **Request Headers**. The **Request Line** is a three-part field, consisting of the method, the resource, and the HTTP-version. The **Request Header** contains a dictionary of additional properties, including the types of files, languages, and encoding types that will be accepted in response. Most of these are not in common usage, so further details can be found in the links in the *Further reading* section:

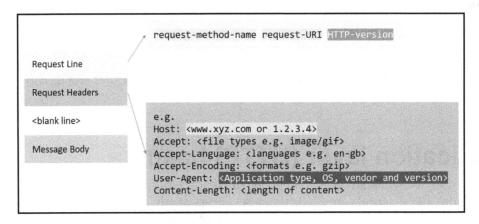

HTTP request message format

For cybersecurity operations, the most important fields to consider are `request-method-name`, URL, and HTTP-version from the **Request Line**, and **User-Agent** from the **Request Headers**. These will be covered in more detail in the following sections.

Request method name

There are a number of different methods associated with HTTP requests, the most common being GET, HEAD, and POST. To find out whether a server will accept each type of request message, the HTTP **OPTIONS** request header can be sent. If the server accepts GET messages, it will also accept HEAD messages, although this is not always listed in the response to the OPTIONS message. Let's go over these methods:

- **GET:** The GET method is used to request a web resource (typically a web page or directory). The response message will include the header and all the associated content. The response message structure is discussed in the *Response* section.

- **HEAD:** The HEAD method is similar to the GET method, but the response returns without the body content. This could be useful in examining the header content before retrieving the content itself. This can be particularly useful if you're verifying a number of GET requests and checking their responses without having to consume too much bandwidth in order to download the whole page each time. This could also be used for verifying that resources actually exist.
- **POST:** The POST method is used to send data to the server. This could be HTML form data, or a file being uploaded. The data being sent is encoded in the request body. GET can be used for the same purpose, but the POST method can send data of an unlimited size since it is in the request body instead of in the header.

The POST query string is not shown on the address box of the browser, as is the case for GET messages, but it is still transmitted to the server in clear text, which means that it isn't secure against packet capture software.

URI

The Uniform Resource Identifier is used to refer to a specific resource (file/application/directory). These can be unique globally, or might be a relative indication. A URL is a globally unique location, which might be the location of a specific file, or the location of a specific host; this could, therefore, take the form of an IP address/socket or a domain name (for example, `packtpub.com`).

HTTP will generally split the URI into a relative identifier in the **Request Line**, and a host in the **Request Headers**.

HTTP version

The HTTP version has evolved a number of times since it was developed in 1989. The most common version is HTTP/1.1, although some sites are using HTTP/2 and successor protocols. The methods, status codes, header fields, and URIs in HTTP/2 have been maintained from HTTP/1.1, so the information in this section is still accepted.

User-Agent

The **User-Agent** (UA) field contains information about the application type, operating system, software vendor, and version of the requesting system. User-Agent helps web servers know what content to send in response to a general request; for example, whether they should be the desktop or mobile versions, what scripting is supported, and which image types are available.

The UA string is normally in the following format:

```
Mozilla/<version> (<system-information>) <platform> (<platform-details>)
                            <extensions>
```

Mozilla is common to all common browsers now, since browser engines are generally an evolution of Mosaic Netscape, or designed to emulate it (in the case of Internet Explorer-derived browser engines).

The system information generally lists the operating system, and in later browsers there are also device details. The platform is the engine that's being used, as well as any qualifiers (see the following examples). The extensions specify any enhanced features that are available (such as add-ons in Chrome):

User-Agent string	Description
`Mozilla/5.0 (Windows NT 6.1; Win64; x64; rv:47.0) Gecko/20100101 Firefox/47.0`	Mozilla Firefox 47 on a computer running 64-bit Windows 7 (Windows NT 6.1). The layout engine is Gecko, which is designed and built by Mozilla. `20100101` indicates that this is running on a desktop (non-mobile device).
`Mozilla/5.0 (iPhone; CPU iPhone OS 10_3_1 like Mac OS X) AppleWebKit/603.1.30 (KHTML, like Gecko) Version/10.0 Mobile/14E304 Safari/602.1`	Safari 10 on an Apple iPhone running iOS 10.3.1. Available features are all those supported by `AppleWebKit`, which operates like Gecko (the Mozilla Firefox engine).

`Mozilla/5.0 (Linux; U;`
`Android 4.4.2; zh-cn;`
`GT-I9500 Build/KOT49H)`
`AppleWebKit/537.36`
`(KHTML, like`
`Gecko)Version/4.0`
`MQQBrowser/5.0 QQ-URL-`
`Manager Mobile`
`Safari/537.36`
	QQ Browser on a Samsung Galaxy S4 (GT-I9500) running Android 4.4.2 (KitKat).
	The Layout Engine is `AppleWebKit`.

`Mozilla/5.0`
`(Macintosh; Intel Mac`
`OS X 10_11_4)`
`AppleWebKit/601.5.17`
`(KHTML, like Gecko)`
`Version/9.1`
`Safari/601.5.17`
	Safari 9.1 running on macOS X.
	The layout engine is `AppleWebKit`.

`Mozilla/5.0`
`(compatible; MSIE 9.0;`
`Windows Phone OS 7.5;`
`Trident/5.0;`
`IEMobile/9.0)`
	Internet Explorer Mobile 9 on a Windows Phone 7.5.
	The layout engine is Trident, which is a Microsoft proprietary engine that has been discontinued.

`Mozilla/5.0 (X11;`
`Linux x86_64; rv:45.0)`
`Gecko/20100101`
`Thunderbird/45.8.0`
	Thunderbird 45.8 on a computer running 64-bit Linux in the GUI (X11).
	The layout engine is Gecko, with `20100101` indicating that it is running in desktop mode.

It is important to look for unexpected strings in the traffic (for example, an IE UA string on a system that only has Chrome installed). This could show that another application is masquerading as Internet Explorer (in order to access more complex content features).

Response header

When a server receives the request, it will respond with a **Status Line** and **Response Headers**, plus the optional **Message Body**. The **Status Line** is a three-part field, with **HTTP-version** being much the same as in the request. **status-code** and **reason-phrase** are the more important parts of the line.

The **Response Headers** have a variety of options, the most notable of which are the **Connection** and **Keep-Alive** fields. A number of other headers are also possible. The **Message Body** is a field with no fixed size and so it would contain, for example, the HTML contents of the requested web page:

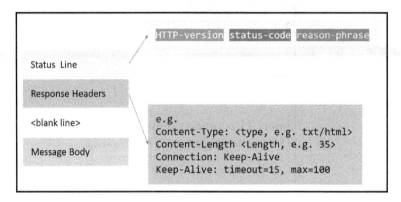

HTTP response message format

The status codes are among the most important for cybersecurity operations centers and researchers, as they indicate what is happening on the server side. It is fairly common to see the 404 error, but other codes do exist, the most common of which are shown in the following table:

Status code series	Code	Description
1xx (Informational): Request received, server is continuing the process	100	**Continue**: The server received the request and is in the process of giving the response.
2xx (Success): The request was successfully received, understood, accepted, and serviced	200	**OK**: The request has been fulfilled.
3xx (Redirection): Further action must be taken in order to complete the request	301	**Move permanently**: The resource that's been requested has been permanently moved to a new location. The URL of the new location is given in the response header, called Location. The client should issue a new request to the new location. The application should update all the references to this new location.
	302	**Found and redirect (or move temporarily)**: The same as 301, but the new location is temporarily in nature. The client should issue a new request, but applications don't need to update the references.
	304	**Not modified**: In response to the If-Modified-Since conditional GET request, the server notifies that the resource requested has not been modified.

4xx (Client Error): The request contains bad syntax or cannot be understood	400	**Bad request**: The server could not interpret or understand the request, probably due to a syntax error in the request message.
	401	**Authentication required**: The requested resource is protected and requires the client's credentials (username/password). The client should resubmit the request with their credentials (username/password).
	403	**Forbidden**: The server refuses to supply the resource, regardless of the identity of the client.
	404	**Not Found**: The requested resource cannot be found in the server.
	405	**Method not allowed**: The request method that was used, for example, POST, PUT, or DELETE, is a valid method. However, the server doesn't allow that method for the resource that's been requested.
	408	Request timeout.
	414	Request URI too large.
5xx (Server Error): The server failed to fulfill an apparently valid request	500	**Internal server error**: The server is confused, which is often caused by an error in the server-side program responding to the request.
	501	**Method not implemented**: The request method that was used is invalid (could be caused by a typing error, for example, **GET** misspell as **Get**).
	502	**Bad gateway**: A proxy or gateway indicates that it receives a bad response from the upstream server.
	503	**Service unavailable**: The server cannot respond due to overloading or maintenance. The client can try again later.
	504	**Gateway timeout**: The proxy or gateway indicates that it receives a timeout from an upstream server.

Different browsers may react to certain error codes in different ways, including different visualizations of the error. However, any captured packet stream will present the data simply as a text stream, with the status line being first.

Summary

Using a layered model of networking (either OSI or TCP/IP) allows protocols to be mixed and matched. In a typical network transfer, the application data is encapsulated in a transport layer frame (either TCP or UDP) that facilitates multiple simultaneous network connections. This segment/datagram is further encapsulated in a network layer frame (normally IP) that coordinates routing, and is then wrapped in an Ethernet frame for transmission over the physical medium between two devices.

At each level, headers are added that track the two ends of the session (source and destination). The way that the source and destination are identified varies depending on the layer, in order to ultimately identify a single application on a single host to a single application/resource somewhere else in the network. When addresses are modified (on the device or in the header), this can open up problems with data going to the wrong people – and possibly to a threat actor.

Sometimes, headers provide functions such as error checking, recorded delivery, and connection establishment. These flags can assist in the reliable transfer of data, but can also be manipulated to create opportunities for attackers, particularly for denial-of-service.

In this chapter, we have learned about the key features of network headers at each layer. Understanding what is normal is key to identifying abnormal data in the network header, and therefore potential signs of infection.

Questions

1. Which addresses are used at which layer?
    1. Layer 2: Physical Address | Layer 3: MAC Address
    2. Layer 2: IP Address | Layer 3: MAC Address
    3. Layer 2: Logical Address | Layer 3: Physical Address
    4. Layer 2: MAC Address | Layer 3: Logical Address
2. How do switches know which interface to send a frame out of to reach a given MAC address?
    1. MAC address table
    2. Interface list
    3. ARP table
    4. Routing table
3. What is the function of CRC?
    1. To check for intentional changes made in the application layer
    2. To check for accidental damage to frames in transit
    3. To check for intentional changes made to UDP datagrams by an attacker
    4. To check for segments arriving out of order in TCP

4. How does IPv6 prevent packets persisting on the internet (for example, in a routing loop)?
    1. Time-to-Live field
    2. Hop limit
    3. Extension headers
    4. Sequence number

5. Which application can use either TCP or UDP on port 53?
    1. Dynamic Host Configuration Protocol
    2. Domain Name Service
    3. Hypertext Transfer Protocol
    4. Post Office Protocol version 3

6. The TCP segment has the source port 51523 and a destination port of 22. Which of the following statements could be true?
    1. The segment is coming from a registered port
    2. The segment is a request to start an SSH session
    3. The segment is the server sending a certificate request
    4. The segment contains data in clear text

7. A developer has created a short script for testing a web resource. The script produces HTTP requests and records the status of the response. Which of the following is true?
    1. The Request Line POST /index.html HTML/1.1 will return status 501
    2. The Request Line GET /index.html HTML/1.1 will always return status 100
    3. The Request Line HEAD /index.html HTML/1.1 will return the same status as GET /index.html HTML/1.1
    4. The Request Line Post /index.html HTML/1.1 will return status 200

The next three questions refer to the following scenario.

A user is struggling to follow a hyperlink to a web resource at `https://www.packtpub.com`, and receives the following error:

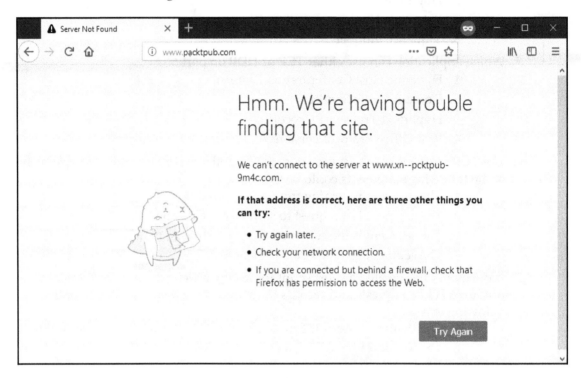

Problem following a link

The user followed a previous link to `https://www.packtpub.com/tec` and received the following error:

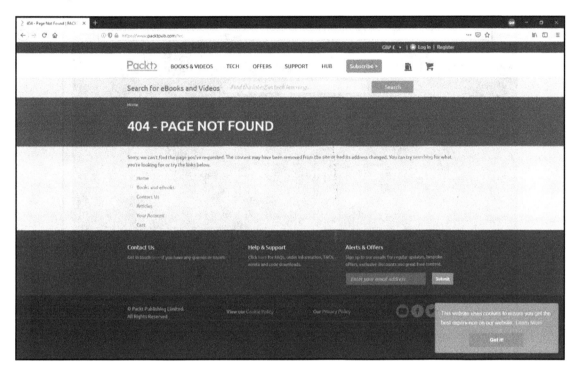

Previous errors

The administrator has conducted a test from the affected computer and received the following response:

```
Command Prompt                                        —   □   ×

Microsoft Windows [Version 10.0.17134.376]
(c) 2018 Microsoft Corporation. All rights reserved.


C:\Users\Admin>ping packtpub.com

Pinging packtpub.com [83.166.169.231] with 32 bytes of data:
Request timed out.
Reply from 83.166.169.231: bytes=32 time = 27ms TTL=121
Reply from 83.166.169.231: bytes=32 time = 26ms TTL=121
Reply from 83.166.169.231: bytes=32 time = 26ms TTL=121

Ping statistics for 83.166.169.231:
    Packets: Sent = 4, Received = 3, Lost = 1 (25% loss),
Approximate round trip times in milli-seconds:
    Minimum = 26ms, Maximum = 27ms, Average = 26ms
```

Ping success message

8. What protocol has been used to successfully reach `packtpub.com`?
    1. POP3
    2. ICMP
    3. DHCP
    4. SNMP

9. What is the cause of the error when navigating to `https://www.packtpub.com/tec`?
    1. The server for `packtpub.com` has not been resolved to an IP address
    2. There is no SSL version of `www.packtpub.com`
    3. The `tec` directory doesn't exist on the server of `www.packtpub.com`
    4. The `tec` directory is behind a paywall, so the user needs to resubmit the request with their username and password

10. What could be the cause of the original DNS not resolved problem, given the other evidence?
    1. The `packtpub.com` server is offline
    2. The domain name includes a rogue character that appears normal but is incorrect
    3. The DNS server for the host is offline
    4. The IP address for the host has been incorrectly configured

Further reading

- The IEEE 802.3 standards (Ethernet) are available through the IEEE GET program. Registration for this program can be carried out at `https://ieeexplore.ieee.org/browse/standards/get-program/page/series?id=68`.
- Nanyang Technological University (Singapore) has an excellent, comprehensive HTTP guide. This is available at `https://www.ntu.edu.sg/home/ehchua/programming/webprogramming/HTTP_Basics.html`.
- Mozilla has also produced a very detailed guide on HTTP headers. This is available at `https://developer.mozilla.org/en-US/docs/Web/HTTP/Headers`.

Network Security Data Analysis 6

Network security data comes in from a number of different sources. Packet captures are important ways of identifying an intrusion into a system, but there are other systems that detect, defeat, and deter threats. This data is vital to see what is being sent across the network, by and to whom, but most importantly, to determine what is causing this.

We will look at different network security files and identify different bits of information. This is always a question in the 210-255 exam and an important part of the job of a SOC.

The following topics will be covered in this chapter:

- PCAP files and Wireshark
- Alert identification
- Security technologies and their reports
- Evaluating alerts
- Decisions and errors

PCAP files and Wireshark

In the last chapter, we looked at network headers and what they might indicate. Ordinarily, though, the network headers are not revealed to the end user; when a user visits a web page, they are presented with the results: the application payload or response body. To view the header (and other network fields), cybersecurity workers must inspect the packets as they appear **on the wire**.

Packet capture software allows cybersecurity workers to do this. The most common applications are tcpdump (which works on the command line) and Wireshark (which includes analysis tools and a **graphical user interface (GUI)**).

PCAP files are the standard format for storing captured network data. Identifying the headers in each layer is a key skill for cybersecurity investigators.

The following sections are based on the captured TCP stream of an HTTP session. The imagery will all relate to Wireshark, as the 210-255 specification requires candidates to be familiar with the Wireshark menu structure.

Viewing packet details

Wireshark can be used to capture data, but can also be used to open PCAP files from other sources (for example, tcpdump). You open a PCAP file through **File | Open**, which will reveal the list of frames that were captured. The following screenshot is a captured DNS request for www.packtpub.com, which is being submitted to the name server (UDP port 53) at 208.67.220.220 (OpenDNS). The **Packet Details** pane (highlighted) separates out all the details into the appropriate layers, with each one expandable using the arrows on the left-hand side of the section header:

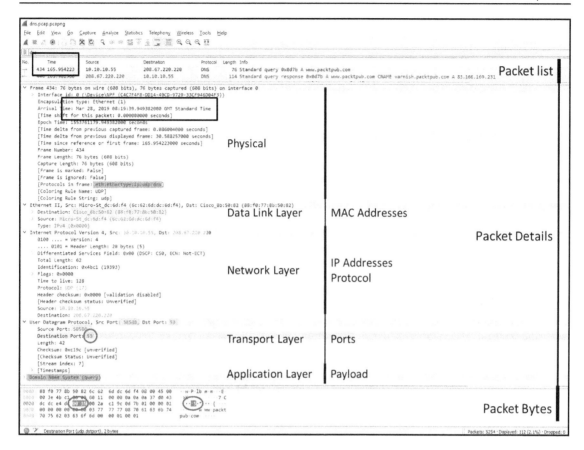

Wireshark main window

The addresses, ports, protocols, and payloads fields under each layer are highlighted (color coded as per the previous chapter); notice how the details in each header are presented as a **header: value** pair. This allows the operator to easily establish what each data point refers to.

When each item is selected, the relevant section in the **Packet Bytes** pane (bottom) is also highlighted, so the operator can see the continuous data stream in hexadecimal format or the dissected data with related labels. Three instances of the destination port are highlighted. In the **Packet Details** pane, Wireshark correctly displays this as an integer value (53). In the **Packet Bytes** pane, the value is 00 35 (53 in hex), and in the ASCII version, it is −5 (the 0 character is a special character, and the 53 character is the 5 digit).

`tcpdump` can present data on the command line, although this is, of course, less user-friendly than the Wireshark GUI. The following screenshot is one `tcpdump` view of the same DNS request as we saw in the preceding section (equivalent to the **Packet Bytes** pane). Notice that there are some formatting differences between `tcpdump` and Wireshark. One noticeable difference is how the data link layer information is presented in the line rather than in the hex and ASCII representation as it is in Wireshark.

More importantly, compare the `08:19:39.949382` timestamp in `tcpdump` to the `165.954223` timestamp in the Wireshark **Packet list** pane. This is because in the **Packet list** pane, the timestamps are relative time stamps, whereas the `tcpdump` timestamp is the actual time of capture. In Wireshark, you can verify this in the **Packet Details** pane (compare the two boxed values), as shown in the following command-line view:

```
[ac@VUbuntu]~$ tcpdump -ns 0 -eX -r dns.pcap
08:19:39.949382 6c:62:6d:dc:6d:f4 > 88:f0:77:8b:50:82, ethertype IPv4 (0x0800),
length 76: 10.10.10.55.58588 > 208.67.220.220.53: 3451+ A? www.packtpub.com. (3
4)
        0x0000:  4500 003e 4bc1 0000 8011 0000 0a0a 0a37  E..>K..........7
        0x0010:  d043 dcdc e4dc 0035 002a c19c 0d7b 0100  .C.....5.*...{..
        0x0020:  0001 0000 0000 0000 0377 7777 0870 6163  .........www.pac
        0x0030:  6b74 7075 6203 636f 6d00 0001 0001       ktpub.com.....
```

Command-line view of a PCAP in hex and ASCII view (-X) using tcpdump. Color coding has been applied to match the highlights from the preceding Wireshark screenshot

Notice that achieving this specific view requires some tweaking of the parameters provided to `tcpdump`. This is beyond the scope of this course; the `tcpdump` man page is listed in the *Further reading* section.

Extracting data using Wireshark

Wireshark can also extract data from a number of different TCP streams. This is particularly important for cybersecurity analysts from HTTP and TFTP, although **Server Message Block (SMB)** information can also sometimes be useful.

To extract data from a stream, the **File** | **Export Objects** | (**HTTP...** | **TFTP...** | **SMB...**) menu option allows users to select a file from the stream and reconstitute it from the packet data. The following screenshot shows the process of extracting a portable executable file (PortRptr.exe) from an HTTP stream:

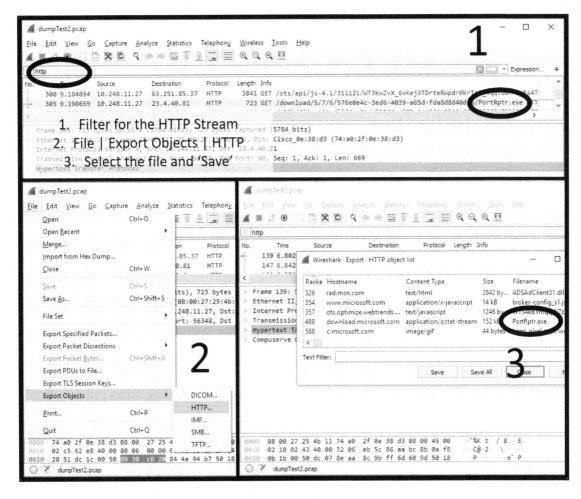

Extracting data from a TCP stream

Notice that this feature allows any text, image, or application to be extracted from the entire PCAP file. Where there is a long stream with multiple files, the packet ID help us to find the item or the text filter box can be used to search for a given filename.

Alert identification

There are a variety of different ways in which an alert can be identified. Different types of incidents will tend to be associated with different artifact elements, which can be used to identify them. This section will cover some of the common artifacts associated with alerts, and what they can be used to indicate.

Remember those artifact elements are only an indication and can have greater or lesser degrees of accuracy and precision.

Network indicators

This section discusses identifying features of threats in network headers. These do not require inspection of the payload. While detecting threats and alerting system administrators is never done in isolation, the split between network indicators and payload indicators can be useful for beginners in the field.

IP address (source/destination)

IP addresses are a useful artifact to note because the public IP address does not change from the source to the destination host. When the source/destination is within the network, **Network Address Translation** (**NAT**) or **Port Address Translation** (**PAT**) may be in operation, but the public routable addresses would remain unchanged.

When threats are identified and classified, the details of these threats are updated and shared in relative real time with other users. In the case of Cisco **Firepower Management Center** (**FMC**), this is either via the cloud or direct updates, depending on an organization's security posture and settings.

IP addresses are logical and hierarchical. The IP address of a given host, therefore, reveals information such as the country of origin, internet service provider, and other information. Certain IP address ranges have a history of being linked with threats, with VPNs, or other undesirable locations. Therefore, requests to/from these locations can be rapidly characterized and filtered. Even if the IP address is not known to be linked to specific threats or undesirable uses, an IP address from a country in which the organization does not typically do business could be an indicator of suspicious traffic. A lot of communication with an IP address in Frankfurt might be typical for a company with a branch there, but for an organization based elsewhere, it might be suspicious. In the following screenshot, three different IP addresses in the same range have been communicating with multiple PCs in the network after a suspected iframe exploit:

srcIP	dstIP	prot	srcPort	dstPort	octets	packets
▒.▒.232.172	62.4.84.45	6	3585	80	71107	388
▒.▒.174.14	62.4.84.53	6	3587	80	74828	499
62.4.84.45	▒.▒.174.14	6	80	3585	65723	7
62.4.84.53	▒.▒.232.172	6	3587	80	15760	201
62.4.84.53	▒.▒.174.14	6	3587	80	91267	848
▒.▒.178.45	62.4.84.45	6	3585	80	74347	168
62.4.84.41	▒.▒.232.172	6	80	3586	56610	374
62.4.84.45	▒.▒.232.172	6	80	3585	56611	447
▒.▒.232.172	62.4.84.41	6	3586	80	2626	764
62.4.84.41	▒.▒.178.45	6	80	3586	71703	423
▒.▒.232.172	62.4.84.53	6	3587	80	53257	904
62.4.84.45						
▒.▒.177.16						
62.4.84.53						
62.4.84.45						
62.4.84.53						
62.4.84.41						
▒.▒.174.14						
▒.▒.177.16						
▒.▒.177.16						
62.4.84.41						
▒.▒.178.45						
▒.▒.174.14						
▒.▒.178.45						

Geolocation data from ipinfo.io (Product: API, real-time);IP2Location (Product: DB6, updated on 2019-3-1);DB-IP (Product: Full, 2019-3-2)

IP Address	Country	Region	City
62.4.84.41 62.4.84.45 62.4.84.53	Germany 🇩🇪	Hesse	Frankfurt am Main

ISP	Organisation	Latitude	Longitude
AS13237 International euNetworks GmbH	euNetworks GmbH (eunetworks.com)	50.1165	8.62975

Net flows to a German IP address during a suspected iframe exploit

The number of hosts involved in the internal network (at least four shown here) communicating with the same three IP addresses is suspicious, particularly with the context of a suspected exploit in progress. This might be corroborated by the fact that these IP addresses have not appeared in the logs prior to the exploit.

In Cisco FMC, the **Intrusion Events** tab can be used to list the intrusion attempts by source and destination IP.

Client and server port identity

The ports associated with the client and server can also be used for threat detection. Ports may be used to identify the protocols in use. There are also instances during which a specific (non-well known nor registered) port is used and held open by a specific application. This is typical of applications for gaming consoles and torrent clients.

When there is high traffic to and from a given port, this can be a sign that data is being extracted or malicious applications are being downloaded. Alternatively, **command-and-control** servers might use non-standard ports that allow them to cloak their supported protocols. Cisco FMC security intelligence events can give an insight into known command-and-control servers based on DNS intelligence and previous incidents.

URI/URL

The **Uniform Resource Identifier (URI)** and **Uniform Resource Locator (URL)** can be used to uniquely identify and locate a specific file in a publicly addressable space. There are a number of ways in which these can be used to identify a threat.

Top-level domains can be a useful indicator. The most common sites for most organizations will be hosted at .com or at national domains. Frequent visits to sites out of a locale may indicate a problem, especially if they are in country codes that have less stringent regulations.

Another indicator is the use of randomly generated domain names. These are very common for command-and-control servers, or for when malware checks whether it is in a sandbox environment. A caveat to this, though, is the use of extended sequences of numbers. These are often used in the Far East to remove transcription and/or transliteration issues.

A URL or URI may be associated with specific files on the internet that have previously been identified as malicious. When a file is detected as malware, the endpoint or network protection systems may add the URL or URI to a banned list. To use a non-computing example, it would be like a shop placing a ban on orders from a certain address if they have a history of non-payment.

Payload indicators

Malicious payloads may, or may not, originate from a malicious site. There are plenty of instances in which sites have been hijacked or corrupted by malicious actors. More complex attacks are, in fact, more likely to target trusted organizations as people and systems become better at detecting and blocking dangerous ones.

Inspecting the payload requires the network traffic to be de-encapsulated up to the application layer for analysis. This is obviously a slow process and, to a certain extent, reduces the utility of a layered network model. However, it is only seeing what the payload *is*, and potentially what the payload *does*, that will confirm or deny a threat. The following elements are the broad categories of indicators that might flag a payload as dangerous.

Process (file or registry)

Malware is often considered to be the infected file or files. However, it is often the case that the executable file leaves remnants of itself (which are still dangerous). One method that malware can use to hide is to launch processes rather than run as its own application.

Processes run in the background, and are often named cryptically; Nvidia GeForce Experience driver (**nvxdsync**) is not as obvious as it could be! This allows malware to hide away. Even if the user knows that malware has started a rogue process, it may be tricky to differentiate between malware and legitimate processes.

An example of this is `csrss.exe`, which is an essential subsystem (client/server runtime subsystem) in Win32 (mostly XP and 32-bit Windows 7). The `W32/Spybot.worm.gen` malware often appears as the similarly named `scrss.exe`; worse still, the `W32/Nimda.gen@MM` malware can appear as `csrss.exe` in the process list. The only method of differentiation is that the legitimate `csrss.exe` process is run from the `C:\Windows\System32` folder.

To further hide malware actions, a more recent innovation has been to run malware as a Windows service. The service is run at system startup. Windows can directly launch applications as services in which case the file launching the service will be listed in the `HKEY_LOCAL_MACHINE\SYSTEM\CurrentControlSet\Services\<servicename>` registry entry under the `ImagePath` value. Services can also package themselves as dynamic-link libraries (`.dll` files rather than `.exe`), which cannot operate on their own. A process called `svchost.exe` can be used to host these services, and these will appear in the task manager as the `svchost.exe` process and not the actual application name.

`Svchost` is an important process with many legitimate uses. It is, therefore, important to investigate the underlying `.dll`, which is listed at `HKEY_LOCAL_MACHINE\SYSTEM\CurrentControlSet\Services\<servicename>\Parameters` under the `ServiceDll` value. Each of these variations is shown in the following composite screenshot:

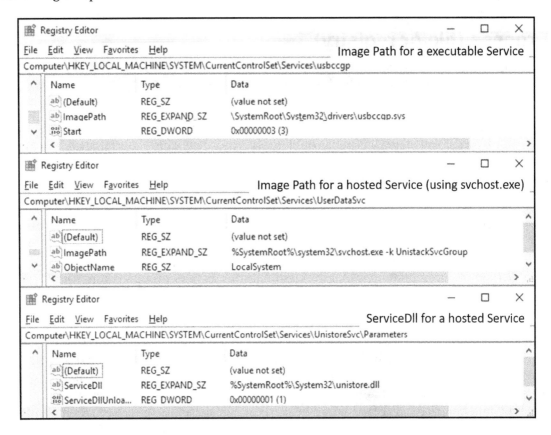

Composite screenshot showing (top) services run as their own executable, (middle) services run through svchost.exe, and (bottom) the ServiceDll run through svchost.exe

The **ControlSet** is the complete configuration used to launch services and other features in Windows. There are always at least two types of ControlSets—one or more numbered ControlSets (for example, ControlSet001) and `CurrentControlSet`, which is effectively the current running configuration on the machine. `CurrentControlSet` is conceptually not stored after a system shutdown. It is a mirror of the loaded numbered ControlSet, which might be the `Default`, `Failed`, or `LastKnownGood` ControlSet. The relevant number identifiers are in the registry under `HKEY_LOCAL_MACHINE\SYSTEM\Select` as individual values as shown in the following screenshot:

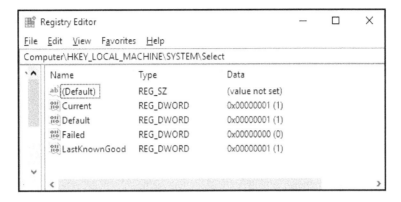

ControlSet registry values

In the sampled system, there is only one numbered ControlSet (ControlSet001); there have been no failed launches on the machine so far, so the value is 0x00000000.

System (API calls)

Malware is now increasingly obfuscated in order to avoid detection. One way of doing this is by packing the payload with other information, or within a compressed file (for example, gzip). The malware can self-extract and reorganize immediately prior to use. The payload might also be encrypted, or a combination of encryption and packing could be employed.

It can often be easier to identify malicious files from their behavior when run. An **application programming interface** (**API**) is the method by which applications interact (through the operating system) with the base hardware. An application (legitimate and otherwise) will typically run through API calls rather than interacting directly with the hardware. This allows the application to function on a greater range of hardware platforms.

Viewing API calls is, therefore, a method that can be used to characterize what the application or file actually does. There is a huge range of APIs that do similar things, but the overall sentiment of the API calls can help to indicate whether a file is malicious or not.

Examples of suspicious activity might include calls to IsNTAdmin, which could be used to check if the user has administrator privileges; MapVirtualKey, often used in keyloggers; WinExec, which can be used to execute another program; or SetFileTime, which can be used to modify the creation, access, or last modified time for a file, and conceal malicious activity on those files.

Again, these API calls have legitimate uses alongside their use in malware. Removing or denying the API call would impact on normal users' behavior; it is the combination of API calls in a malicious way that must be detected.

Hashes

When malware is analyzed (for example, within a sandbox environment) and found to be a confirmed threat, the file itself is hashed using SHA-256, or similar, and that hash is added to the list of known malware. This hash can be uploaded and stored in the cloud to assist other users to detect the dangerous files. With Cisco **Advanced Malware Protection** (**AMP**), a local cache is held, which allows faster processing. If no match is found in the local cache, the FMC can check its own cache. If again, no match is found, FMC can query the cloud. The hash allows for rapid comparison of the file with known threats, even if things like metadata or filenames have been changed.

A parallel could be drawn between hashes and identity verification in casinos. A banned player may attempt to return with a fake name and disguise, but facial recognition would still identify the individual and bar entry.

With the WannaCry example used previously, the domain name that was used to check for sandbox environments was `iuqerfsodp9ifjaposdfjhgosurijfaewrwergwea.com` and, when registered, limited the malware's progress.

There are times when a signature/hash is not a match to known threats but is still dangerous. The Cuckoo sandbox screenshot in `Chapter 1`, *Classifying Threats*, is a clear example of this; the threatening file would not have been detected by every supplier (32/46 at the time of that screenshot).

Security technologies and their reports

There is no panacea in cybersecurity. There are certainly better and worse systems out there, but defending against cyber incidents (ranging from intentional attack to accidental breaches) requires a principle derived from the military: defense in depth.

In the 90s, many organizations were unprotected, but those that were protected typically relied on being behind a firewall. This is a static defense; I liken this to the idea of a fortress or castle wall. The story of the fall of Troy is an example of how this system can go wrong. Once the attacking force was within the wall, they had freedom of action across the entire city.

Instead, defense in depth works to create little pockets of detection and resistance. There are still firewalls, access control lists, and the like, but also antivirus software on the endpoints, intrusion detection, and prevention systems at the boundary and within the sub-networks of the system.

In this section, you will learn to define the different components of layered network defense, and how each technology can contribute information regarding a security event.

There is often a cross over between the different technologies and defense types, so while each is considered independently, some events may fall into several technologies and categories. Several of these technologies use elements specifically mentioned in the previous section, *Alert identification*. If you are unsure about any references, switch back and forth between the sections to consolidate the learning.

Network indicators

As before, this section is split into network indications and payload indications. This should assist in matching technologies to the elements that a cybersecurity operator may be looking to identify. Again, you'll notice that significant amounts of crossover exist between technologies; cross-referencing network and payload indicators, along with other contextual information, will always be the most effective means of identifying threats.

NetFlow

NetFlow is a system that accounts for how and where traffic flows (by IP address and by port). NetFlow allows administrators to measure network usage (particularly peak and average load) and can also be used to provide usage-based billing. New flows are created for each new source/destination socket pair. This means that each communication session should generate two flows (a request and a reply).

NetFlow can be exported for greater readability (as in the image for **Alert Identification** | **IP Address**). The main benefit of NetFlow is to show anomalies. These anomalies could be new IP addresses/ports being used, high traffic volume from certain hosts, or high traffic volume in a given protocol. This can provide some simple IDS capabilities. NetFlow exports will list the source and destination IP address and ports, transport protocol, packet, and byte counts.

Proxy logs

A proxy server is often used to speed up internet access as well as implement access and bandwidth controls. A proxy server is also useful to cybersecurity operators because it is an intermediary step between end users and the internet, specifically for web browsing.

Since all requests to the internet are first made to the proxy server's cache, a log of incoming requests is a single point of capture for every request made by all users. If the resource requested is not already in the proxy server's cache, the server itself then repeats the request to the larger internet. This means that each resource should only be requested once, such that oft-requested data only needs to be inspected once, too.

For these reasons, proxy logs contain significant amounts of HTTP data. There are four key areas in which warning signs might appear:

- **Unusual protocol version**: The bulk of modern web traffic uses HTTP/1.1 and some newer applications may use HTTP/2. HTTP/1.0 traffic may be used by some legacy applications, so it needn't be blocked out of hand, but requests and responses on HTTP/1.0 certainly warrant further inspection.
- **User agents**: As described in Chapter 5, *Warning Signs from Network Data*, a user agent string, which does not correspond with the applications and operating systems known to be present on the host or network, can flag the need for further investigation.
- **HTTP request methods**: HTTP has three main request methods (GET, HEAD, and POST), which were discussed in the last chapter. There are other methods, but their use is rare (although not unheard of). A potential alert could be set for other request methods (for example, CONNECT or PUT).
- **Length of content response**: The length of content can be a useful flag for cybersecurity operators. Extremely large content can be a concern as it can indicate a large download, which might consume a lot of resources, or, potentially, a large upload, which could be the removal of sensitive documentation.

Repeated content of the same size could also be a warning sign. This could indicate malware beaconing out to control servers or it could be some other coordination signal.

Payload indicators

If the data originated from a believable source or managed to hide in the volume of legitimate traffic, the threat may still pass through the network level monitors. To actually protect the end user, payload analysis can be conducted at a variety of opportunities throughout the network. With the following three technologies, we work in order from the user device out towards the network boundary.

Antivirus

Antivirus software can sit on the end-user device and typically operates in one of three ways:

- **Signature-based detection**: The traditional antivirus software leverages signature-based detection. This relies on *hashes* of known threats. This method is increasingly constrained as malware authors create code that can disguise itself.
    - **Oligomorphic**: Oligomorphic malware refers to an encryption/decryption system in which the malware chooses from a number of variations to encrypt and decrypt itself. This could be combated by producing multiple signatures, one for each of the variations.
    - **Polymorphic**: Polymorphic malware refers to a system in which the malware chooses the encryption and decryption keys at random (or by using an algorithm) so that each iteration has a separate key. This can still be combated, as the software must be decrypted in order to run itself. At this point, it can still be profiled.
    - **Metamorphic**: Metamorphic malware is the largest threat to signature-based detection. This type of code can rearrange and restructure itself with each iteration, so the content of the code is different each time.
- **Sandbox detection**: Cuckoo Sandbox, discussed in `Chapter 1`, *Classifying Threats*, is an example of this type of detection. By running the file in a closed environment, sandboxing antivirus software can look at the actions initiated by it. This could include revealing a file with a known hash or signature (for example, after the polymorphic malware has decrypted itself), by a process, or API calls. This process is slow and is therefore rarely used at the endpoint, or for applications that require real-time intervention.

- **Data mining techniques**: An intermediate stage between reliance on known threats and detecting new threats in a sandbox, data mining techniques can be used to try to classify the file that is given file features extracted from the file itself. As these techniques are increasingly determined by machine learning, these techniques are a powerful tool for cybersecurity operators but are also dangerous because they are opaque and might not have the rigor required for evidential purposes.

Intrusion Detection Systems/Intrusion Prevention Systems

Intrusion Detection Systems (IDS) monitor the network and determine whether it is currently under attack. This is done by diverting a copy of the traffic to the device for analysis. An IDS does not interrupt the flow of traffic, which allows the end user to access the data from the network immediately on demand, rather than having to wait for the IDS to process it. However, this also means that the attacker can immediately reach the different assets and an attack may initiate in the time between the attack traffic arriving, the IDS creating an alert, and administrators taking the required actions to stop it.

Intrusion Prevention Systems (IPS) run in line with network traffic. As traffic enters the system, it passes through the IPS before passing on to its eventual destination. This allows intrusions to be prevented without external action. Where the traffic is identified as a threat, the packets are dropped.

IDS and IPS both leverage signature-based detection and statistical anomaly detection, which randomly sample network traffic and compare it to a pre-calculated baseline. Anything outside a normal range will initiate an alert/blocking action.

Firewall

A traditional firewall leverages stateful inspection. This means that it looks principally at network headers, including states, ports, and protocols. However, newer systems have started to integrate features of other, payload-based information, which is why it is considered here.

A **Unified Threat Management** (**UTM**) firewall combines stateful inspection with intrusion prevention and antivirus.

Next-generation firewalls (**NGFW**) additionally integrate a system for upgrades, typically also leveraging the cloud for new virus and malware definitions. Application awareness (as described here) can also be added to provide more granular control.

The threat-focused NGFW is one of the newer advancements, as they can not only detect and block threats in progress but can also make changes to the policies on the inbound interface to prevent similar attacks in the future.

Network application control

Bringing together network and payload indicators, Cisco **Application Visibility and Control** (**AVC**) assists administrators to be aware of applications being used on the network, their location, and their impact on productive network use. AVC brings together information from application recognition systems based on deep packet inspection and network performance data from NetFlow to characterize normal traffic as well as identify abnormal traffic.

This is further combined with management tools such as Cisco Prime Infrastructure, which can be used to control and optimize network utilization using things such as the **quality of service** (**QoS**) to prioritize one application over another.

Network application control overcomes one of the key limitations of protocol-based control; protocols can be used for more than one purpose. HTTP traffic can be productive, recreational, malicious, or a combination. Blocking all HTTP traffic would not be appropriate, but nor would allowing unfettered HTTP traffic.

Evaluating alerts

Having identified an alert, it is important for a cybersecurity operator to prioritize the alert, particularly in terms of the impact it might have on the organization. Remember that in CVSS v3.0 there were three elements: exploitability, impact, and scope. If an alert has been generated, the *exploitability* element has really passed and the exploit is likely to be in process. It, therefore, has an impact, which is of most importance at this time.

Cisco Firepower provides a collection of network security and traffic management products either as a software solution or onto Cisco hardware. A typical deployed system has a series of managed devices, which sense and monitor traffic for analysis and a manager. This section will look at the impact flag generated by Firepower Management Center.

This guide will not unlock the full potential of the Firepower Management Center. The Cisco Firepower support area (from which manuals for each deployment type can be downloaded) is linked to in the *Further reading* section. It will, however, give you enough information to calculate the impact flag for examination purposes.

Impact flags

The impact flag is used to indicate where the alert was detected (in relation to the network) and what the impact of it was (in relation to the network/server/device). The impact flag is an 8-bit field in the impact event alert message. The meaning of each bit value is given in the following table:

Bit pattern	Hex	Description
XXXXXXX1	0x01	Source or destination host is in a network monitored by the system.
XXXXXX1X	0x02	Source or destination host exists in the network map.
XXXXX1XX	0x04	Source or destination host is running a server on the port in the event (if TCP or UDP) or uses the IP protocol.
XXXX1XXX	0x08	There is a vulnerability mapped to the operating system of the source or destination host in the event.
XXX1XXXX	0x10	There is a vulnerability mapped to the server detected in the event.
XX1XXXXX	0x20	The event causes the managed device to drop the session (used only when the device is running in inline, switched, or routed deployment). It corresponds to the blocked status in the Firepower System web interface.
X1XXXXXX	0x40	The rule that generated this event contains rule metadata setting the impact flag to red. The source or destination host is potentially compromised by a virus, Trojan, or other pieces of malicious software.
1XXXXXXX	0x80	There is a vulnerability mapped to the client detected in the event (version 5.0+ only).

Table of Firepower impact flag bit values

Each bit value in the flag works independently, as a single event may match several of the alert criteria. The X against the other bits underlines the idea that they can have any value (0 or 1). A score may have one or more bit flags associated with it, so the end value of the flag can be anything from 0 to 255, although certain combinations are unlikely.

Firepower Management Center priorities

The Firepower Management Center prioritizes alerts based on the impact flag values (among other measures). The impact flag can be used to categorize an alert into one of five groups. Again in the table, the character X indicates that the value can be 0 or 1:

Color code	Impact level	Description	Bit pattern
Gray	0	Unknown	00X00000
Red	1	Vulnerable	XXXX1XXX X1XXXXXX 1XXXXXXX
Orange	2	Potentially vulnerable	00X0011X
Yellow	3	Currently not vulnerable	00X0001X
Blue	4	Unknown target	00X00001

Table of impact levels

Notice that some of the bit values are very similar. Ensure that you know which bits to look out for in the flag. For example, the difference between being potentially vulnerable versus currently not vulnerable is bit 2 (00x00**1**1x vs 00x000**1**x).

Analyzing a network and host profile

The following screenshot contains a network diagram for a medium-sized business. Not every host is shown; this is just for simplicity of the network diagram. The green section is inside the company's network, and the white section is external to the company. Each server is listed by IP address and port:

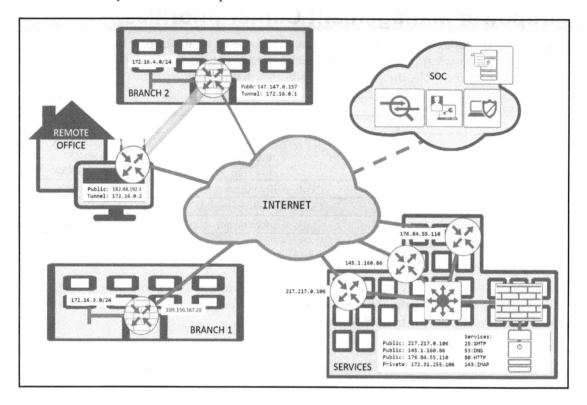

Example network diagram

The alert data is shown in the following screenshot. This alert has been detected as a buffer overflow attack using SMTP. Notice the IP addresses and ports involved, and how they relate to the network map:

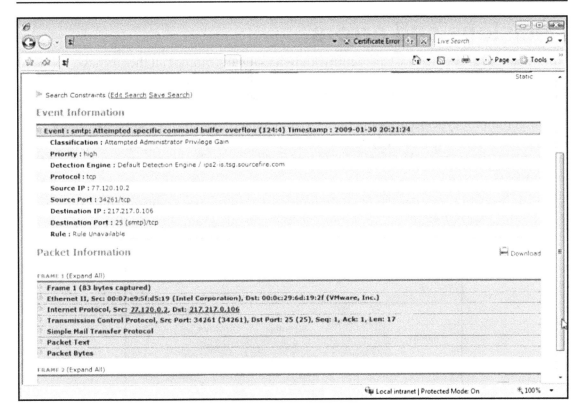

Example alert data

With this data, we can calculate some of the impact flags. For cases in which the detail is unknown, we will flag it with a 0.

The destination host for the attack is the SMTP server within the network. This means that the first 3 bits will be a 1 (it is within the network map and running a server on the designated port). There is no information stating whether there is a vulnerability on the SMTP server's operating system or the server software itself, so bits 3 through 5 are a 0. There is, again, no information regarding whether there is a virus, Trojan, or other malicious software within the destination, and since the source is outside the network, there isn't much to be done about that. Therefore, bits 6 and 7 are also 0.

The final impact flag score is 00000111, which suggests that the impact level will be yellow: potentially vulnerable.

Decisions and errors

Up-to-date security software can identify known malware, but not all threats have defined signatures; threat actors amend their tactics constantly, new malware is developed, and new domains and IP addresses are registered and used.

It is important for cybersecurity operators to understand that security software cannot 100% definitively classify activity into the binary malware/non-malware groups. This fact that sometimes software classifies activity incorrectly means that there are four different categories.

The four different categories are often thought about in terms of a table dividing the actual threat against the software classification. The following diagram shows a different interpretation of this setup:

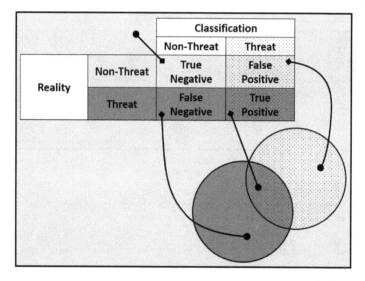

System activity classified as True Negatives/True Positives; False Negatives and False Positives are a concern for cybersecurity operators

In an ideal world, the hatched circle (classified threat) should overlap totally with the red section (actual threats). It is also worth noting that the vast majority of traffic is legitimate, so it is important for a balance to be made between protecting and restricting users.

True Positive (red and hatched)/True Negative (green and unhatched)

When an activity is correctly identified as malware, it is known as a **True Positive**. When an activity is correctly identified as a normal activity, it is known as a **True Negative**. There is no impact on normal, legitimate users, and the activity of threat actors is halted.

False Positives (green and hatched)

If the system is too sensitive, it may classify legitimate data as a threat and, thus, legitimate users' activity is prevented. This effectively creates a situation in which the security systems actually creates a denial of service. The impact of this could be that users cannot do what they need to, but they might also be tempted to turn off systems that are designed to protect them.

False Negatives (red and unhatched)

If the system is too lax, it may incorrectly classify malware activity as no-threat and allow it through. This activity poses a threat to the system. False negatives are particularly dangerous because users (and administrators) may have misplaced confidence in their safety. A threat that is incorrectly classified as safe will have longer to affect the system.

Summary

There is a huge range of cybersecurity products on the market, with many having overlapping or similar aims and capabilities. In this section, we looked at different network security technologies and the information that they capture.

Having a range of different data is vital in establishing what is being sent across the network and by whom. If we consider this in terms of previous chapters on evidence and attribution, the range of different data helps cybersecurity operators by providing corroboration to their interpretations.

Many systems provide decision making in isolation, although companies are increasingly providing suites of interconnected systems that can share information to make better decisions. However, there is always a risk of making incorrect decisions. Where a threat is incorrectly permitted, this is called a false negative; when legitimate traffic is incorrectly blocked, this is called a False Positive. Both of these errors can create issues for the end user. Users could be exposed to threats or prevented from being productive.

Questions

1. How can PCAP files be opened in Wireshark? (Select two.)
   1. Using the **File** | **Open** menu option
   2. Using the **File** | **Import** from **Hex Dump...** menu option
   3. Using the **File** | **Open** | **Filetype libpcap** menu option
   4. Dragging and dropping the PCAP file into Wireshark

2. What would be the value given in the Wireshark Packet bytes pane for port `80` (HTTP)?
   1. `0050`
   2. `0080`
   3. `---P`
   4. `80`

3. What is the content type of a `.exe` file extracted from an HTTP stream in Wireshark?
   1. `application/octet-stream`
   2. `application/exe`
   3. `application/pe`
   4. `executable/microsoft-exe`

4. An administrator is checking the registry for suspected malware. Which entry in `HKEY_LOCAL_MACHINE\SYSTEM\CurrentControlSet\Services\BasicDispl ay` might be an expected normal value for this system service?
   1. `ImagePath = \SystemRoot\Program Files\system.exe`
   2. `ImagePath = \SystemRoot\.system32\BasicDisplay.exe`
   3. `ImagePath = \SystemRoot\System32\drivers\BasicDisplay.sys`
   4. `ImagePath = \SystemRoot\.System32\svchost.exe -k BasicDisplay`

5. Which of the following entries from a proxy log may require further investigation?
    1. HTTP Request header: CONNECT index.html HTTP/1.0
    2. HTTP Request header: GET index.html HTTP/1.1
    3. HTTP User-Agent: Mozilla/5.0 (Windows NT 5.1; rv:36.0) Gecko/20100101 Firefox/36.0
    4. HTTP User-Agent: Mozilla/4.0 (compatible; MSIE 6.0; Windows NT 5.1)

6. A traditional, signature-based antivirus fails to detect a file as malware. Which of the following statements is most true?
    1. This is a False Positive.
    2. This is a False Negative.
    3. This is caused by a polymorphic malware.
    4. This is part of a zero-day attack.

7. IP addresses can be used to determine which countries traffic is originating from. Which is not a feature of IP addresses that facilitates this?
    1. IP addresses can be assigned dynamically using DHCP.
    2. Internet routable address ranges are registered with IANA.
    3. IP addresses are retained from source to destination host except for NAT and PAT.
    4. IP addresses are hierarchical, so the large classes were generally bought up by countries and ISPs.

The following three questions relate to the following network and scenario:

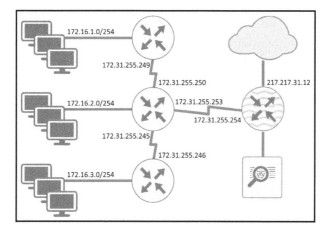

Network Diagram

A user reports that their computer has started to work very slowly after clicking a link in an email. The IT team has reviewed the NetFlow records for that individual. They have found some flows that they believe to be suspicious. They have sent the suspicious NetFlows to the SOC as seen in the following screenshot, but not their reasoning:

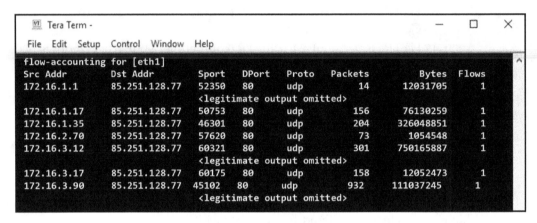

Filtered NetFlow

8. Which of the following is a concern?
   1. Large amounts of data are being sent out of the network.
   2. Large amounts of data are coming into the network.
   3. A high volume of packets is coming into the network.
   4. A high volume of packets is being sent out of the network.

9. Which of the following is a concern?
   1. The IP address being communicated with is outside the country.
   2. The IP address being communicated with is inside the network.
   3. A single internal address is communicating with multiple external addresses in a similar IP address range.
   4. There are multiple internal addresses communicating with the same external address.

10. Which of the following is a concern?
    1. The port used is associated with HTTP, but the transport layer protocol is UDP.
    2. The port used is associated with SSL, so the traffic cannot be decrypted and inspected.
    3. The port used is a non-standard port, so the application layer protocol cannot be determined.
    4. The ports used to indicate a Telnet session, which allows non-encrypted connections.

Further reading

- The Wireshark user guide can be found at `https://www.wireshark.org/download/docs/user-guide.pdf`.
- The tcpdump man page can be found at `https://www.tcpdump.org/manpages/tcpdump.1.html`.
- The Cisco Firepower support section (from which manuals for each platform can be downloaded) can be found at `https://www.cisco.com/c/en/us/support/security/defense-center/tsd-products-support-series-home.html` for hardware deployments, and `https://www.cisco.com/c/en/us/support/security/defense-center-virtual-appliance/tsd-products-support-series-home.html` for virtual (software only) deployments.
- `malwarebytes.com` includes some good examples of analyzing malware by API calls on their blog. It is accessible from `https://blog.malwarebytes.com/threat-analysis/2017/10/analyzing-malware-by-api-calls/`.
- A list of common functions in malware analysis can be found from InfoSec Institute at `https://resources.infosecinstitute.com/windows-functions-in-malware-analysis-cheat-sheet-part-2/#article`.
- An article about common registry key anomalies from virus affected hosts is listed by Symantec and can be found at `https://www.symantec.com/connect/articles/most-common-registry-key-check-while-dealing-virus-issue`.

Section 3: Incident Response

3

Incident response is one of the core business areas for a **Security Operations Centre** (**SOC**). Identifying vulnerabilities, threats, and attacks in progress are worth nothing unless the organization (informed by the SOC and others) does something about it.

There are national guidelines for identifying individual and team responsibilities during an incident response, but the 210-255 course centers around the American **National Institute of Standards and Technology** (**NIST**) guidelines. This is because Cisco is an American company, but also because the NIST guidelines are fairly internationally recognized as a baseline. National guidelines tend to supplement, rather than contradict, the NIST guidelines.

NIST has defined the stages of incident response (pre-, during-, and post-incident); the teams that exist and how they interact (national, company, industry, software, and manufacturer); and the different tasks individuals and teams have at each of the different stages. These guidelines contribute to and are supplemented by regulatory and industry guidance. Each organization must be compliant and part of an SOC's responsibilities may be to provide assurance to the board that this is the case.

The following chapters are included in this section:

- Chapter 7, *Roles and Responsibilities During an Incident*
- Chapter 8, *Network and Server Profiling*
- Chapter 9, *Compliance Frameworks*

7
Roles and Responsibilities During an Incident

The **National Institute of Standards and Technology** (**NIST**) Special Publication 800–61 Revision 2 (*NIST.SP 800-61 Revision 2*) is 79 pages worth of recommendations by the NIST on the subject of computer security incident handling. A link to the original source document is listed in the *Further reading* section.

Planning for incident response is an important function of any organization's cybersecurity function, and is the responsibility of everyone within the organization (including organizational management and the end user) to comply with the plan. This will require education programs, but also appropriate restrictions to prevent users from operating outside the plan.

At each of the four stages of incident response (as described in *NIST.SP 800-61 Revision 2*), different individuals and teams have different responsibilities. It is important to know this to minimize the duplication of effort and prevent gaps in protection.

The following topics will be covered in this chapter:

- The incident response plan
- The stages of an incident
- Incident response teams

The incident response plan

The incident response plan is the first action required to minimize risk. It is naive to assume that just building the wall is enough to deter any and all attacks materializing. In sport, an incident response plan might be referred to as a **playbook** in other situations, it might be called contingency planning. Whatever the terminology, every organization should have one, and those that don't should be creating one. When joining an organization as a security operator, knowing where the plan is and any stated responsibilities of the role should be a priority.

In this section, we will look at elements that should be included in an incident response plan.

An incident response plan outlines the basic requirements for incident response, including key personalities, responsibilities, and accountability. The aim of the plan is to stimulate action within the organization toward managing incidents responsibly. Most importantly, it underlines the importance of incident response to the organization's strategic aims and objectives.

Each of the key elements (highlighted in bold) of an incident response plan, as listed in *NIST.SP 800-61 Revision 2 § 2.3.2*, are discussed briefly in the following sections.

Organizational priorities

Organizational priorities drive how incidents are responded to, and hence the teams and capabilities to be put in place. The organization's **mission** will guide the boundaries for incident response. For example, if IT is a support function to the mission, is it possible to separate the network from the internet either pre-emptively (air-gapping) or reactively to limit the spread of an infection/attack? In the case of the WannaCry attack on the UK's National Health Service, many hospitals decided to disconnect, as the core mission was to treat the patients as best they could.

However, if the core mission is to provide 24/7 capability, disconnecting would not be an option. For example, a stock exchange or banking group would sustain massive losses through a loss in connectivity. Organizations such as these may well have a much larger team on standby for incidents so that any loss in connectivity was for as short a time as possible.

The organization's **strategies and goals** should be guided by, and in line with, the mission. These will impact the incident response plan, as they dictate the priorities for the response. Potentially there are sections of the organization that *must* be secured, where others would result in losses that were considered acceptable.

It is important for organizations to recognize **how the program fits into the overall organization**. Times have moved on since plans for incident response were a **bolt-on** or afterthought. Incident response is fundamental to how many businesses operate, and must be considered and evolved through an organization's life cycle.

Incident response requirement and capability

The **organizational approach to incident response**, which outlines the size, capability, and responsibilities for incident response, should be in line with the priorities, so an organization whose stated requirement is for zero loss of connectivity (for example, the stock exchange), it might be inappropriate to have a distributed, part-time incident response team. Clearly having an on-site team might be resource intensive in terms of finance and personnel, so it is important to strike a balance.

The plan should provide a way of measuring effectiveness. Metrics might include the speed of response to an incident or exercise, the speed and extent of data recovery, or even the financial impacts of an attack. **Metrics for measuring incident response capability and its effectiveness** are difficult because the effectiveness of incident responses is normally the prevention of loss rather than any tangible gain.

A plan should also include a **roadmap for maturing incident response capability** as companies can change size, market share, or exposure, or may have learned lessons from exercises or incidents. As one of the largest impacts of cybersecurity incidents is on customer confidence, an effective incident response may be less important to a highly agile start-up than to a well-established company; customers are often more forgiving of a small business. As the company gets more established, the *prestige* as a target also increases, meaning it is more likely to be the subject of an attack.

Command-and-control

Command-and-control is very important in incident response. Ownership of incident response needs to be at a level appropriate to the importance of incident response within the organization, and the kind of actions that will be required. It would be very difficult for an IT engineer to tell board members that they cannot use their computers that day. Some organizations are beset by cultural differences between the IT department and other staff, as the chain of command has not been adequately established and/or communicated. This is a problem on both sides, as staff may ignore security critical instructions, or IT staff could overstep and impact upon business-critical activity.

The NIST guidelines recommend that a plan receives **senior management approval**. This enables an incident response team to have the right amount of authority and agency, in line with business aims. The senior manager is responsible for implementing and reviewing the plan, as well as empowering the team.

Command-and-control is also required to manage the handover from incident response to a normal routine. It is very difficult to sustain a war footing in the medium and long term; it is resource intensive and has significant impacts on staff morale. It is important for the incident response team to communicate effectively, and plans should include **how the incident response team will communicate with the rest of the organization and with other organizations**. This allows feedback to be provided, but also a consistency of messaging. The 2015 attack on TalkTalk in the UK attracted the then largest fine from the information commissioner's office, but the company's media relations limited the effect on consumer confidence. The attack was estimated as having cost $77 million. An attack on Ashley Madison (also in 2015), but which took much longer to reveal, may cost up to $498 million once lawsuits are settled.

The stages of an incident

In this section, we will learn to define the stages of analysis. For each stage, you will learn to identify the elements that should be referenced and the organizational stakeholders who are involved in, and subject to, the plan. This understanding of NIST.SP800-61 Revision 2 links specifically to topics 3.2 and 3.3 of the 210-255 syllabus.

Implementing Cisco Cybersecurity Operations (210-255) Topic List:

3.2 Map elements to these steps of analysis based on the NIST.SP 800-61 Revision 2
3.2.a Preparation
3.2.b Detection and analysis
3.2.c Containment, eradication, and recovery
3.2.d Post-incident analysis (lessons learned)

3.3 Map the organization stakeholders against the NIST IR categories (C2M2, NIST.SP
800-61 Revision 2)
3.3.a Preparation
3.3.b Detection and analysis
3.3.c Containment, eradication, and recovery
3.3.d Post-incident analysis (lessons learned)

As you can see from the topic list, the four incident response categories/steps of analysis are the same for topic 3.2 and 3.3, reflecting the NIST Incident response life cycle, which is shown in the following diagram:

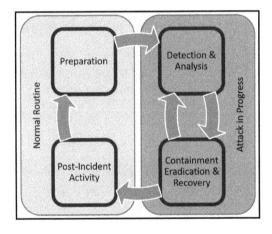

The incident response life cycle

This section will be split into these four stages, mapping the respective elements and organizational stakeholders side by side. Through this process, recall that the system is a life cycle. Many depictions will show these four stages in a line, and although an arrow returns to the start, the reality of incident response is that incidents may be long and drawn out, or there may be several incidents within a short space of time. The normal routine half of the diagram must still continue, even when an incident is ongoing.

Preparation

In the preparation phase, which is hopefully the bulk of the time, the general objectives sit in three categories: preventing attacks, training, and procurement.

Preventing attacks is the primary aim of this stage. The key stakeholders, including senior management, **Computer Security Incident Response Team (CSIRT)**, IT support, information assurance, and the legal department must work towards the organization being as compliant as possible, and to repel attacks before they become incidents.

The CSIRT and other members of the organization must be trained for incident response. They must be comfortable with all the kit and equipment so that they are ready with all the skills needed to detect and react to an incident. During this phase, they should also be documenting and gaining an understanding of the existing infrastructure, so there is a baseline for recovery, as well as staying up-to-date with any guidance from manufacturers and service providers (for example, about updates).

If any part of the response is carried out by untrained personnel, there is a risk that evidence may be mishandled (and hence lose its integrity), or that important information is missed. Either of these outcomes might hamper efforts to hold the perpetrators responsible, or even to fully remedy the situation (for example, if a component of the attack is not fully removed).

The preparation phase is also where the organization purchases and maintains the kit and equipment required for prevention, detection, and response.

Detection and analysis

Detecting an incident could be from automated detection systems, such as antivirus software or an IDS, user reports, incident precursors and indicators, or third-party reporting (for example, white hats).

During this phase, the CSIRT is responsible for confirming or denying the existence of an incident. This will require collection and analysis of event data (both network and endpoint) and previous data along with intelligence reports.

Once the suspicion of an incident is validated, the CSIRT must react to notify the appropriate individuals.

This phase, again, mainly focuses on the CSIRT, but depending on the source of the incident, other personalities may be required (even if the incident has not yet been confirmed). It is like hearing the fire alarm; the fire might not be evident yet, but it is a good idea to take steps towards protection before the fire reaches the door.

Stakeholders may include public affairs and media relations departments, facilities management and physical security providers, or partner organizations.

Containment, eradication, and recovery

Containment ensures the incident does not continue. The playbook should detail a range of different incidences and scenarios, and what to do about each. During this phase, the CSIRT provides advice and guidance along with the senior management to ensure that staff throughout the organization take the required action to contain the incident. Every individual within the organization is a stakeholder during this phase.

Eradication requires the identification of all hosts that need fixing and the removal of all the effects of the security incident. It is important that the CSIRT leads with eradication, and that it is carried out from within the team. This could be done centrally, or on each individual host, but it is important that no user can **skip** the updates or interrupt the process. Ultimately, the systems cannot remain in the **contained** state indefinitely if the organization is to work towards its overall mission. The CSIRT must be able to provide assurance that eradication steps have been completed.

The recovery of hosts may require clean backups or complete rebuilding with installation media. It is important that any exploited vulnerabilities are patched and corrected before the incident is considered **over**.

Post-incident analysis (lessons learned)

After the incident has been resolved or, at least, controlled, the organization should perform an **after action review** (**AAR**) to discuss the events that took place, the actions of all the stakeholders, and what could be learned from it. This process should include all four stages, from lessons not learned/solutions not implemented from past incidents, through to changes required in the planning phase, through to ways of speeding up detection, reaction, and remediation.

The post-incident analysis is less about *how did this happen;* this should be well understood in order to contain, eradicate, and recover, and should be more about *how we prevent/react/recover better/stronger/faster.*

During this phase, data should be collected to determine the cost of the incident, the effectiveness of the CSIRT, and highlight any possible weaknesses. A policy should also be generated about how, and for how long, evidence should be retained. There may be other industry-specific requirements for reporting or investigations required for regulatory purposes. This should also be prepared for at this stage.

Incident response teams

There is a layered system of **Cyber Security Incident Response Teams** (**CSIRT**) that support organizations. This reflects a threat's severity, likelihood, and sphere of operation. Broadly speaking, CSIRTs support organizations with common interests (for example, companies, industries, research areas, national interests, and so on). A representation of this is shown in the following diagram, although there can be variations on this:

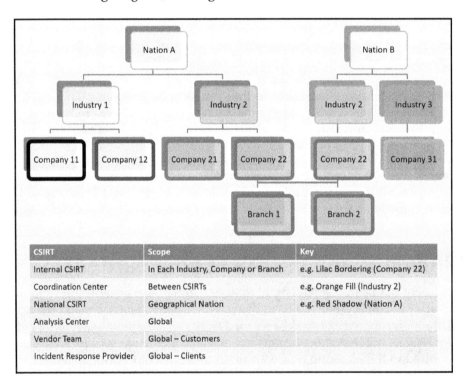

CSIRT	Scope	Key
Internal CSIRT	In Each Industry, Company or Branch	e.g. Lilac Bordering (Company 22)
Coordination Center	Between CSIRTs	e.g. Orange Fill (Industry 2)
National CSIRT	Geographical Nation	e.g. Red Shadow (Nation A)
Analysis Center	Global	
Vendor Team	Global – Customers	
Incident Response Provider	Global – Clients	

Hierarchy and jurisdiction of incident responders

NIST.SP 800-61 Revision 2 lists six different incident response teams. In this section, we will learn how to describe the goals of each team and explain how they differ.

The overall aim of a CSIRT is consistent: to respond to cybersecurity incidents. This means reducing the technical impact, but also the impact on user confidence, customer engagement, and public opinion. In short, the CSIRT must be engaged in every element before, during, and after an incident.

Internal CSIRT

An internal CSIRT is entirely within the organization being protected. The staff may be dedicated, or part-time, but they are employees of the company.

Realistic aims of an internal CSIRT are linked to their size and employment model, but the primary aim is providing reactive services (things that happen in the **detection and analysis**, and **containment**, **eradication**, and **recovery** phases). As the team increases in size and dedication, they may provide proactive services such as creating security tools and improving IDS/IPS/firewall policies. These proactive services allow the organization to react more effectively.

Finally, larger CSIRTs may also move into the preparation stage, providing quality management services such as risk analysis, disaster recovery planning, and education and training.

Coordination centers

Coordination centers are typically utilized in very large organizations, or in multi-disciplinary teams with a common interest. In large organizations, the coordination center may have a command relationship to provide direct assistance. This might be in the central CSIRT for a multinational bank, or a central governmental CSIRT assisting different ministries and departments. Alternatively (particularly for teams with a common interest), the coordination center may only be able to provide advice. They might provide high-level event data analysis capacity, or suggest recovery and mitigation strategies. Examples of this might include a research network consisting of several universities. Each university CSIRT has a common interest in group protection, but one cannot impose their solutions directly on another.

The goal of a coordination center is to coordinate and provide impartial advice to members of the community it serves. It has a dedicated staff, which allows it to provide focused, dedicated action towards coordinating incident response. Most of all, coordination centers aim to protect the overall community, which may include ensuring that one organization's actions do not adversely affect another organization within the group.

National CSIRT

A national CSIRT handles incidents within the geographic boundaries of a country. It may be used as a coordination center for attacks across a broad frontage within the country, or as a *CSIRT of last resort*, where an incident occurs against an organization for which no CSIRT of sufficient scale exists. This might be, for example, an attack on critical infrastructure, academia, or small- and medium-sized enterprises if there is the possibility of the problem spreading to other national infrastructures.

A national CSIRT response may come from incidents other than attacks on the nation-state (for example, an attack on the power grid or telephony), or from *state-on-state* activity (for example, actions taken in kinetic or economic war). The only requirement is that the incident affects some organization that is entirely, or in part, within the geographic boundaries of the nation.

Analysis centers

Analysis centers collect data from various sources to determine trends in incident activity. This information can be used to help predict future activity or to provide early warning. Analysis centers may provide this for free to enable them to collect more data, or as part of a paid-for service. This might include the provision of a next-generation firewall, with analysis centers providing distributed, machine-learned malware definitions or intelligence-led profiles of potential attacks to augment policies on the fly.

The role of the analysis center is to provide analysis that could not be handled in-house, or even as part of a national CSIRT. This analysis helps organizations to adapt to the changing cybersecurity picture.

Vendor teams

Vendor teams render services relating to specific products that they offer. A vendor may be a manufacturer, developer, or service provider. Cisco, for example, has a vendor CSIRT, as do other large services providers (for example, Microsoft or Amazon). The purpose of this type of CSIRT is to mitigate the impact of vulnerabilities associated with their products from affecting their clients. This may be in pre-emptive action (for example, pushing updates) or learning lessons from one attack to advise other customers.

Managed Security Service Providers

If a company is unable to staff their own CSIRT (either for personal or financial reasons), they may buy in services from a **Managed Security Service Provider** (**MSSP**). Cisco interchangeably uses the term incident response provider for the same organization.

An MSSP may support many different companies or organizations. Each organization only needs to supervise and oversee the provider's work. Using an MSSP allows an organization to receive support that is both scalable and available on demand.

Summary

Incident response is the visible side of cybersecurity. It is often the case that no-one knows what a **Cyber Security Incident Response Team** (**CSIRT**) is doing when there isn't an incident in progress.

In this chapter, we saw that there are, in fact, four stages of incident response, and only two of these occur while an incident is in progress. The **National Institute for Standards and Technology** (**NIST**) have produced guidance on how to produce and enact a plan for incident response. It is centered on the four stages: preparation; detection and analysis; containment, eradication and recovery; and post-incident analysis (NIST calls this post-incident activity).

We have also learned the different types of CSIRT and their different aims and objectives. Sitting at different levels of an organization, the CSIRT collective effort is aimed at keeping users safe from vulnerabilities and attack. In the most part, they are collaborative, working together for the general good; at other times, CSIRTs cooperate to protect the common interest. Incident response can also be provided as a service through **Managed Security Service Providers** (**MSSP**).

Questions

1. Why is mission a key element of an incident response plan?
   1. The IT team mission will dictate when a CSIRT is mobilized away from their day-to-day roles.
   2. The organization's mission will dictate which actions cannot be taken.
   3. The CSIRT mission will dictate what the team's priorities are.
   4. Every CSIRT's mission is the same, so including it in the plan informs senior management of this.

2. NIST guidelines suggest that metrics are included in the incident response plan. What are these metrics there for?
   1. To measure the effectiveness of the plan
   2. To measure the severity of the incident before triggering the plan
   3. To measure the risk associated with the plan
   4. To quantify the value of the CSIRT

3. Which of the following are actions within the preparation stage of incident management?
   1. Collecting and documenting evidence
   2. Training the CSIRT on the systems and technologies in use
   3. Fixing damaged host machines
   4. Recovering data from backups

4. Which of the following CSIRTs contains staff who are directly employed by the affected organization?
   1. Internal CSIRT
   2. Analysis Center
   3. Vendor CSIRT
   4. Incident response providers

5. Who is responsible for the implementation of the incident response plan?
   1. Senior management
   2. Information assurance team
   3. IT support team
   4. Public relations team

6. At which stage of an incident are host computers restored from an image?

   1. Preparation
   2. Detection and analysis
   3. Containment, eradication, and recovery
   4. Post-incident analysis

7. Which of the following is an example of a vendor CSIRT activity?

   1. Cisco responding to a denial of service attack on `cisco.com`
   2. Cisco providing emergency updates for older routers
   3. Cisco briefing the media about new trends in cybersecurity
   4. Cisco providing security as a service

The following three questions are related to the following scenario.

The HQ building for HACME Bank is accessible by any HACME employee using an RFID tag inside their ID card. Users from branches can use the computers at HQ to access all the same things that they could if they were in the branch.

Recently, a previously convicted fraudster was caught by police with a list of user IDs and passwords for HACME Bank employees. The IT manager is informed and notices that a number of large transfers were made from HQ, where the member of staff who was logged in was also logged in at their branch offices, and whose ID card had not entered the HQ building on the day that the transfers were made.

8. Which of the following actions would you expect the bank to now take in the detection and analysis phase?

   1. Log out all sessions for the listed users.
   2. The incident is already verified; containment should now begin.
   3. Change all the listed users' passwords and inform their managers of the new passwords by secure communications.
   4. Change the policy that allows users to be logged in on multiple machines simultaneously.

9. Which of the following actions would you expect the bank to do in the containment, eradication, and recovery phase?

   1. Change the password rules so that passwords are less easy to guess.
   2. Change the username rules so that they are less easy to guess.
   3. Suspend all the listed users' accounts.
   4. Change the login rules at HQ so that only those users who are in the building (by ID card scan) are able to log in.

10. Which of the following does the CSIRT need to be able to answer before entering the post-incident phase?
    1. How did the fraudster acquire the information?
    2. Are the affected users' accounts now secured?
    3. How many frauds have been carried out?
    4. Can we ensure that the fraudster cannot access the HQ building again?

Further reading

- The NIST SP 800-61 Revision 2 can be accessed online at `https://nvlpubs.nist.gov/nistpubs/specialpublications/nist.sp.800-61r2.pdf`.
- To read more about the costs of data breaches, and hence the importance of incident response to business strategy, head to `https://www.egnyte.co.uk/blog/2017/06/how-much-does-a-data-breach-cost-a-business/`.

Network and Server Profiling

8

Network and server profiling is used to establish **normal** traffic on a network and server and, therefore, to help identify incidents in action. Profiling also allows administrators to identify any potential future problems, such as a lack of redundancy, or bottlenecks in the system.

Profiling is a fundamental network security task. Knowing what **normal** is allows us to better identify what isn't **normal**, and sets us on the path to defeating a threat.

The following topics will be covered in this chapter:

- Network profiling
- Server profiling

Network profiling

Networks are all different, carrying variable amounts of data in variable numbers and lengths of a session. If we, as cybersecurity operators, work on the assumption that having an infected host is an exception rather than the usual status of the network, the ability to detect anomalous traffic will help to detect an attack in progress. Network profiling is used to establish the normal *pattern of behavior* for a network.

There are a number of different metrics that should be collected during network profiling. In this section, we will identify the elements that are useful for network profiling, looking at the technologies that can facilitate collection, and know what to look for in each metric.

Network profiles should be collected periodically to stay relevant, but consideration should also be given to temporal variation, whether daily (for example, lunchtime with peak traffic, compared with overnight), weekly (for example, weekends), or seasonal (for example, holiday shopping/summer vacations, and so on). A company's usage may also vary over time, with periods of growth perhaps associated with increased user and traffic volume.

Cisco's 210–255 specifically identifies four features to be considered during network profiling. These are discussed separately in the following sections.

Total throughput

Throughput is a measure of how much transport successfully passes through a single point in the network during a given time period. It is often thought about as the **speed** of data transmission, although this is a flawed idea. A good parallel to this is looking at a motorway. A car might be able to travel at 70 mph (110 km/h) but can only carry five people. A bus that travels at 50 mph (80 km/h) but carries 50 passengers results in higher throughput than the car, despite traveling at a lower speed. In addition to this, some of the vehicles are actually lost and effectively create congestion without getting to where they want to go.

Measuring network utilization (how much traffic is on the network and being delivered successfully per unit time) is a useful metric, but it is limited; network utilization does not show what is consuming the bandwidth, or why packets might be failing. Effectively, network utilization is the equivalent of a picture of slow-moving traffic. The observer cannot tell whether this has been caused by a traffic accident ahead, because everyone is on their way to work, or simply that the speed limit on that road has been reduced.

Gaining more insight into the situation requires more data. NetFlow can be used to gain further insight as it separates outflows by port (allowing protocol to be inferred). NetFlow allows us to know that the bulk of the people on the road at that time are destined for work, which gives us a better understanding of the traffic. NetFlows may, for example, show big changes in the destination country (by IP address) as the company's staff communicate with Asian, European, and American markets at different times of the day. If the company doesn't have multinational dealings, flows to a variety of countries may be more of an anomaly.

Capturing full packets allows the SOC to analyze the full contents of the traffic. However, this has considerable drawbacks; the storage required for full packet captures, and then the processing to analyze the data and create alerts is much more resource intensive than using NetFlow.

The following screenshot shows a side-by-side comparison of the same set of traffic data (collected over only 41 seconds). The NetFlow presents a summary, which, although it is still a lot of data, is much smaller than the 693 full packets captured in Wireshark; full packet capture collects more data but at the expense of processing and analysis time:

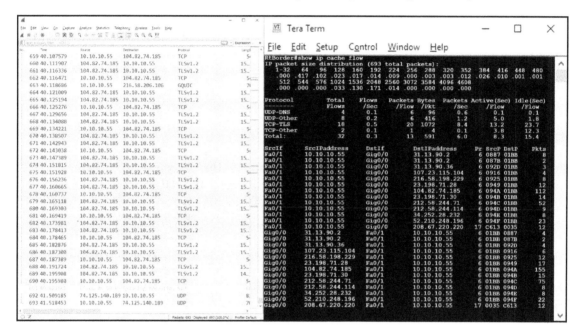

Full packet capture compared with NetFlow

Hybrid systems do exist, with Cisco's Stealthwatch technology collecting and analyzing NetFlow data, before transitioning to full packet capture if an anomaly or alert is triggered.

Session duration

Measuring or calculating session duration is important to see how usual working patterns affect the network. This might include how devices join and then leave the network in short order (causing IP address depletion), or how much each resource is accessed through the course of the day (for example, cloud-based virtual machines left running).

This information can be used to guide rules on session timeouts. An example of this might be to see that devices at a train station have very short session times, as travelers traverse the platform, or check timetables, and so on. Consideration should be given to a short DHCP lease time compared to the lease time when on board the train's Wi-Fi.

Session duration is not always an immediately available metric. There are a number of software packages that can calculate this, normally through a combination of SNMP outputs.

Ports used

Ports in the network profiling context are not the same as the ports used at the transport layer. Network utilization based on the protocol (and hence TCP/UDP port) is covered in *throughput* and *session duration*. In the network profiling context, ports used refers to the physical interfaces on switches and routers. During the network build, network designers should have planned and documented which interfaces go to, and from, which other interfaces; they produce and maintain a network diagram, updating as and when devices are added/removed/moved. A device that can access the network, particularly via a physical (and normally unsecured) connection, could pose significant threats to the system. They would appear to be already within the trusted internal network.

On Cisco equipment, individual interfaces may be activated or shut down, which makes it more difficult to insert a further device onto the network. In addition, things such as *port-security* can be used to lock interfaces to specific MAC addresses, or to a certain number of devices. Cisco devices can produce alerts on a strange device attempting to connect or take automatic action such as shutting down the interface or dropping incoming packets.

Cisco also utilizes **Cisco Discovery Protocol (CDP)**, or **Link Layer Discovery Protocol (LLDP)**, to advertise themselves and receive advertisements, and to build a representation of what types of device are connected to each interface. This would allow, for example, swapping two network devices (with differing MAC addresses), while still alerting administrators if an unexpected device type appears on a link.

The following screenshot shows the output from CDP and LLDP from the routers in the basic network shown. Notice how the network diagram could be derived from the CDP output. This obviously increases in difficulty with network complexity:

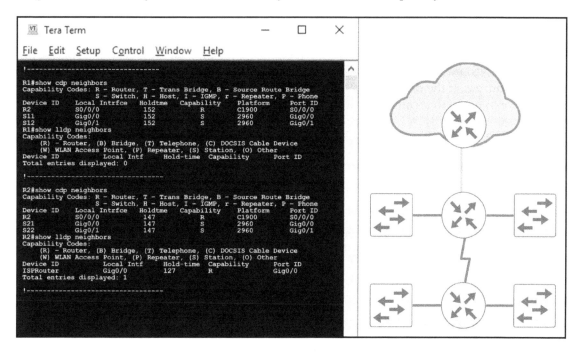

CDP and LLDP output from routers in the network diagram

Network access control (**NAC**) is an enhancement of these methods, in which the network attempts to identify the type of device as it connects to the network, as well as who is using the device. This user identity then is given access to the relevant resources, VLAN, and so on regardless of their physical location. NAC reduces the administrative burden of fixing interfaces and devices. Portability and flexibility are built into the NAC system.

Critical asset address space

Addressing in the IP system works on the assumption that there are no duplicates in the network. With static addressing, this is controlled by network administrators and designers, but as the network grows in size, this becomes an increasingly complex task. DHCP can be used to reduce this burden by assigning addresses dynamically.

Some interfaces will still require fixed addressing. The interfaces of the default gateway, web servers, or management interfaces, for example, should always be fixed, so other devices know how to access those resources. In order to do this, in DHCP (for IPv4) these addresses could be reserved, or removed from the pool and the interfaces statically assigned.

In **stateless address autoconfiguration** (**SLAAC**) (for IPv6), the client will send a **neighbor solicitation** (**NS**) message to discover whether any other device is already using the intended address. If the device receives a **neighbor advertisement** (**NA**) message in reply, it will have to move to an alternate address.

Critical assets that might need to be accessed from the public internet (for example, a web server) may also benefit from a dedicated global (public) address too, rather than sharing a pooled address for **Network Address Translation** or **Port Address Translation** (**NAT/PAT**).

Administrators can take critical asset address allocation in combination with port use, and equipment identification on the network to help combat threats such as rogue DNS or DHCP servers, ensuring the appropriate device is providing the correct services from the right address.

Server profiling

Server profiling is, again, used to create a picture of normal operation. While it is still broadly expected that server performance and operations will evolve over time, server profiles tend not to vary as rapidly or as markedly as network profiles.

In this section, we will look at five elements that are important to server profiling. Ports, related to the protocols connecting to them, is an obvious cross over between network and server metrics, but the other elements are more similar to those investigated in endpoint threat analyses.

Under the next five headings, we will look at each of these five elements independently. We will look at the technologies and processes that can be used to collect and monitor each data set, and some things that can be inferred from the elements, either in isolation or in combination.

Listening ports

We have previously discussed at length how TCP and UDP ports relate to different provided services. If a server is providing services over the network, it is necessary for a port to be left permanently available for inbound connections. This state is called **listening**. When a client wishes to establish a session, it generates a pseudo-random port on the client end and connects to the listening port. It is, therefore, not possible to entirely shut down all ports on a device if it is also to be functional.

An unauthorized active listening port is a good indicator of an intrusion, or poor network design and administration. If an unauthorized active listening port leads to an exploited system, a malicious entity could gain access to it from outside the network.

On the server itself, the netstat command can be used to review which connections are established. To check on those that are listening as well, the -a option can be used, which displays both established and listening ports.

The following screenshot shows an extract from netstat on a server that is providing DNS and HTTP services. Notice that port 53 (DNS) is in the listening state, whereas port 80 (HTTP) has a number of established connections. If each of these connections were to be ended, the port would re-enter the listening state:

```
Microsoft Windows [Version 10.0.17134.376]
(c) 2018 Microsoft Corporation. All rights reserved.

C:\Windows\System32>netstat -an

Active Connections

  Proto  Local Address          Foreign Address        State
  TCP    0.0.0.0:53             0.0.0.0:0              LISTENING
  TCP    0.0.0.0:80             0.0.0.0:0              LISTENING
  TCP    0.0.0.0:443            0.0.0.0:0              LISTENING
  TCP    10.10.10.254:53        0.0.0.0:0              LISTENING
  TCP    10.10.10.254:80        10.10.10.17:51328     FIN_WAIT_1
  TCP    10.10.10.254:80        10.10.10.17:51342     ESTABLISHED
  TCP    127.0.0.1:8307         0.0.0.0:0              LISTENING
  TCP    127.0.0.1:28380        0.0.0.0:0              LISTENING
  TCP    127.0.0.1:28385        0.0.0.0:0              LISTENING
  UDP    0.0.0.0:54307          *:*
```

Output from the netstat -an command on a server

On Cisco IOS devices, netstat does not work; the equivalent command is show control-plane host open-ports.

A port could be put into a listening state from the inside (via an internal network or physical access), literally opening a doorway into the server. Alternatively, an external actor may scan the ports to see which are open, which might lead to a service that they can compromise.

Common port scanning tools include Nmap, which can be used from the command line. Nmap can operate in a number of ways. The simplest scan technique is to attempt a connection (`nmap -sT`). This gives a lot of information, but does mean that the target logs the session. Imagine ringing random phone numbers, and asking for the name of whoever picks up the phone. If the call is picked up, you know that the number is live, and if they answer the question, you know who is by that phone.

A TCP SYN scan (`nmap -sS`) does not establish a connection. It resets the connection halfway through the three-way handshake, using the reply as an indication of the port status. For this type of scan, imagine ringing the random phone numbers again, but only allowing it to ring once. If the call rings, the number is live; if the number says unregistered, the number is not live; if the number gives an engaged tone or goes to voicemail, the caller is either on the phone or the phone may be switched off. Without revealing yourself, you have done some reconnaissance of the target.

It is often useful for a network administrator to scan the network themselves, both from the inside and from the outside, to have a good handle on the profile of the server during normal conditions. This should be repeated as and when new services are added.

Logged in users/service accounts

It is important to know who normally logs into which physical host device for a number of reasons. This can be broadly broken down into three areas of interest: who is logging in to which host, where are users logging in from, and what privileges do these users have/need/use.

Which users are present?

It is important to know who is on the system at any one time, as well as whether there are multiple users logged into a single host, or single hosts logged into multiple hosts (at the same time). Multiple login sessions can be (but are not always) a sign that the user's account details have been compromised, and that another individual was using their credentials. It is much easier to know whether specific users, multiple user sessions, or multiple session users are normal or not if a profile is taken of the server and/or hosts.

Knowing who is logged in can assist network security in a number of ways. It helps to attribute events; linking a specific user to an IP address and hence to traffic. Tracking the movements of a logical user among the physical landscape of the network can also be important. If a user has used the same terminal in the London branch every work day for five years, it would be an anomaly for them to log in in Berlin or New York. While this may well be legitimate, it is definitely out of the ordinary, and something to check.

Where are users located?

Users can log in either locally (physically on the machine) or remotely (via a remote desktop or SSH). When users are physically logged into a machine, the query application (`query user /server:<server_name>`) can be used in Command Prompt, or `w` for Unix.

Remote access is increasingly common, particularly with cloud services. If we consider the case of remote access to a physical host, the most common methods are through **Remote Desktop Services** (which can be monitored using **Remote Desktop Services Manager**) or via other remote desktop solutions, such as RealVNC. These are often used for things such as remote assistance and servicing, but could equally be leveraged with malicious intent.

Virtual desktop infrastructure is a different way of considering a host. In this case, the bulk of the users access remotely, even if remotely is still on the premises. Services such as Citrix or VMware can provide on-premises functionality. This is often more cost effective than real machines (which will often be dormant) but adds complexity to the security picture. The Citrix Access Management Console can list users with an open session, individual applications, and desktops.

What privileges and access rights are available?

In general, the key feature of managing logged in users is the type of user and their associated privileges. It is generally considered good practice to give only the minimum access rights required to perform the job. However, this often translates to minimum access possible. This creates a situation in which security measures end up being discarded or sidestepped.

A low-level example of this was from the retail sector. A cashier could process purchases but needed a manager's key to process a refund. This might seem reasonable, but at some times (for example, post-Christmas returns), the manager's key would end up fairly permanently left in the cash register. The access rights were not sufficient to *perform the job*.

In a similar way, if members of the IT team aren't ordinarily set up as administrators, they will often have to change between accounts of different privilege. This inevitably leads to multiple login sessions to reduce login times, or permanently simply sitting in the administrator account.

Running processes, tasks, and applications

Identifying which processes, tasks, and applications are running on a system is important to network security. Whilst malicious entities may attempt to disguise their activities, a good knowledge of what ordinarily runs on the system will help to identify malware.

If there is direct access to the running machine, the task manager can be used to identify what is running on the system (Task Manager on Windows, System Monitor in Linux, or Activity Monitor in macOS). In an SSH (command-line only) session, the Windows `tasklist` command and `ps -e` on Linux and macOS can achieve similar functionality.

In some distributed models (for example, Citrix), unified application monitoring tools may be included, which allow the aggregation of this information and its communication back to a (semi) remote monitor.

If direct access is not possible (or is unwarranted), the system can still determine information about running applications from the network traffic. Port numbers and protocols can hint at the kind of application that is being run, albeit only a general hint. Mechanisms such as **Network-Based Application Recognition** (**NBAR**), which uses deep packet inspection, can identify the layer-seven information and give better insight into the source application. This is particularly useful for BYOD environments if monitoring software cannot be implemented by the systems administrators.

Summary

Establishing the normal, or expected, activity on a network or server is crucial to identifying when there is abnormal activity. There are a number of data points that can be used to objectively measure the activity on a network. These should be sampled over time to create a baseline of normal data.

We have learned that on a network, the key factors are throughput, session duration, ports (interfaces) used, and critical asset address space. On a server, the key factors are listening ports, logged in users/service accounts, running processes, running tasks, and applications.

Profiling a network or server is a continuous task. Normal differs based on a number of different factors, so knowledge of the operating conditions is vital to effective anomaly detection.

Questions

1. Under which of the following scenarios might an organization try to create a new network profile?
    1. A change in company workforce planning to create two shifts a day instead of a regular 9-5 working day
    2. Changes in employee hours to accommodate daylight savings time
    3. Members of staff going on parental leave
    4. One of the branches moving to BYOD

2. Which of the following elements from network profile data is the best indication of vulnerability allowing confidential data out of the network?
    1. Increase in total throughput
    2. Decrease in internal traffic
    3. Additional traffic out of the network, outside of work hours
    4. Network congestion at 9.30 am

3. Which multi-vendor supported protocol allows network devices to share their own identity and abilities?
    1. LLDP
    2. CDP
    3. Port security
    4. Port forwarding

4. Which of the following is an example of why critical asset address space should be profiled?
    1. Preparing for IPv6
    2. Protection against man-in-the-middle attacks by default gateway hijack
    3. Detection of high network use by a single host in a denial of service attack
    4. Data exfiltration to external networks

5. Which command can be used to check what ports on a Linux server are in listening or connected mode from outside the network?

    1. `netstat -a`

    2. `nmap -sT`

    3. `show control-plane host open-ports`

    4. `netstat`

6. Which of the following is a principle that helps limit the risk of confidentiality breaches?

    1. Users should be given the minimum possible access.

    2. Users should be given the maximum possible access to prevent multiple logins.

    3. Users should be given the minimum access rights required to perform their job.

    4. Users should be grouped to profile what they should be accessing.

The following four questions are related to the scenario in the following screenshot. Further information is included in the individual questions where required.

An organization has a single branch in Gdansk, with a public facing web server. The web server uses HTTP and HTTPS:

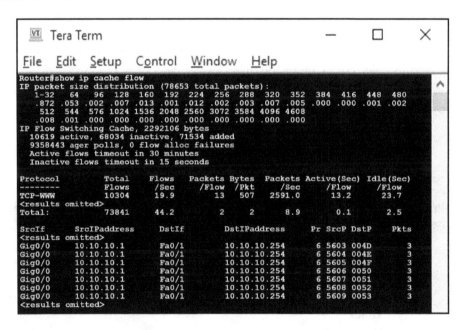

7. The network administrator sees that the session duration for some of the NetFlows is very short. What might this suggest?

    1. The server is malfunctioning.

    2. The lease times are too short.

    3. Port scanning is in progress.

    4. The network is suffering from high congestion.

8. In the next NetFlow scanning period, the NetFlows in the following screenshot were collected. Which of the following is the biggest concern from this new information, and why?

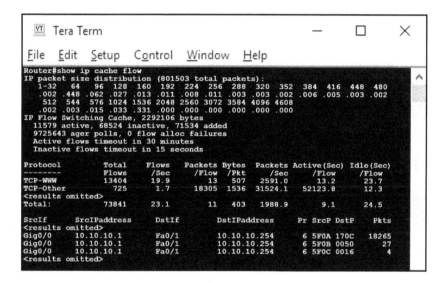

    1. The amount of data that is leaving the server on port 80

    2. The extended, high volume session on the unknown port

    3. The low number of sessions being established

    4. The number of HTTP sessions being established

9. The profile for host `172.16.201.15` is reviewed. This is a Linux PC used by one of the software development team. The developer is currently at a conference overseas and has previously used RealVNC to log into the computer. How could an administrator with physical access to this machine confirm that the developer was the only person logged into the machine?
     1. Using Remote Desktop Services Manager
     2. Using the `whoami` command from the command line of the host
     3. Using the `query user` command from the command line of the host
     4. Using the Access Management Console

10. What other actions could be taken to further secure the network in the future?
     1. Using a VPN to create a secure connection for the developer
     2. Adding the external IP address to a whitelist
     3. Allowing the developer to use internet-based collaboration tools so he can access from anywhere
     4. Preventing remote access to devices

Further reading

- Guidance for Cisco IOS port utilization commands can be found through the Cisco support site:
    - **CDP**: `https://www.cisco.com/c/en/us/support/docs/network-management/discovery-protocol-cdp/43485-cdponios43485.html`
    - **shutdown**: `https://www.cisco.com/c/en/us/td/docs/switches/lan/catalyst2960/software/release/12-2_55_se/command/reference/2960_cr/cli3.html`
    - **port-security**: `https://www.cisco.com/c/en/us/td/docs/switches/lan/catalyst4500/12-2/25ew/configuration/guide/conf/port_sec.html`

- Infosec Institute's guide to Nmap gives more detail on some of the other scan types. This can be accessed at `https://resources.infosecinstitute.com/nmap/#gref`.

Compliance Frameworks

Some industries have legal and regulatory frameworks that dictate how they must conduct their cybersecurity business. This section is 8–10% of the 210-255 exam, but more importantly, failing to adhere to these frameworks has a significant impact on an organization's ability to operate in that industry again, or could even cause corporations or individuals to face criminal charges.

The following topics will be covered in this chapter:

- Payment Card Industry Data Security Standard
- Health Insurance Portability and Accountability Act 1996
- Sarbanes Oxley Act 2002

Payment Card Industry Data Security Standard

The **Payment Card Industry Data Security Standard** (**PCI DSS**) is a set of rules that dictates what data must be protected and the steps that must be taken to protect it, for organizations involved with financial transactions. This does not just mean banks and finance businesses; it means any organization that handles money in any way – basically every business!

Transaction data covered under PCI DSS can expose legitimate owners to theft and financial loss. This can be through unauthorized transactions undertaken on the card itself, or through identity theft, which can have larger implications and costs.

In this section, we will be identifying the data elements that are protected under PCI DSS and the actions required by the standard. This is specifically referred to in topics 3.7a and 3.8 of the 210–255 topic list:

Implementing Cisco Cybersecurity Operations (210-255) topic list:

3.7 Map data types to these compliance frameworks
3.7.a PCI

3.8 Identify data elements that must be protected with regards to a specific standard (PCI DSS)

We will separate the section into two parts: the data elements that are protected under PCI DSS and the actions required.

Protected data elements

PCI DSS protects information required to carry out a transaction. This data is divided into card information and authentication information. If this data were to be attacked and stolen, this could lead to fraudulent transactions.

Card or account information identifies the card used. The **primary account number** (**PAN**) is the minimum requirement to qualify as cardholder data. This is because the cardholder name, expiration date, and service code could be gained by other means (for example, delivery address or behavioral indicators).

Authentication data includes the full track data on a magnetic strip or a chip, card security numbers (CAV2/CVC2/CVV2/CID/CSC), and PINs/PIN blocks.

To protect these data elements, the PCI DSS standards apply to all the other processes in the chain of a transaction, even if they are not specifically involved in that transaction, as stated in PCI DSS v3.2, page 10. PCI DSS standards still apply even if the data is encrypted:

PCI DSS v3.2, page 10:

PCI DSS security requirements apply to all system components which are included in or connected to the people, processes, and technologies, which store, process, or transmit cardholder data or sensitive authentication data.

A guide to whether systems are in or out of scope is given in the following diagram. Unless it is clear that the system is definitely out of scope, it is better to assume that it is in scope. Steps taken to achieve compliance are generally good for overall security, so should be considered anyway:

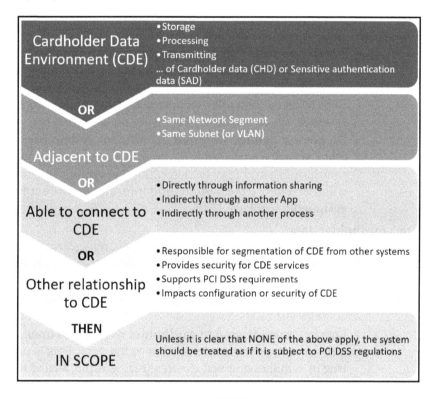

Scope of PCI-DSS

Imagine a conventional restaurant setup. The customer service agents take orders and potentially takes payments. They then pass the order to the kitchen who process the order, returning with the cooked food. It seems obvious that the scope of PCI DSS extends to the payment system and to the agents who process the card payment.

Imagine now that the restaurant upgrades its systems so users can order and pay for their meals. It seems obvious that this system would need to comply with PCI DSS. If this system then shares the order details (but not the payment details) with the kitchens directly, the scope of PCI DSS now also extends to the communication system between the tills and the kitchen.

Required actions

There are 12 requirements of PCI DSS, designed to maintain security on systems within the scope of PCI DSS. These are outlined in more detail within the PIC DSS v3.2.1 document, which is linked in the *Further reading* section. These 12 requirements are as follows:

- **Build and maintain a secure network and systems**:
  - **Install and maintain a firewall configuration to protect cardholder data** because public systems (for example, the internet) is out of scope for PCI DSS, and organizations must, therefore, take steps to isolate the internal network from publicly accessible systems.
  - **Do not use vendor-supplied defaults for system passwords and other security parameters** because these are well known by hacker communities and may be determined via public information. This will then expose the systems and information the equipment was designed to protect.
- **Protect cardholder data**:
  - **Protect stored cardholder data** so that any successful intrusion doesn't expose the data to the attackers. Does the cardholder data even need to be stored? Can it be truncated, encrypted, or masked? How secure is the software being used to carry out any masking or encryption?
  - **Encrypt transmission of cardholder data across open, public networks** to prevent interception of the data. This is particularly true of wireless-enabled devices (for example, a card reader used at the table in a restaurant, or a phone app-based card reader).
- **Maintain a vulnerability management program**:
  - **Protect all systems against malware and regularly update antivirus software or programs** in order to keep system vulnerabilities as few and as minor as possible.
  - **Develop and maintain secure systems and applications** including the timely application of patches and updates in order to minimize exposure to vulnerabilities.

- **Implement strong access control measures**:
    - **Restrict access to cardholder data by the business's need to know** to ensure critical data can only be accessed by authorized personnel, systems, and processes. This will limit the scope of PCI DSS by segmenting the system based on sharing the minimum data and privileges needed to perform the job.
    - **Identify and authenticate access to system components** to reinforce the idea of individual accountability for actions.
    - **Restrict physical access to cardholder data** so that cardholder data cannot be viewed accidentally or in passing.
- **Regularly monitor and test networks**:
    - **Track and monitor all access to network resources and cardholder data** to reinforce access control measures and to determine the cause of and contributing actions toward a breach for future procedure review.
    - **Regularly test security systems and processes** to ensure security controls continue to reflect the changing environment.
- **Maintain an information security policy**:
    - **Maintain a policy that addresses information security for all personnel** to ensure that they are aware of the sensitivity of data and their responsibility for protecting it.

These 12 requirements are a minimum and may need to be augmented and evolved over time. The PCI Security Standards Council, therefore, also lists 10 recommended best practices for Maintaining PCI DSS as of January 2019. These are outlined as follows:

- **Develop and maintain a sustainable compliance program**, which is designed to maintain the security of cardholder data, not simply attaining compliance.
- **Develop program, policy, and procedures** that includes people, process, and technology to help drive proper behavior and repeatable, sustainable business practice.
- **Define performance metrics to measure success**, which allocates the right resources in the right areas to minimize risk occurrence.
- **Assign ownership for coordinating security activities** at an appropriate level to maintain accountability, resource allocation, and buy-in from other departments.
- **Emphasize security and risk management to attain and maintain compliance** in order to focus minds on the security of cardholder data and not just compliance.
- **Continuously monitor controls** to ensure that policies remain able to secure cardholder's data.

- **Detect and respond to control failures** to minimize the impact of an incident, restore controls, repair the system, and ensure future defense.
- **Maintain security awareness** throughout the organization to defend against the changing threat landscape.
- **Monitoring compliance of third party service providers** to ensure they remain compliant and that the systems remain secure.
- **Evolve the compliance program to address changes** in business structure, new innovations, and changes to the threat landscape.

Health Insurance Portability and Accountability Act, 1996

The **Health Insurance Portability and Accountability Act (HIPAA)** 1996 focuses on the security of healthcare data. Healthcare data is sensitive for a number of reasons. Protecting and securing healthcare data is important to ensure patients get the right care (considering things such as pre-existing conditions or medication). Additionally, securing this data is important for protecting individuals from discrimination based on healthcare or genetic issues (or perceived issues) and protecting providers (and insurers, including the state) from identity theft and those resultant costs.

In this section, we will identify the data elements that are protected under HIPAA. This is specifically referenced in topic 3.7b of the 210–255 syllabus:

> *Implementing Cisco Cybersecurity Operations (210-255) topic list:*
>
> *3.7 Map data types to these compliance frameworks*
> *3.7.b HIPAA (Health Insurance Portability and Accountability Act)*

In this section, we need to consider the entities covered by HIPAA and the types of safeguards that must be in place.

Protected health information and covered entities

HIPAA covers information related to transactions for which the United States Department for **Health and Human Sciences (HHS)** has adopted a standard. This means that the information covered may, and likely will, evolve over time as more standards are agreed.

Protected health information *relates to the past, present, or future physical or mental health or condition of an individual; the provision of healthcare to an individual; or the past, present, or future payment for the provision of healthcare to an individual* (§2791(b)(2) of the Public Health Service Act 1944, Title 42 United States Code). Protected health information by definition must, therefore, by be identifiable as relating to an individual.

There are 18 features that can be used to identify, contact, or locate an individual. When any one (or more) of these are combined with health information, that information becomes identifiable and is therefore protected:

- Names (full or last name and initial)
- All geographical identifiers smaller than a state, except for the initial three digits of a zip code if this defines an area containing at least 20,000 people
- Dates (other than year) directly related to an individual
- Phone numbers
- Fax numbers
- Email addresses
- Social security numbers
- Medical record numbers
- Health insurance beneficiary numbers
- Account numbers
- Certificate/license numbers
- Vehicle identifiers (including serial numbers and license plate numbers)
- Device identifiers and serial numbers;
- Web **Uniform Resource Locators (URLs)**
- **Internet Protocol (IP)** address numbers
- Biometric identifiers, including finger, retinal, and voice prints
- Full face photographic images and any comparable images
- Any other unique identifying number, characteristic, or code except the unique code assigned by the investigator to code the data

An organization must comply with HIPAA if they are a **covered entity**. Covered entities are defined as being either a healthcare provider, a health plan, or a healthcare clearinghouse (an intermediary company working between healthcare providers and insurance companies), as shown in the following table:

Health Care Providers	Health Plans	Health Care Clearinghouses
e.g. • Doctors • Psychologists • Dentists • Nursing Homes • Pharmacies	e.g. • Health insurance companies • HMOs • Company health plans • Government programs that pay for health care (Medicare, Medicaid, military and veterans health care programs)	e.g. • Entities that process nonstandard health information into a standard format or vice versa.

Covered entities as defined for HIPAA

Organizations that are not covered entities may still need HIPAA-compliant systems if the PHI is sourced from a covered entity. It makes sense that this covers medical research in which the PHI is sourced from a hospital or physicians are involved with a clinical trial; however, this includes looser interactions such as HR departments' storage of occupational health emails, managers' storage of sick notes, or lawyers' storage of files after litigation.

Safeguards

HIPAA incorporates a number of different elements, including the **security rule** that focuses on e-PHI. The security rule defines a series of safeguards that are loosely designated as administrative, physical, and technical. These are inter-linked to provide layers of security. For example, if access to the systems processing e-PHI were strictly and correctly enforced 100% of the time, it would not be necessary to restrict access to the building (with respect to e-PHI). However, having both of these safeguards is insurance against one of these failing or being subverted.

Administrative safeguards

Administrative safeguards refer to the policies and actions taken at an organizational system level to maintain security for PHI (and e-PHI):

- **Security management process** should identify risks to PHI and e-PHI and contain an action plan to reduce the vulnerability.
- **Security personnel** should be identified and made responsible for developing and implementing an action plan.
- **Information access management** should be used to enforce the least privilege to PHI and e-PHI to minimize those with access, and therefore the potential for access controls to be subverted.
- **Workforce training and management**, which allows those in contact with PHI and e-PHI to understand their roles and responsibilities for this information.
- **Evaluation** against the HIPAA security requirements to ensure that changes, where necessary, are rolled out, and otherwise, that compliance assurances can be given.

Physical safeguards

Physical safeguards are those elements of the security plan that protect the environment around the systems holding PHI:

- **Facility access control** restricts access to the site to authorized individuals and organizations. This includes having secure access to the building and identity checks in offices.
- **Workstation and device security** restrict access to the systems. This may include not placing PHI terminals in shared spaces, or restricting them to specific locations (separate offices, and so on).
- **Device and media controls**, which can be used to track hardware and electronic media moving into, out of, and around the facility. This also covers policies for maintenance and disposal of workstations, devices, or storage.

Technical safeguards

Technical safeguards are implemented on the devices, workstations, and systems themselves:

- **Access control**, which restricts data access to only authorized persons.
- **Audit controls**, which record and evaluate access and other activity within systems containing e-PHI.
- **Integrity policies**, which ensure that e-PHI isn't improperly altered or destroyed. This will include maintaining backups and differentiating users with read-only from those with read-write access.
- **Transmission security** mechanisms to protect e-PHI during transit over electronic networks, restricting the systems and users who can access the data, and preventing interception of data.
- **Person or entity authentication**, which can be used to verify that a person or entity is who they claim to be. This should include techniques that integrate *out-of-band* authentication.

Sarbanes Oxley Act, 2002

The **Sarbanes Oxley** Act, 2002 (**SOX**) provides oversight on the financial reporting of companies. All companies that are publicly held in America and any international organizations that have registered equity or debt securities within the US Securities Exchange Commission must comply with SOX.

SOX was designed to verify internal processes to combat corporate fraud. In this section, we will identify the key data elements that are protected under SOX and the correct actions required by the standard. This relates to topic 3.7c in the 210-255 specification:

Implementing Cisco Cybersecurity Operations (210-255) topic list:

3.7 Map data types to these compliance frameworks
3.7.c SOX

While SOX focuses on senior managers reviewing annual reports, signing off deficiencies, and reporting fraudulent behavior, this is based on trust in the internal policies and controls. If all the paperwork and accounts add up, this is worthless unless the signing officers and auditors can be sure of the data's integrity.

For information to be truly auditable, all systems, including computers, network equipment, and other infrastructure, which have contact with financial data, must provide assurance. A SOX audit will, at minimum, review the policy and technology that impact on the truthfulness of the financial data produced. These could include the following:

- **Access controls**, which define users that have physical and electronic access to financial data, and how much access each of these users has. This also includes the management of former employees, contractors, and other system users.
- **IT security policies**, which prevent the loss of sensitive data and maintain their integrity. In most other scenarios, the biggest threat is data leaks, but a ransomware situation would mean that the organization would be non-compliant with SOX, with all the consequences that would bring.
- **Logging** of changes to users, infrastructure, IT assets, and the financial data itself, which will provide assurance of the data's integrity.
- **Backups** of the financial data and any logs must be protected in case data recovery is required. SOX compliance includes data stored offsite or by a third-party data storage provider. The policy regarding backups should also be clear about how often backups are taken, and how to ensure that different versions of the data are controlled.

Summary

In this chapter, we looked at three frameworks detailing the minimum expected standards for maintaining data, and the types of data that must be protected.

PCI-DSS covers card holder detail and authentication data for any organization that handles payment card processing, even if this is outsourced.

HIPAA covers **electronic protected health information (ePHI)** for any organization that is involved with transmitting, generating, or accessing health information in electronic form.

SOX covers the safeguarding of information related to auditing and accounting, focusing on the integrity of the information held.

While these three legislative and regulatory frameworks are created specifically with the USA in mind, other countries will have frameworks of their own, and international countries will often have to comply with a number of different frameworks simultaneously. Frameworks are, therefore, a minimum standard.

Questions

1. Which of the following runs counter to the requirements of PCI-DSS?
    1. Using the out-of-box settings for the firewall
    2. Installing a firewall to protect CDE systems from public systems (for example, the internet)
    3. Applying only vendor-supplied patches and updates
    4. Using custom passwords and settings

2. Which of the following is a recommended best practice under PCI DSS but could also be applied to all the other frameworks?
    1. Impose strict access controls.
    2. Maintain and evolve security awareness across the organization.
    3. Use third-party software to reduce the scope.
    4. Maintain training programs to ensure standards do not slip.

3. Which of the following is the best method for preventing exposure of cardholder data?
    1. Masking cardholder data
    2. Encrypting cardholder data
    3. Storing only the data required
    4. Truncating cardholder data

4. Which of the following name formats would not count as an identifiable feature under HIPAA?
    1. Mr. John Doe
    2. Mr. J Doe
    3. Mr. Doe
    4. J Doe

5. Which of the following controls is listed in PCI DSS, HIPAA, and SOX?
    1. Audit controls
    2. Encryption
    3. Data expiration
    4. Maintenance of backups

The following five questions are related to the following scenario. Additional details may be provided in the questions.

A new start-up has launched in Florida, which links customers with providers of therapies such as pharmacy services, massage, and acupuncture. Their app allows users to record their symptoms and any other relevant health information, book appointments, and pay for them through the app, either through their insurance companies or by credit card. The therapy providers are also paid through the app.

6. The company, as a start-up, is privately owned. Which of the following statements is true?
    1. SOX does not apply until shares are issued publicly.
    2. SOX does not apply at the current time.
    3. SOX may still apply if the company has registered debt securities.
    4. SOX will still apply because the company is operating in the US.

7. The start-up is planning an upgrade that would allow customers and therapists to call each other through the app rather than the current system, which shares customers' phone numbers with providers. Which of the following statements is true?
    1. Both the systems are in scope for HIPAA because they store identifiable health data.
    2. The present system is out of scope for HIPAA because phone numbers are not identifiable data elements.
    3. The proposed system, which would remove the requirement for phone numbers would be exempt from HIPAA as the data would be unidentifiable.
    4. The use of a privacy and sharing article in the terms and conditions of service exempts the system from HIPAA.

8. The system used a third-party provider to certify that they were compliant with PCI DSS. Which of the following is true?
    1. The system, now certified, will always be compliant with PCI DSS.
    2. The system should be re-checked annually as per PCI DSS regulations.
    3. The system should be continuously monitored as it is good practice.
    4. The system must be regularly monitored as this is a specified requirement.

9. The company wants to move to a new site. The proposed office would be an open plan, hot-desking environment. Which of the following is true?
    1. This layout would not comply with the *workstation and device security* physical safeguard under HIPAA.
    2. The company could comply with the *workstation and device security* physical safeguard under HIPAA by locking away its servers so that the people in the open plan office cannot physically access them.
    3. This layout would not comply with the *restrict physical access* requirement under PCI DSS.
    4. The company could comply with the *restrict physical access* requirement under PCI DSS by moving all the devices in the open plan environment to a different subnet to the CDE and ensuring no data is shared between the two systems.

10. The company has decided that complying with HIPAA is too difficult and that it no longer wishes to store patient symptoms on the app. Which of the following is true?
    1. The company still needs to comply with HIPAA because individuals are being connected to covered entities.
    2. The company still needs to comply with HIPAA because it processes payments in relation to healthcare provision for individuals.
    3. The company would no longer need to comply with HIPAA because they are only relaying information about service providers to its customers.
    4. The company would still need to comply with HIPAA for its backups and historical data only.

Further reading

- Detailed guidance on PCI-DSS is provided by the PCI Security Standards Council at https://www.pcisecuritystandards.org/pci_security/.
- Detailed guidance on HIPAA is provided by the U.S. Department of Health & Human Services at https://www.hhs.gov/hipaa/for-professionals/security/laws-regulations/index.html.
- Detailed guidance on SOX can be found from Addison-Hewitt Associates at http://www.soxlaw.com/.

Section 4: Data and Event Analysis

4

Cyber security operators should be able to analyze data from multiple sources and make relevant conclusions about a security event. They should also be able to prioritize events and use common security frameworks. Readers will look at a range of data sources, from network logs, packet captures, intrusion detection systems, intrusion prevention systems, and host-based detection systems and draw conclusions about what type of event is happening, its severity, and how likely it is to happen again.

Most importantly, the cyber security operator must be able to communicate the findings of these processes with high-level management (most of whom are non-technical). The analysis and presentation of these results must, therefore, build a narrative with various logs providing context for each other in a coherent format.

This section covers the process of bringing together information from various sources and drawing conclusions from this.

The following chapters are included in this section:

- Chapter 10, *Data Normalization and Exploitation*
- Chapter 11, *Drawing Conclusions from the Data*

10
Data Normalization and Exploitation

Cybersecurity data comes in from many different sources. Identifying security events is dependent on bringing all these data sources together and relating one piece of data to another. Creating a common format and putting the data into this format is vital for the identification of threats. Once this has been done, data points can be linked to each other, which helps to maintain the data's integrity and reduce duplication. This process is called **data normalization**.

Cybersecurity operators must be able to normalize data to identify attacks and conduct investigations.

The following topics will be covered in this chapter:

- Creating commonality
- Using the IP 5-tuple
- Pinpointing threats and victims

Creating commonality

In Chapter 1, *Classifying Threats*, we looked at the need for common naming and rating systems so that data could be communicated between organizations. Here, we will address the need for standardization within the organization.

In this section, we will look at how to standardize the data into a universal format, and how to normalize the storage of data. We will then look at how these processes can help to give a better insight into what is happening on the network or system.

These subject areas are specifically referenced as topics 4.1 and 4.2 in the 210-255 syllabus:

> *Implementing Cisco Cybersecurity Operations (210-255) topic list:*
>
> *4.1 Describe the process of data normalization*
> *4.2 Interpret common data values into a universal format*

Organizations increasingly employ a range of defensive systems, typically from a range of suppliers. There are a number of reasons for this, ranging from the distrust of a supplier (consider the controversies over Huawei providing 5G infrastructure in some nations), or different specialisms among security firms, to simply providing redundancy. Although many vendors provide a single dashboard for their own systems, fewer systems draw in data from multiple vendors.

Most questions posed to cybersecurity operators will require information from a number of different sources. To service this answer, the operator must trawl through every log separately. The problem arises when multiple services have logged the same event; a IDS may log a potentially malicious file, which is then quarantined and logged by the antivirus system. Would this count once or twice when posed the question of *how many security incidents have there been this month*?

Worse still, let's say that the IDS classified the malicious file as a **medium risk** but the antivirus system classified it as **high risk** (both on arbitrary, vendor-specific scales). Would the risk of the event be high or medium in the report back to management? Should the IDS be made more stringent, or should the antivirus be made more lenient?

If instead, all the separate logs were instead combined into one database, this would yield much more representative results.

This has led to **security information and event management (SIEM)** tools to emerge; Splunk and SolarWinds are among the most well-known packages with SIEM features. These software packages can directly collect data themselves, instead of drawing in data from other providers. This allows a modular system, with different (and sometimes overlapping) defensive systems feeding a single administrator view.

Standardized formatting

The human brain is far better at processing a narrative or story than it is at looking at individual data points. Grouping data assists in providing context to, and the corroboration of, a story. Consider the reveal in a detective show; the detective explains the crime as a timeline, from the motive through to the actions, to any cover-ups. Several streams of physical evidence, witness testimony, and other information need to be brought together to form the story, almost all of which is given to the viewer; however, until it is presented as a story, it barely makes sense.

One of the best examples of standardizing formatting occurs with time stamping. In Chapter 6, *Network Security Data Analysis*, we saw how Wireshark and tcpdump displayed different date and time stamps for the same PCAP file. The reason for this, and the reason that both systems were able to generate valid and reasonable results from the same data, is that human-readable date and time stamps are inefficient in terms of memory and processing; computers store dates, instead, as a number on a continuous scale, translating these numbers back to times and dates on demand.

A number of different time systems exist in the world. Calendars that have a different **Year 0** include the Jewish calendar starting in 3761 BCE or the Japanese era names starting with each new emperor; various calendars (particularly lunar calendars) vary in year length. The common date/time systems in the computer domain are the Unix **epoch** time (counting seconds since 00:00 1 Jan 1970) and Windows GetSystemTimeAsFileTime (which counts 100-nanosecond intervals since 00:00 1 Jan 1601). Storing timestamps as integer values are much more efficient than in RFC 8601 (YY-MM-DD hh:mm:ss) format, which makes it perfect for log files, which may have thousands of entries very quickly.

The Unix (and Linux) CLI strftime command can be used to reformat the integer string from a Unix timestamp to human readable formats. The most common commands are strftime("%c",<time>) and strftime("%F",<time>), where %c denotes **current locale** representation, %F denotes RFC 8601 formatting, and <time> is the timestamp in Unix time. The awk command can be used to separate out the fields around a field separator (most commonly a comma (,), semicolon (;), space ( ), or pipe |).

In the following code, the `awk` command is used to separate the fields in a `orig_log.csv` (`{FS=OFS=","}`). The Unix time in the 2 (`$2`) field is then replaced (using the `strftime` function) with the RFC 8601 date (`%F`), and 24-hour time with seconds (`%T`), and outputting it to the `new_log.csv` file. For brevity, we have used a tail to show just the last five lines of the file on the screen. The `awk` command will have carried out the replacement on the entire contents of the original file:

```
[ac@VUbuntu]~$ cat orig_log.csv | tail -n 5
INFO ,1556636630,pool-1-thread-1 ,fma.update.UpdaterEngine ,Starting Wrapper.
INFO ,1556636663,pool-1-thread-1 ,fma.update.UpdaterEngine ,Finishing installation.
INFO ,1556636694,pool-1-thread-1 ,fma.update.UpdaterEngine ,Installation 1798831 completed.
ERROR,1556636902,pool-1-thread-1 ,fma.update.UpdaterEngine ,Failed to report (END,false,null).
INFO ,1556636910,pool-1-thread-1 ,fma.update.UpdaterEngine ,Uploading log file.
[ac@VUbuntu]~$
[ac@VUbuntu]~$ awk 'BEGIN {FS=OFS=","}{$2=strftime("%F %T",$2)}{print}' orig_log.csv > new_log.csv
[ac@VUbuntu]~$
[ac@VUbuntu]~$ cat new_log.csv | tail -n 5
INFO ,2019-04-30 16:03:50,pool-1-thread-1 ,fma.update.UpdaterEngine ,Starting Wrapper.
INFO ,2019-04-30 16:04:23,pool-1-thread-1 ,fma.update.UpdaterEngine ,Finishing installation.
INFO ,2019-04-30 16:04:54,pool-1-thread-1 ,fma.update.UpdaterEngine ,Installation 1798831 completed.
ERROR,2019-04-30 16:08:22,pool-1-thread-1 ,fma.update.UpdaterEngine ,Failed to report (END,false,null).
INFO ,2019-04-30 16:08:30,pool-1-thread-1 ,fma.update.UpdaterEngine ,Uploading log file.
[ac@VUbuntu]~$
```

Changing a log file from Unix to human-readable timestamps

Time is just one of the many discrepancies that can appear between different system logs. In `Chapter 4`, *Identifying Rogue Data from a Dataset*, we also looked at the different MAC address representations. A similar process could be done here using `pcregrep` to remove any formatting in the source or to reformat it for the desired output.

Standardized formatting should be as generic as possible. As we have seen, the Unix epoch time can be converted into a number of different formats; a MAC address with no formatting or delimiters can be extracted into any number of formats as required.

Normalizing data

Normalizing data is about creating a single format and point of reference for all the data in the system. This data can then be visualized, analyzed, or extracted by different systems without affecting the source data. This allows the maintenance of a single version of the truth. Normalized and standardized data are not equivalent terms. Normalized data relies on the standardization of data, but standardization does not require the data to be normalized. The aim of normalization is to have the minimum redundancy (duplicates) possible. This aids integrity, although it can be at the cost of processing and memory during reading and updating.

There are a number of normal forms; there is not enough detail to go through all of them, although a good reference is included in the *Further reading* section of this chapter. In this section, we will look at the first three normal forms (after which data is generally considered normalized.

Original data

The following diagram shows a number of logs that have been consolidated into one big table. At present, the data is not in any normal form:

Time	Service IP address	Device	Source	Action	UserID	User Name
09:18:02	10.10.10.251	SysLog Server	10.10.10.2	Port F0/5 Up	Nil	Nil
09:18:03	10.10.10.254	DHCP Server	2D76.241A.C5CB	Assigned 10.10.10.21	Nil	Nil
09:18:05	10.10.10.253	Log On Server	10.10.10.21	Log On Success	AA001	Aaron Adams
09:19:02	10.10.10.253	Log On Server	10.10.10.21	Password Change, Log On Success	AA001	Aaron Adams
09:19:04	10.10.10.252	Web Proxy	10.10.10.21	Access Web Link	AA001	Aaron Adams
09:23:23	10.10.10.253	Log On Server	10.10.10.21	Log Out Success	AA001	Aaron Adams
09:53:12	10.10.10.253	Log On Server	10.10.10.21	Log On Success	BB002	Bob Bryant
09:55:23	10.10.10.252	Web Proxy	10.10.10.21	Access Web Link	BB002	Bob Bryant
09:55:23	10.10.10.21	Host Device	End Point Antivirus	Virus Detected	admin	Administrator

Original data (not normalized)

This data is not normalized as more than one value is stored in a single attribute (such as the actions in entry 4).

First normal form

In the **first normal form** (**1NF**), the data should be atomic, and each record/row in the database should be unique.

Atomic data representation means that each cell must contain a single value. In the original data, the actions **Password Change** and **Log On Success** both happen at the same time, and all the other fields are the same. Although it feels like it is a backward step, a further record needs to be created to separate out these actions, as follows:

Time	Service IP address	Device	Source	Action	UserID	User Name
09:18:02	10.10.10.251	SysLog Server	10.10.10.2	Port F0/5 Up	Nil	Nil
09:18:03	10.10.10.254	DHCP Server	2D76.241A.C5CB	Assigned 10.10.10.21	Nil	Nil
09:18:05	10.10.10.253	Log On Server	10.10.10.21	Log On Success	AA001	Aaron Adams
09:19:02	10.10.10.253	Log On Server	10.10.10.21	Password Change	AA001	Aaron Adams
09:19:02	10.10.10.253	Log On Server	10.10.10.21	Log On Success	AA001	Aaron Adams
09:19:04	10.10.10.252	Web Proxy	10.10.10.21	Access Web Link	AA001	Aaron Adams
09:23:23	10.10.10.253	Log On Server	10.10.10.21	Log Out Success	AA001	Aaron Adams
09:53:12	10.10.10.253	Log On Server	10.10.10.21	Log On Success	BB002	Bob Bryant
09:55:23	10.10.10.252	Web Proxy	10.10.10.21	Access Web Link	BB002	Bob Bryant
09:55:23	10.10.10.21	Host Device	End Point Antivirus	Virus Detected	admin	Administrator

First normal form

There are now two entries at 09:19:02, but each record only relates to a single event.

Second normal form

In the **second normal form** (**2NF**), we need to remove partial dependencies. To do this, we must look at the things that uniquely identify each record. In this case, we can see that the time and action uniquely identify single records. In data normalization terms, we call the time and action fields a composite key; together, they uniquely identify each record.

A partial dependency exists where a field's value depends solely on one field within the composite key and no other. In this case, the **Device** and **Service IP address** is dependent on the **Action**, but not on the time. To arrive at 2NF, we will extract the **Service IP address**, **Device** type, and **Action** into another table, identifying a server with a unique ID, as follows:

Time	Source	Action ID	UserID	User Name
09:18:02	10.10.10.2	1	Nil	Nil
09:18:03	2D76.241A.C5CB	2	Nil	Nil
09:18:05	10.10.10.21	3	AA001	Aaron Adams
09:19:02	10.10.10.21	4	AA001	Aaron Adams
09:19:02	10.10.10.21	3	AA001	Aaron Adams
09:19:04	10.10.10.21	5	AA001	Aaron Adams
09:23:23	10.10.10.21	6	AA001	Aaron Adams
09:53:12	10.10.10.21	3	BB002	Bob Bryant
09:55:23	10.10.10.21	7	BB002	Bob Bryant
09:55:23	End Point Antivirus	8	admin	Administrator

Action ID	Action	Service IP address	Device
1	Port F0/5 Up	10.10.10.251	SysLog Server
2	Assigned 10.10.10.21	10.10.10.254	DHCP Server
3	Log On Success	10.10.10.253	Log On Server
4	Password Change	10.10.10.253	Log On Server
5	Access Web Link	10.10.10.252	Web Proxy
6	Log Out Success	10.10.10.253	Log On Server
7	Access Web Link	10.10.10.252	Web Proxy
8	Virus Detected	10.10.10.21	Host Device

Second normal form

This reduces updating errors because each service is hosted at a single IP address. Although these logs would have been mostly created automatically, having data in the second normal form reduces the risk that a `Log on Server` at `10.10.10.25` might be created by mistake. The consistency of the data is much more secure.

Third normal form

In the **third normal form** (**3NF**), any columns that are not dependent upon the primary key are removed. The **UserID** and **User Name** fields are dependent on each other, rather than being independent entities within the main table. Equally, the **Device** and **Service IP addresses** are dependent on each other rather than the **Action**; in this setup, the **Log On Server** is always at `10.10.10.253`, regardless of whether it is processing a log on, log out, or password change.

In 3NF, we separate the device and users into separate tables as follows:

Time	Source	Action ID	UserID
09:18:02	10.10.10.2	1	Nil
09:18:03	2D76.241A.C5CB	2	Nil
09:18:05	10.10.10.21	3	AA001
09:19:02	10.10.10.21	4	AA001
09:19:03	10.10.10.21	2	AA001
09:19:04	10.10.10.21	5	AA001
09:23:23	10.10.10.21	6	AA001
09:53:12	10.10.10.21	3	BB002
09:55:23	10.10.10.21	7	BB002
09:55:23	End Point Antivirus	8	admin

Action ID	Action	Service ID
1	Port F0/5 Up	1
2	Assigned 10.10.10.21	2
3	Log On Success	3
4	Password Change	3
5	Access Web Link	4
6	Log Out Success	3
7	Access Web Link	4
8	Virus Detected	5

Service ID	Device	Service IP address
1	SysLog Server	10.10.10.251
2	DHCP Server	10.10.10.254
3	Log On Server	10.10.10.253
4	Web Proxy	10.10.10.252
5	Host Device	10.10.10.21

UserID	User Name
Nil	Nil
AA001	Aaron Adams
BB002	Bob Bryant
admin	Administrator

Third normal form

The advantage of removing transitive dependence is reducing duplication, which improves data integrity as in 2NF. The greater benefit of 3NF is reached because data that was additional is now much more structured.

Criticisms

There are some criticisms of data normalization, including added processing time and complexity spent drawing in data from multiple sources. There are schools of thought that argue that the prioritization of data recall over data update or creation can sometimes be justified. In the case of cybersecurity, the vast volumes of data and the fact that the data is leveraged in many different forms, including making custom views that may not be normalized in and of themselves, make normalization a very complex business. Normalization is often not completed, which poses some redundancy and data integrity issues, but this is offset by the speed of operation and flexibility of the dataset.

One other issue with highly normalized data is that the data is very rigid. Imagine, for example, if there was another log on server added at a different IP address. To allow the above 2NF and 3NF data models to work, there would need to either be duplication of the **Action** field, or the relationship between the service and the IP address would be broken.

The IP 5-tuple

The IP 5-tuple is a collection of five features (protocol plus source and destination IP addresses and ports) that identify a TCP/IP connection. A tuple is immutable, which means that it's structure and its values *cannot* change (as opposed to a variable, even if the value *doesn't* change). The IP 5-tuple is unchanged throughout its journey from the source device to the destination device. This means that it can be tracked as it moves around the system. Where there are multiple network devices producing NetFlow data, for example, a packet can be seen traversing the network.

In this section, we will identify how the IP 5-tuple can be used to group events by host devices, and how we can isolate a compromised host in a grouped set of logs using this 5-tuple. This section relates to topics 4.3 and 4.4 of the 210–255 specification:

> *Implementing Cisco Cybersecurity Operations (210-255) Topic List:*
>
> *4.3 Describe the 5-tuple correlation*
> *4.4 Describe the 5-tuple approach to isolate a compromised host in a grouped set of logs*

The IP 5-tuple is one of the most important tools for system and network administrators for tracking a packet through the system, and hence for identifying compromised host devices.

5-tuple correlation

The IP 5-tuple can be used to identify the destination and host IP address and port. Many systems (for example, Cisco ASA, Firewalls, NetFlow, IDS, and IPS) will use the 5-tuple to identify events as it is easy to differentiate between devices. With the 5-tuple differentiating between the traffic flow in both directions, this can be used to gain information such as the amount of data uploaded compared with the amount of data downloaded (NetFlow). It can also be used to identify whether data is establishing a connection or is referring to an existing connection (Cisco ASA).

IDS and IPS can establish the origin of detected threats and the destination of data exfiltration.

Isolating compromised hosts

The IP 5-tuple includes source and destination IP addresses and ports, in addition to the protocol being used. Previously we have discussed the use of well-known or registered port numbers to distinguish between the different protocols being used; it is more important here to consider the impact of **Port Address Translation (PAT)**.

If detection devices are placed at, or near, the exit point from the network (the border router), events may contain translated addresses instead of the addresses configured on each device. This may skew the findings, particularly if there is a small pool of addresses available for the network.

Even when NAT or PAT are used, the inclusion of the ports in the 5-tuple allows for cross-referencing with the NAT and PAT logs to determine the final host. This can be exceptionally useful for isolating a compromised host.

Isolating compromised hosts is a real demonstration of the importance of collating and normalizing data. If the right information is available, a lot of information can be brought together. This will be demonstrated through the scenario questions for this chapter.

Pinpointing threats and victims

As we saw in Chapter 1, *Classifying Threats*, attributing actions to threat actors is an important cybersecurity task. Additionally, pinpointing machines that were targeted is important to the containment idea from the NIST incident response plan guidelines from Chapter 7, *Roles and Responsibilities During an Incident*. This is particularly important if the target has actually been compromised.

In this section, we will learn how to describe the retrospective analysis method to find a malicious file or to identify compromised hosts in a network based on reports that arise from network monitoring tools and threat analyses. This will be, specifically, in the guise of an AMP threat grid, which we saw in Chapter 1, *Classifying Threats*. This links to objectives 4.5 and 4.6 in the 210–255 topic list:

> *Implementing Cisco Cybersecurity Operations (210-255) topic list:*
>
> *4.5 Describe the retrospective analysis method to find a malicious file, provided file analysis report*
> *4.6 Identify potentially compromised hosts within the network based on a threat analysis report containing malicious IP address or domains*

In the aftermath of an incident, the CSIRT will be receiving a multitude of analysis reports. Rapid operator analysis can be the difference between having to contain and recover one host or every host on the network.

Malicious file identification

Malicious files are consistently evolving, and won't always be spotted by IDS, IPS, or the other systems involved in the layered defense. There is considerable research that suggests that threats often go undetected for many days, weeks, or even months.

Files may be identified as malicious, using systems such as Cisco TALOS, sandbox systems, security researchers, or end-user reports. These files may have already spread through the network, and may or may not have completed their nefarious activities.

While anti-virus systems may be able to update and search for new threats, this may not be possible on all systems, particularly legacy systems or device-specific control systems. The retrospective analysis describes the process of applying the new threat intelligence data to existing logs, to identify whether an infection or intrusion had occurred. This is particularly useful if the threat intelligence data has specific signatures or behaviors to look for.

Host identification

With a retrospective analysis, there may have been a number of different files on various hosts to seek and track down. Host identification can, therefore, be very time-consuming. It can sometimes be easier to track the movement of files through the system, from host to host. This could be particularly useful to look at a mutating threat (for example, files changing names or locations).

Again, the use of centralized, normalized, and searchable data will help in host identification. Cisco **Advanced Malware Protection** (**AMP**), combined with AMP for endpoints and visualized with network file trajectory can massively assist the process.

Summary

Cybersecurity data comes in from many different sources. While we have already discussed systems that provide (relatively) real-time protections, significant data from previous attacks suggests a delay of some weeks and months from breach to detection.

Using the whole suite of available tools and available data helps to improve our ability to detect threats, both in real time and retrospectively. To do this, information needs to be brought together in a common place and format. To improve searchability, and data integrity, normalization should be carried out. This reduces redundancy (hence becoming resource efficient) and helps to relate one log to another.

One key field for relating one entry with another is the time stamp, which can vary in format from one system to another. The other is the IP 5-tuple, which can be used to identify connections between endpoints, both within and external to the network.

Questions

1. Which of the following will output the GMT time 2009-01-20 16:00:00?
   1. `strftime(%F, 1232467200)`
   2. `strftime(%c %T, 1232467200)`
   3. `strftime(%F %T, 1232467200)`
   4. `strftime(%c, 1232467200)`

2. Which of the following CLI commands is used to separate the fields in a serial file?
   1. `pcregrep`
   2. `awk`
   3. `grep`
   4. `split`

3. What is the aim of normalization?
   1. Maximizing redundancy
   2. Minimizing duplication of data
   3. Maximizing log file space requirements
   4. Minimizing processing during updating

4. What does the term **atomic** mean in relation to data normalization?
   1. The contents of each field must be unique.
   2. Each field title must be unique.
   3. The contents of each record must be unique.
   4. Each field may only contain a single value.

5. Which of the following systems is capable of using the IP 5-tuple to identify whether incoming data relates to an existing connection, or is establishing a new connection?

    1. Cisco ASA

    2. Cisco AMP

    3. NetFlow

    4. Firewall

The following five questions relate to the following scenario. Additional details may be provided in the questions.

A company has a number of different security software packages, none of which have recorded any security events within the last few days. An industry insider has alerted them to a potential threat, which may have affected them.

6. The log file from the PAT log is shown in the following screenshot. The date/time field is the second listed field and is in Unix time format:

```
[ac@VUbuntu]~$ cat orig.log | tail -n 25
Pro Time         Inside_global            Inside_local         Outside_local          Outside_global
tcp 1470481221 81.173.237.255:54610 10.10.10.39:54610 52.114.75.79:443   52.114.75.79:443
udp 1470481221 81.173.237.255:55777 10.10.10.37:55777 216.58.210.194:443 216.58.210.194:443
udp 1470481222 81.173.237.255:58065 10.10.10.39:58065 216.58.206.110:443 216.58.206.110:443
udp 1470481222 81.173.237.255:59918 10.10.10.42:59918 219.83.193.158:80  219.83.193.158:80
udp 1470481222 81.173.237.255:59919 10.10.10.40:59919 208.67.222.222:53  208.67.222.222:53
udp 1470481223 81.173.237.255:61937 10.10.10.43:61937 208.67.222.222:53  208.67.222.222:53
udp 1470481223 81.173.237.255:61938 10.10.10.44:61938 216.58.212.67:443  216.58.212.67:443
udp 1470481224 81.173.237.255:63200 10.10.10.43:63200 216.58.204.68:443  216.58.204.68:443
udp 1470481225 81.173.237.255:63568 10.10.10.45:63568 216.58.206.67:443  216.58.206.67:443
udp 1470481225 81.173.237.255:63889 10.10.10.47:63889 216.58.210.193:443 216.58.210.193:443
udp 1470481226 81.173.237.255:64707 10.10.10.45:64707 216.58.206.67:443  216.58.206.67:443
udp 1470481226 81.173.237.255:64710 10.10.10.44:64710 216.58.204.68:443  216.58.204.68:443
udp 1470481226 81.173.237.255:65355 10.10.10.41:65355 172.217.169.38:443 172.217.169.38:443
tcp 1470481228 81.173.237.255:2528  10.10.10.18:2528  64.202.112.51:443  64.202.112.51:443
tcp 1470481228 81.173.237.255:2533  10.10.10.27:2533  18.153.11.11:443   18.153.11.11:443
tcp 1470481231 81.173.237.255:2538  10.10.10.25:2538  2.21.184.8:443     2.21.184.8:443
tcp 1470481231 81.173.237.255:2550  10.10.10.26:2550  185.33.223.206:443 185.33.223.206:443
tcp 1470481233 81.173.237.255:2562  10.10.10.38:2562  199.166.0.24:443   199.166.0.24:443
tcp 1470481234 81.173.237.255:2563  10.10.10.42:2563  175.185.216.10:443 175.185.216.10:443
tcp 1470481236 81.173.237.255:2566  10.10.10.43:2566  175.185.216.10:443 175.185.216.10:443
tcp 1470481237 81.173.237.255:2568  10.10.10.44:2568  175.185.216.10:443 175.185.216.10:443
tcp 1470481239 81.173.237.255:2569  10.10.10.47:2569  175.185.216.10:443 175.185.216.10:443
tcp 1470481239 81.173.237.255:2570  10.10.10.48:2570  175.185.216.10:443 175.185.216.10:443
tcp 1470481240 81.173.237.255:2571  10.10.10.51:2571  175.185.216.10:443 175.185.216.10:443
[ac@VUbuntu]~$
```

Rearrange the following statements to give a suitable Unix command that will replace the Unix date/time format with a human-readable date/time.

1. `{$2=strftime("%c %T",$2)}`
2. `awk '`
3. `{print}`
4. `' orig.log > new.log`

7. The same command is applied to another log from the same day by another operator in the company, but the times don't quite match up. What could be the problem?

   1. The logs were generated on Microsoft time instead of epoch time.
   2. The NTP settings were incorrect.
   3. The local time settings on the other operator's computer do not match.
   4. The logs were recorded with the wrong time zone.

8. The operations center is informed that users of an affected web page during the summer of 2016 were made to download a file from the `219.83.193.152/29` subnet. This file is now assessed to be further malware. The following screenshot shows an extract from the partial PCAP for August 6, 2016:

```
1 1470481222 IP 109.144.5.192.80 > 81.173.237.255.53780: Flags [F.], seq 1728581233, ack 3173337657, win 237, length 0
2 1470481222 IP 104.83.167.20.80 > 81.173.237.255.53794: Flags [P.], seq 1:589, ack 1, win 260, length 588: HTTP: GET
/downloads/install-2.3.7.exe HTTP/1.1
3 1470481222 IP 96.6.6.15.443 > 81.173.237.255.53794: Flags [F.], seq 31, ack 1, win 264, length 0
4 1470481222 IP 104.82.226.140.80 > 81.173.237.255.53702: Flags [F.], seq 301519585, ack 1374806929, win 283, length 0
5 1470481222 IP 104.82.247.154.80 > 81.173.237.255.53781: Flags [F.], seq 1887142500, ack 2902455664, win 237, length 0
6 1470481222 IP 81.173.237.255.53780 > 109.144.5.192.80: Flags [.], ack 1, win 259, length 0
7 1470481222 IP 81.173.237.255.53727 > 96.6.6.15.443: Flags [P.], seq 2753157:2753188, ack 4184794, win 264, length 31
8 1470481222 IP 81.173.237.255.53702 > 104.82.226.140.80: Flags [.], ack 1, win 736, length 0
9 1470481222 IP 81.173.237.255.53781 > 104.82.247.154.80: Flags [.], ack 1, win 256, length 0
10 1470481222 IP 219.83.193.158.80 > 81.173.237.255.59918: Flags [S.], seq 4053836452, ack 4117794138, win 16060, options
[mss 1448,nop,nop,sackOK,nop,wscale 1], length 0
11 1470481222 IP 81.173.237.255.59918 > 219.83.193.158.80: Flags [.], ack 1, win 260, length 0
12 1470481222 IP 81.173.237.255.59918 > 219.83.193.158.80: Flags [P.], seq 1:589, ack 1, win 260, length 588: HTTP: GET
/156258b8da831b85/install-2.3.1.exe HTTP/1.1
13 1470481222 IP 219.83.193.158.80 > 81.173.237.255.59918: Flags [.], ack 589, win 8618, length 0
14 1470481222 IP 219.83.193.158.80 > 81.173.237.255.59918: Flags [.], seq 1:1449, ack 589, win 8618, length 1448: HTTP:
HTTP/1.1 200 OK
15 1470481222 IP 219.83.193.158.80 > 81.173.237.255.59918: Flags [P.], seq 1449:1461, ack 589, win 8618, length 12: HTTP
16 1470481222 IP 81.173.237.255.59918 > 219.83.193.158.80: Flags [.], ack 1461, win 260, length 0
17 1470481222 IP 219.83.193.158.80 > 81.173.237.255.59918: Flags [.], seq 1461:2909, ack 589, win 8618, length 1448: HTTP
18 1470481222 IP 219.83.193.158.80 > 81.173.237.255.59918: Flags [.], seq 2909:4357, ack 589, win 8618, ength 1448: HTTP
19 1470481222 IP 219.83.193.158.80 > 81.173.237.255.59918: Flags [.], seq 4357:5805, ack 589, win 8618, length 1448: HTTP
20 1470481222 IP 219.83.193.158.80 > 81.173.237.255.59918: Flags [.], seq 5805:7253, ack 589, win 8618, length 1448: HTTP
```

Which extracts from the 5-tuple are correct for the file download that originated from this address?

    1. Destination IP: `219.83.193.158`

    2. Destination port: `59918`

    3. Protocol: UDP

    4. Source port: `443`

9. Using both of the log files, what is the inside local IP address of the host that sent the HTTP `GET` message?

    1. `81.173.237.255`

    2. `10.10.10.40`

    3. `219.83.193.158`

    4. `81.173.237.255:59918`

10. Which system, if installed, could be used to track the location, activity, and spread of the file?

    1. SIEM

    2. Splunk

    3. QRadar

    4. AMP

Further reading

- Splunk, one of the most well-known security incident and event management tools, produced a 2018 white paper on moving incident and event management away from just data collating to data analysis, which is available at `https://www.splunk.com/pdfs/white-papers/the-seven-essential-capabilities-of-analytics-driven-siem.pdf`.

- The manual pages for the Unix CLI commands listed can be found as follows:
    - `strftime`: `http://man7.org/linux/man-pages/man3/strftime.3.html`
    - `awk`: `http://man7.org/linux/man-pages/man1/awk.1p.html`

- A good resource on the normal forms can be found at `https://www.guru99.com/database-normalization.html`.
- A good article by SS8 COO Faizel Lakhani to the commission on enhancing national cybersecurity on retrospective analysis can be found at `https://www.nist.gov/sites/default/files/documents/2016/09/16/ss8_rfi_response.pdf`.

11
Drawing Conclusions from the Data

Gaining data is the **easy bit** of cybersecurity. Even once data is normalized, sorted, and categorized, there is still a requirement to analyze, interpret, and draw conclusions from it. Spotting the patterns and drawing conclusions from the data is one of the primary reasons that human operators are still required for cybersecurity operations. While this is only 10-12% of *210-255*, it is the greatest cybersecurity skill.

The following topics will be covered in this chapter:

- Finding a threat actor
- Deterministic and probabilistic analysis
- Distinguishing and prioritizing significant alerts

Finding a threat actor

In Chapter 3, *Computer Forensics and Evidence Handling*, we looked at the idea of threat actor attribution. In this section, we look more specifically at how we can utilize network (DNS and HTTP logs) and threat intelligence data to find a threat actor. This is specifically referenced in topics 4.7 and 4.8 in the 210-255 specification:

> *Implementing Cisco Cybersecurity Operations (210-255) Topic List.*
>
> *4.7 Map DNS logs and HTTP logs together to find a threat actor*
> *4.8 Map DNS, HTTP, and threat intelligence data together*

DNS and HTTP services are fundamental to many network applications, particularly those that operate over the internet. This means that they are services that very close to 100% of organizations will have permitted on their networks. For an attacker, this means that the likelihood of data successfully traversing the trusted/untrusted boundary is higher when using DNS and HTTP than for rarer protocols (for example, FTP or Telnet). DNS and HTTP are therefore common protocols leveraged by attackers for both data upload/download, and command and control messages.

In the previous chapter, we looked at pinpointing threats and identifying malicious files. Malicious files can mutate very quickly, in some instances changing with every iteration. URL (in HTTP traffic), DNS, and IP information changes much more slowly.

Routable (public) IP addresses must be bought or assigned from the available pools; it is often difficult to obtain an address outside the geographic area. Even using the Tor network or a **virtual private network** (**VPN**), exit points are often still known or registered. While the actor's own address may be obfuscated to the casual user, the use of a VPN or Tor exit point can even be a greater indicator of a threat.

To help obscure the end location, multiple domain names could be used to point to the same ultimate IP address. Again, domain names must be registered. Domain name servers must know the addresses associated with each name; if they did not, the URL would not point to the correct location anyway.

Deterministic and probabilistic analysis

When an event occurs, the cybersecurity operator only ever sees the symptoms or consequences of the event, rather than the actions themselves. Like a medic, the cybersecurity operator has two tasks: mending the symptoms and treating the cause. Unlike a medic, operators cannot ask the patient questions about the events leading up to the symptoms starting; the data has either already been collected or it is gone.

To figure out what has happened – in order to establish, and hence to find treatments for, the cause – the operator can choose from two paths, or a combination of both. These two different approaches to analysis are called deterministic and probabilistic. The ability to compare and contrast between these approaches is topic 4.10 in the 210-255 specification:

> *Implementing Cisco Cybersecurity Operations (210-255) topic list:*
>
> *4.10 Compare and contrast deterministic and probabilistic analysis*

In this section, we will outline the similarities and differences between the two techniques in key areas, before looking at examples of each technique.

Data required

Deterministic analysis requires the information to be concrete facts that can be compared against the standard. It is therefore dependent on the data requirement being known ahead of time; if the facts of the matter have not been collected, they cannot be analyzed. In the example of the patient and doctor, there is no scope for obtaining information that *didn't seem important at the time*.

Probabilistic analysis does not require as much data; if the facts aren't available, the investigator can just think about what is most likely to have happened. The investigator has some agency to just fill in the gaps, reducing the confidence levels to reflect this. The probabilistic analysis model compensates for holes in the data by assuming the likelihood that something will or has happened, even if it is not known exactly when, or how, or even if it has happened or will happen.

Scope

Deterministic analysis is generally restricted to events that occur frequently. This is because of the amount of data that must be collected ahead of the event, as well as the overheads incurred in processing to pinpoint the cause. If you think about doing a science experiment, there are more things that happen around the experiment than are directly caused by it. You have to know what to look for in order to make good judgments on cause and effect. The same is true for cybersecurity incidents. The artifacts created by a security incident must be seen a few times before it can be definitively stated that evidence X proves incident Y.

Probabilistic analysis can be applied to a much wider range of activities, including activities that have never been seen before (but that are theoretically possible). As probabilistic analysis improves, particularly if similar incidents occur repeatedly, a larger body of evidence can be created. Policies can evolve to look for other expected features, which might then enable deterministic analysis for this type of incident in the future.

Results

Deterministic analysis yields factual, explainable results. The cause will be specific, and there are low numbers of false positive reports.

Probabilistic analysis does not yield definitive results. With larger datasets, the accuracy increases, but probabilistic results will never reach the accuracy of deterministic analysis. Probabilistic analysis normally highlights more suspicious events, but some of these will be False Positives.

When a probabilistic analysis is conducted, the operators must decide what they think the cause is, and therefore how to prioritize the incident. To do this, they must decide what is the most likely threat, but also which is the most dangerous threat that fits with the observed symptoms (and everything in between). They can then look at the risks involved (severity combined with likelihood).

Examples

The best example of deterministic analysis is signature-based antivirus software. As we have discussed previously, signature-based antivirus software works by taking confirmed viruses and making a signature that references it. If the antivirus finds a match to the signature of MegaVirusA, there is close to a 100% chance that this is the case (a very, very unlikely situation would be another file that had an identical 256-bit hash).

Now let's say that the attacker changes the virus slightly each time (either manually or through an algorithm). A signature-based, deterministic antivirus would not catch a subsequent attack. A probabilistic analysis might help in this, however. By comparing the activity of the first antivirus to the activity of a subsequent attack, we may know that MegaVirusA always attempts to insert itself into a specific file location, let's say `C:\virus`. We could then say that any file that finds its way into the `C:\virus` directory is a virus, and specifically that it is a strain of MegaVirusA.

Let's take this one stage further. Let's say that MegaVirusA doesn't insert itself into the `C:\virus` directory, but that some byproduct of its behavior leaves this directory as a residue. There is no direct evidence that MegaVirusA was present, nor about the event timing or mechanism. The presence of the residue would be indirect evidence, but a probabilistic analysis might conclude that at some point the system was infected by MegaVirusA, and that other, less visible consequences are also likely to have occurred.

Of course, users may have created this folder themselves, or it may have been created legitimately by another process, so there is a chance that a probabilistic analysis might create an alert for an incident that did not exist.

The opposite example would be the process of getting a signature-based antivirus in the first place. Let's say that a company discovers that files are leaving the system from a number of hosts on the network. The IPS, IDS, and antivirus software has not produced any alerts, but it is clear that the activity is out of the ordinary.

The incident response team is able to see that the traffic seems to be originating from an executable file in the system directory. They identify five files that are all on affected devices and not on any of the other (unaffected) devices. A probabilistic analysis might suggest that one or more of these files is either the cause of – or an artifact from – an infection. The files can be put in a sandbox and analyzed. One file exhibits evasive traits, where none of the others do. The likelihood is that this single file is a threat, and the others are either there by coincidence or as a result of the other file.

Looking back at the logs, the file originated from a website that each of the hosts visited. The URL was in the body of an email that was received by many users in the organization. Probabilistic analysis would suggest that this website is a risk to the system, as is the source of the emails.

This initial incident could only be analyzed using probabilistic analysis. Now that a single file, URL, and email sender have been identified, deterministic analysis can occur for any future incidents.

Distinguishing and prioritizing significant alerts

In Chapter 6, *Network Security Data Analysis*, we looked at how individual systems might flag an occurrence as suspicious. Sometimes, however, each individual occurrence is not suspicious on its own. A good example of this is in identifying scams online. The first time you are told you are a winner of $1 million and to click through to tell them which account to pay the money into, this might not seem suspicious – particularly if you were already on a competition site! But when your friend also wins $1 million, and her friend and several other people you know, that would certainly seem suspicious!

When identifying a scam – and when identifying a security alert – having data from multiple sources is often advantageous. Having aggregated the data from multiple sources such as NetFlow, Antivirus, IPS/IDS, and other logs, and normalized the data to minimize contradictions and redundancy, we can use this as effectively a new set of data to draw further conclusions from. There are many management consoles that help to draw conclusions from the data. For 210-255, topic 4.9 specifically references the use of the Firepower Management Center:

> *Implementing Cisco Cybersecurity Operations (210-255) topic list:*
>
> *4.9 Identify a correlation rule to distinguish the most significant alert from a given set of events from multiple data sources using the Firepower Management Center*

In this section, we will look at how to use a management console to find correlations between multiple data sources and distinguish the most significant alerts. We will reference the Firepower Management Center, but will focus on the generic techniques, as the console itself will likely evolve and be updated over time.

A correlation rule combines a number of user-defined features to help identify significant alerts. In an ideal world – where memory, processing power, and licensing was unlimited – every alert would be investigated. As it is, applying too many, multi-condition rules is itself a resource-consuming activity.

Correlation rules and policies can be assigned a priority value from 1 to 5, with 1 being the highest priority and 5 being the lowest. In the 210-255 specification, there is no requirement to know all the possible correlation rule options. There may be a selection of correlation rules, and a set of events, which should be matched to them. The highest priority match would be the correct answer. An example of this is given in the questions at the end of the chapter.

Summary

In the previous chapter, we focused on the need to centralize security data and to cross-reference information coming from multiple sources. We also demonstrated that this was a particularly difficult task! In this chapter, we have looked at some key indicators, particularly the use of DNS and HTTP data, which is less likely to change than file signatures.

We have also looked at the difference between deterministic analysis (100% assurance based on confirmed evidence) and probabilistic analysis (<100% assurance based on likely interpretations of available but incomplete evidence). When the reasons for certain activity is not immediately clear, or even definitive in retrospect, operators must consider the severity (best/worst case) along with the frequency (most/least likely) of those threats in combination to determine the risk.

The Firepower Management Center is equipped with a feature that allows organization defined correlation rules to prioritize alerts based on multiple sources of data. Applying too many, overly granular rules can affect the performance of the system as a whole, so correlation rules must be chosen carefully and reviewed periodically to ensure they work with the organization's business priorities.

Questions

1. Which of the following does not contribute to the prevalence of DNS and HTTP use in cyber attacks?
    1. DNS and HTTP are fundamental to many network applications and therefore are likely to be enabled on corporate networks.
    2. HTTP is a secure method of bulk data transfer.
    3. DNS enables attackers to create code that does not directly reference the destination IP address.
    4. Legitimate HTTP traffic occurs in high volume, so data relating to an incident can be masked.

2. Which of the following would not be useful to an attacker for hiding their location?
    1. Utilizing the Tor network
    2. Utilizing a VPN
    3. Utilizing a public internet location (for example, public Wi-Fi or internet cafes)
    4. Utilizing a spoofed IP address

3. Which of the following statements is true?
    1. In probabilistic analysis, the absence of evidence is direct evidence of absence.
    2. In deterministic analysis, the absence of evidence is direct evidence of absence.
    3. In probabilistic analysis, conclusions can only be drawn from the hard data available.
    4. In deterministic analysis, conclusions can only be drawn from the hard data available.

4. Which of the following is true for deterministic analysis as compared with probabilistic analysis?
    1. Results are specific and factual.
    2. Results indicate how likely they are to be true.
    3. Reports generated have lower numbers of false negatives.
    4. Reports generated have higher numbers of true positives.

5. Which of the following statements is true?
    1. Deterministic analysis is possible for threats that have not yet occurred, while probabilistic analysis is only possible for existing threats.
    2. Deterministic analysis may yield multiple results where probabilistic analysis always results in a single cause being identified
    3. There is a trend towards deterministic analysis now that storage space is more plentiful.
    4. There is a trend towards probabilistic analysis as the rate of malware evolution increases.

6. A correlation policy exists that has a priority of 1. The rules in this policy are set with the default priority, except one rule that is given a priority of 3. Which of the following statements is true?
    1. If the priority 3 rule triggers, the event priority would be 1 as the policy priority takes precedence.
    2. If the priority 3 rule triggers, the event priority would be 1 as the highest priority takes precedence.
    3. If the priority 3 rule triggers, the event priority would be 3 as the rule priority takes precedence.
    4. If the priority 3 rule triggers, the event priority would be 3 as the highest priority takes precedence.

The following four questions relate to the following scenario. Further information may be provided in each question.

The security team receives multiple user reports about devices on the network running slowly over the last week. Unfortunately, some of the network monitoring devices were offline last weekend, so the logs are incomplete.

One of the analysts mentions that a few partner organizations reported incidents last week too. The key symptoms of these incidents were rogue running processes on infected devices, and what appears to be a sandbox checker using a randomly generated (unresolved) domain name.

After checking their logs, the partner organizations (and other agencies) showed that these attacks could be conclusively linked if they originated from one or more of the following Tor nodes:

- `104.131.108.7`
- `104.206.237.24`
- `107.172.42.236`
- `78.192.118.230`

7. Which of the following would be true?
    1. If the security team can find one of these four IP addresses in their logs, they can conclusively link the user reports through to the same attack used against the partner organizations.
    2. As the security team does not have complete logs from last weekend, their analysis will only be probabilistic.
    3. The security team must find either the sandbox checker or the IP addresses to have completed deterministic analysis.
    4. The security team does not need to find the cause of the problem in order to fix it.

8. On further analysis, the attack seems to be able to respawn, appearing on other network devices even a few hours after the attack seemed to be contained. The reports seem to suggest that malware may be duplicating over the network, then lying dormant to avoid detection. The malware appears to beacon using SSL. The SSL certificate appears to be a multi-domain certificate for the `DontTrustMe.Inc` **Organization (O)**.
    Which of the following could be used to create an alert for this beacon?
    1. Using FireSIGHT to block HTTPS traffic
    2. Using FireSIGHT to create a correlation rule specifying SSL certificate subject `DontTrustMe.Inc` **Organization (O)**

    3. Using FireSIGHT to block connections through to
`*.donttrustme.com`

    4. Using FireSIGHT to create a correlation rule for connections to destination port `443`

9. What elements might help to identify the threat actor involved in this attack?

    1. Looking up the corporate registration of `DontTrustMe.Inc`

    2. DNS lookup of `DontTrustMe.Inc`

    3. DNS lookup of `donttrustme.com`

    4. The URL from the HTTPS header in the beacon message

10. Some further investigation reveals that `DontTrustMe.Inc` is actually an organization that provides a number of services from a partner organization. The certificate has been repurposed by the attackers who also bought up and registered some of the unused subdomains. The file that initiates the beacon is a portable executable file, and has been seen with the `.acm`, `.exe`, `.sys`, `.ocr`, and `.efi` extensions. The legitimate process is launched from a `.dll` file. Which would be the best way to organize the correlation rules?

    1. Create a rule for each of the five extensions individually.

    2. Create a rule for all portable executable files, with a white list exemption for `.dll` files.

    3. Keep the rule that alerts on all SSL certificates matching `DontTrustMe.Inc`.

    4. Create a single rule where the file type is a portable executable file and not a `.dll` file.

Further reading

- The banking and finance post has a very basic description of the move from deterministic to probabilistic approaches to cybersecurity in its article from 2018 found here: `https://bfsi.eletsonline.com/from-deterministic-to-probabilistic-approach-in-cyber-threats-using-ai/`. Clients are likely to be influenced by articles such as this one, so a working knowledge of their perceptions will help you to work as a cybersecurity operator within that organization.

- The Firepower Management Center user guide for correlation rules can be found at `https://www.cisco.com/c/en/us/td/docs/security/firesight/541/user-guide/FireSIGHT-System-UserGuide-v5401/Correlation-Policies-Rules.html`.

Section 5: Incident Handling

Incident response describes the immediate actions required of the **Security Operations Centre** (**SOC**). This is principally directed toward stopping an incident from getting worse.

Incident handling is different because it includes non-technical work carried out around the incident. Whereas, in the incident response section, we spoke about how there were other organizations that needed to know things, this section provides details about what the rest of the organization is considering and doing while the SOC is investigating, fighting, and defeating the threat.

In this section, we also look at the classification of intrusion events in the Cyber Kill Chain model and appropriately apply the NIST guidelines to guide the organization's response using standardized (VERIS) terminology.

The following chapters are included in this section:

- Chapter 12, *The Cyber Kill Chain Model*
- Chapter 13, *Incident Handling Activities*

The Cyber Kill Chain Model 12

The Cyber Kill Chain model describes the sequence of activities which occur during a generic attack. This model separates an attack into seven stages, each happening sequentially. The model is derived from a military model of a campaign, and was modified by Lockheed Martin to apply to information security. As such, the sequential nature of the phases might not fit logically in the mind; some steps might occur simultaneously, or loop back and repeat, but this should be accepted as a quirk of the model. The principles in action remain useful.

Although most commentators and resources refer to the Cyber Kill Chain model as the stages of an attack, I have chosen to use the term campaign to describe a structured, sustained, and coordinated activity. There may be one or more attacks, but the overall aim is not simply the defeat of an adversary on a position, but a more strategic defeat. Using this terminology allows the model to scale; currently different models are being used when there is a need to consider advanced persistent threats, such as those involving state sponsorship or international organized crime.

At each stage in the campaign, there are opportunities to detect, opportunities to disrupt, and opportunities defend against it. To underline the importance of considering a campaign rather than an attack, consider the historic case of an attack mounted against a castle. If there is a successful defense of the castle wall, has the problem gone away? The adversary still knows the size and shape and orientation of the walls, and may return with a larger army/bigger guns/better engineers. Subsequent attacks may well be part of the same campaign.

The 210-255 exam requires candidates to classify intrusion events into the correct category. This ability to categorize intrusion events into the right stage of the model is important as the model can provide good guidance as to the actions which occurred previously, and some of the actions still to be detected or are still to come. This helps incident response teams prepare future actions, and to acknowledge remediation steps which may be required.

In this chapter, we will look at a cyber attack from the point of view of a novice attacker – aided by the internet – as it is easier to categorize the activities into discrete phases. To ease understanding, we will divide the seven stages of the Cyber Kill Chain model into the US Army Operations Process' three command activities that are performed during operations:

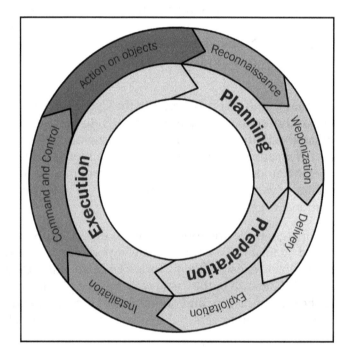

We will cover the following topics in this chapter:

- Planning
- Preparation
- Execution

Planning

There are a number of activities that an attacker conducts before the attack really kicks off. If you think about what would happen in a physical military campaign, people don't just turn up at a castle and hope they can attack it; there are a number of preparatory steps.

In this section, we will discuss the distinguishing features of an intrusion in the reconnaissance and weaponization phases and how to defend against an attack at this point. This is specifically referenced in topics 5.1a and b in the 210-255 topic list.

Implementing Cisco Cybersecurity Operations (210-255) Topic List:

5.1 Classify intrusion events into these categories as defined by the Cyber Kill Chain model
5.1.a Reconnaissance
5.1.b Weaponization

As it is in the topic list, and in the Cyber Kill Chain model, we will look at each stage separately.

Reconnaissance

During the reconnaissance phase, the attacker looks to learn as much about the target as possible. Cybersecurity operator professionals often get caught into the trap of thinking purely in terms of technological vulnerabilities and solutions, but it is worth remembering that the target is a whole system.

If there was a novice hacker (with an inexplicably wide variety of tools available), the reconnaissance phase would involve collecting information about the technology being used, the personnel using the technology, and any defensive systems in place.

In terms of the castle attack example, an attacking force might look at a map of the castle (where it is and where things are inside it). This would be the technological reconnaissance. In terms of personnel, they might also consider who is able to go in and out of the castle, the dungeons, or the vaults. The security measures then intersect with this; when are the gates open, who's on guard when, and what other walls, ditches, and hazards are there.

Technology

The technology being used includes the entire system within the organization – or as much as can be seen from the attacker's current position. This might include the public-facing services (for example, website or mail servers for teleworkers); the worker's terminals – if they can be accessed; the software systems running on servers, worker's terminals, customer interfaces; and even the hardware that's employed and the operating systems running on them.

This information can be found by running port scans, leveraging the `robots.txt` file on a website to discover the areas of the website that search engine's spiders ignore, or looking for CDP or LLDP messages which might escape the system through misconfiguration.

Technological information to note would also include things like the locations of important files – maybe even the prize itself!

To defend against this, organizations should be looking at how to limit the egress of information on the system. Segmentation of the network and associated services is very important, as is enforcing the *need to know* from a technological perspective. CDP, for example, is only really needed for areas of high device turnover. Is the convenience of CDP worth the risk?

Personnel

Personnel are the most overlooked element of a cyber defense. Personnel are a problem because, a lot of the time, they have legitimate access to some or all of the system. Differentiating between a member of staff who is legitimately accessing the data compared to when they are engaged in nefarious activity may be very difficult indeed.

In addition to the insider threat, things like social media and an individual's public persona are important sources of information. A hacker may use this information to blackmail individuals to assist them, or discern passwords. In 2008, a hacker was able to access a Yahoo! account belonging to vice-presidential candidate Sarah Palin by using open source biographical data to conduct a password reset. Often, things like dates of birth, mother's maiden name, place of birth, and other details that are used as security information can be found freely on social media profiles.

Other valuable pieces of information might be found through researching the key figures within the organization. Who are the people who might have the highest levels of access? Who are the people who designed and built the systems being used? What are their areas of expertise, and, therefore, what are they most likely to have implemented?

Even things like gaining a list of workers and coworkers may be useful in successful social engineering, such as making an email appear to come from a real contact rather than a computer generated one!

Combating the threat to/from the personnel is particularly difficult, but could include internal education programs, utilizing stranger security questions, or requiring certain direct questions for access. In the UK, banks have begun asking customers to name a recent transaction on the account as a security measure against telephone banking fraud.

Defenses

The defensive technologies that are being employed by the system are an obvious source of information. These technologies include physical security, but will effectively inform the attacker about which risks they face when conducting their attack. For example, if NetFlow is being used, they may need to consider masking their own IP addresses and hence location. If a certain antivirus is being used, they may want to pre-scan their tools to see if it will get through.

Imagine someone attempting to attack a building. If they know that there are metal detectors being used, they know that certain attacks are unlikely to work.

Weaponization

In reality, an attacker won't find every possible piece of information about a system during reconnaissance. In fact, it is unlikely they will even try to. They are more likely to look for systems which they know have vulnerabilities, which is where the cross-over with weaponization occurs.

An attacker will want to know the easiest, least costly, lowest risk path to their aims. In terms of the castle attack, the attacking force may have identified that the castle walls are of a certain construction. The weaponization phase might involve finding that this particular design has shallow foundations, which would allow a tunnel to be dug beneath it.

Again, we need to recognize that the attacker's aims may not just be technological (data theft, compromise, or denial). If an attacker's aim is to discredit the organization, an attack might consist of simply demonstrating that an organization has a security blind spot, even if they don't attempt to leverage it at all.

During weaponization, the attacker looks to find an exploit that might be effective against the vulnerable systems that have been identified during reconnaissance. For example, if the reconnaissance showed up Java files, they may look for exploits for vulnerabilities in Java rather than a hardware vulnerability that might be rarer and harder to access.

A popular tool is the Metasploit framework, which includes a searchable list of vulnerabilities that the attacker can match against the technologies that are found in reconnaissance

Alternatively, Nessus can be used to uncover vulnerabilities during a scan and automatically map possible exploits. Note that, because this system is performing both a scan and identifying exploits, this crosses over between reconnaissance and weaponization.

In terms of personnel, the attacker may already have weapons (for example, incriminating information which could be used to blackmail them), but it's likely they would have to figure out a way to weaponize it. Therefore, an attacker may have discovered that a particularly high-value target often goes to a certain pub. They may then also attend the pub to find more information (still reconnaissance), with the aim of finding a vulnerability (weaponization).

Preparation

With a flaw identified and a plan created, the attacker attempts to get their army ready. This will involve moving them to the right place and stretching the weakness to see if they can indeed get through the castle walls.

In this section, we will explain the distinguishing features of an intrusion in the Delivery and Exploitation stages and how to defend against an attack at this point. These two stages are specifically referenced as topic 5.1c and d in the topic list for the 210-255 exam.

Implementing Cisco Cybersecurity Operations (210-255) topic list:

5.1 Classify intrusion events into these categories as defined by the Cyber Kill Chain model
5.1.c Delivery
5.1.d Exploitation

Again, we will look at the two stages separately. We will also use some examples to help differentiate between the two categories.

Delivery

In order to actually exploit the vulnerability identified during weaponization, the attacker must deliver it to the target. In the case of the castle example, even if we know that the wall is vulnerable to tunneling, we need to get the engineers and shovels to the wall. This activity might be a little bit suspicious!

Having developed a great tool during weaponization that will open a backdoor into any system that executes it, the attacker must get the tool to the right place and get it to execute. Delivery vectors may include tricking someone into opening a connection over the internet (for example, through a rogue link in an email), or through mobile storage devices like USB sticks (for example, a USB drop attack). There are also other vectors, which will be discussed later in this chapter.

To combat threats during the delivery phase, security professionals may consider scanning emails and/or restricting USB drives which may be connected to the system. These will cover many attacks. The difficulty with this is that the security systems themselves may end up being so restrictive that they achieve a denial of service all of their own; might this be achieving the attacker's aim for them?

Remember that, in cybersecurity terms, it isn't possible to monitor activity outside of the network or office. Where defenders in the castle example can look over the wall, and physical security guards can look out or have CCTV, it is very difficult for an organization to monitor outside their logical network. If they were to create a demilitarized zone or buffer between the public internet and their own internal networks, this would just shift the boundary of their network outwards. Even when checking for USB drives connecting to network devices, this relies on direct contact between the USB memory device and the USB port on the network device. In the case of an email, the email has to actually arrive at the email servers to be scanned and categorized.

Exploitation

With the engineers and breaching tools delivered to the castle, exploitation is where the attacker now needs to press the advantage home. The engineers will have to work to get through the wall. They find the area with the shallow foundations and start to dig under it.

The exploitation phase is where security teams generally invest the most time and effort. Detecting and defeating a threat actor in the act of exploitation is very difficult; there are too many potential points of failure in a system to monitor effectively. Checking against every signature in existence would be so slow that it would limit the organization's ability to conduct business as usual. This is particularly important for industries which gain advantage of near real-time service. Such businesses must balance the organization's business priorities against the risks. (We covered this in the *The incident response plan* section of Chapter 7, *Roles and Responsibilities During an Incident*)

Organizations can work proactively to minimize the risk of exploitation by monitoring the threat landscape and deciding which threats may impact the organization's existing and future infrastructure. For example, when new tunneling technology is developed, they can reevaluate the depth of their walls; if new, taller, siege ladders are made, they may review the height of their walls; if a major flaw were found in Java, they might have to find a patch or decrease the viability of these exploit kits by adding further layers of defense.

Execution

With a decent force inside the network, the attacker has invested time and energy, but, as yet, has no reward. The execution phase is where the attacker actually leverages their advantage for their own ends. In the castle scenario, the attacking force defeats the remaining defenders, takes command of the castle, and plunders the treasury.

In this section, we will explain the distinguishing features of an intrusion in the installation, command and control, and action on objectives stages and how to defend against an attack at these points. These are sections 5.1e, f, and g in the 210-255 specification.

> *Implementing Cisco Cybersecurity Operations (210-255) Topic List:*
>
> *5.1 Classify intrusion events into these categories as defined by the Cyber Kill Chain model*
> *5.1.e Installation*
> *5.1.f Command and control*
> *5.1.g Action on objectives*

Once again, we will look at each category in turn. Remember, that for the exam, the requirement is to classify events into the appropriate category.

Installation

During the installation phase, the attacker has two aims: to establish persistence and/or a foothold in the targeted system. In the castle example, persistence can be seen as a way of holding the tunnel open. The attackers may put in support beams and reinforce the tunnel walls, or may seek to open the tunnel up so that bigger and better equipment can be conveyed to the inside of the walls. Similarly, they may use this phase to better camouflage the tunnel. Upon establishing a foothold inside the castle, they might move troops and equipment through the tunnel and hide them among the local population for a later assault.

Establishing a foothold can have different meanings, depending on who is asked. It is often considered that establishing a foothold is analogous to establishing persistence of the exploit. This is not necessarily true; once an attacker has tools *inside the wall*, the initial exploit can be detected, closed, and patched by the defenders without impacting on the attacker. Going back to the castle example, with a small band of attackers inside, what is preventing them from opening the gates from the inside? The exploit isn't always required after the initial break-in.

The principal aim of the incident management team during this phase is to reduce the time to identify, contain, and eradicate the breach, and remediate any after-effects. Estimates for the time between exploitation and discovery range, but an estimate of three months is considered conservative. This is plenty of time for an adversary to accomplish the remaining phases of the kill chain. In fact, it may even be enough for the adversary to loop back through the phases, finding new vulnerabilities from within, and exploiting those too.

Command and control

During the command and control phase, an attacker connects to the system and gains *hands-on-keyboard* access to the system that they wish to attack. This may involve looping back through the system to find the right environment to form up, prior to the final push for the objective.

In the castle example, command and control might involve those *within the walls* getting roles within the gate guard, or working their way up into the royal inner circle. *Hands-on-keyboard* access, while the defining feature of the command and control phase, is a limited term. What is really meant in this phase, is that the attacker has set the conditions for a successful final (decisive) action.

The attacker must have force elements – a sufficient amount– physically located to launch the action (possibly including lateral movement to a suitable host). These elements must have the logical and social position (including privilege escalation) to complete the action. The attacker must be able to coordinate these force elements (using a communications channel), or allow them to be autonomous.

In the classical model of perimeter defenses, the command and control phase is completed fairly quickly. With layers of strong defense, the command and control phase can be considered an entire repeat of the Cyber Kill Chain from within the walls, which means that defenders have opportunities to detect and patch internal vulnerabilities, as well as detect, defeat, and deter movement within the network.

Action on objectives

The action on objectives phase is where the attacker attempts to achieve its aims. This is where the adversary really impacts on confidentiality, integrity, or availability. This phase can be the end of the attack, or can be a small part of a larger attack.

In the castle scenario, an attacker in the final phase might begin to steal the contents of the treasury, or attempt to unseat the castle's commanders. Alternatively, the attacker might destroy the gunpowder or grain stores, weakening the defending force prior to a larger assault. Another alternative might be conducting an action somewhere within the castle grounds with the aim of distracting the defenders from a larger threat elsewhere.

Detecting an attack or breach in the Actions on Objectives phase – while generally considered too late – can still represent an opportunity for defenders. If the attack is part of a larger campaign, they may still prevent the campaign's overall success. If the attack is in the final phase, early detection can mitigate the impact of it.

One method which is increasingly common is the implementation of honey pots within the system. These appear to be attractive targets and tempt the attacker to attack there instead of the real target. This approach has two benefits for the defenders. First, the attacker must expend time and energy on the false target, giving the defenders longer to detect and interdict the attack. Second, if the honey pot is similar enough to the real target, the defenders might gain an insight into what kinds of actions might be attempted in the future, the attacker's aims, and possible disposition.

Summary

The Cyber Kill Chain model is one of the models that's used to represent the phases that an attack moves through to obtain their objective. The phases, derived from the Lockheed Martin and military models, are reconnaissance, weaponization, delivery, exploitation, installation, **command and control** (**C2**), and actions on objectives.

Reconnaissance is about information gathering. This might be about the system in general, but is more likely to be targeted at areas with known vulnerabilities. This can reveal information about the attacker or groups that are involved.

Weaponization is where the attacker links the information that's gathered during reconnaissance with known vulnerabilities and exploits.

The delivery phase aims to get the tools to the right location to enact the exploit. This is often an email or a physical delivery (for example, a USB drop).

Exploitation is where the tool is launched against the perceived vulnerability. This opens an entry point for the attacker to launch the next phase.

During installation, the attacker aims to make the breach persistent. This can include reinforcing the exploit, opening up new entry points, or amassing tools inside the system.

In command and control, the adversary attempts to gain *hands-on-keyboard* access inside the system. They may need to pivot and move laterally to a more capable position, escalate their privileges, and coordinate their activities.

The final stage of the Cyber Kill Chain is actions on objectives. Here, the attacker may extract data, amend or delete it, or deny access to other services.

The Cyber Kill Chain model appears to be linear, but this is not always the case. Some extensions and amendments have been suggested, including spiral, tree, and unified models, among many others. Regardless of the model(s) that is (are) chosen and used, the ability to identify the stages of an attack allow the defender to predict future actions, conduct retrospective analysis on probable prior actions, and contain, delete, and mitigate all of these.

Questions

1. Which of the following is a technique that's often deployed during the reconnaissance phase?
    1. Installing a keylogger
    2. Port scanning
    3. Searching Metasploit
    4. Phishing

2. Which of the following is the most common reason an attacker might focus energy on researching an organization's website?
    1. The website is likely to reveal internal IP addressing
    2. The website might reveal the organization's hierarchy and the highest value targets
    3. A flaw in the website might expose a server, which would be in the organization's trusted domain
    4. The website might reveal addresses that will help in physical penetration

3. Which of the following is a feature of Nessus which makes it a useful tool during weaponization?
    1. PCI compliance checker
    2. Open source security scanning
    3. Automatic mapping of exploits to scanned vulnerabilities
    4. Integral dictionary password attack capability

4. Which of the following actions would not be classified as being in the "exploitation" phase?
    1. An attacker runs a script which opens a backdoor in the system.
    2. An attacker accesses a user's account by guessing their password.
    3. A user clicks on a link in an email, which downloads a rootkit.
    4. Malware accesses the working memory of another process during a buffer overflow attack.

5. Which phase of an attack establishes persistent access to the system for the attacker?
    1. Persistence
    2. Installation
    3. Defense Evasion
    4. Action on Objective

6. Fill in the blank: _____ is the phase in the Cyber Kill Chain model where an attacker might try to match a vulnerability with a feature that's been observed on the target system.
   1. Weaponization
   2. Execution
   3. Delivery
   4. Exploitation

The following four questions relate to the following scenario. Further information will be provided in the question, if it's relevant.

The security team has noticed significant changes in behavior of a user in the network over the past week. The user appears to be working much longer hours, and is generating considerably more requests to the server than normal. The security team conducts an investigation since no alerts have been generated by either the IDS/IPS or other security systems.

On examination, the user appears to be logging out at the end of the working day before logging back in approximately 30 minutes later via a browser-based remote desktop utility. Their second login session each day corresponds with the larger volume of server requests.

7. The server requests appear to be attempts to authenticate as an administrator. The team suspects that this user is attempting to elevate their privileges within the system. At which phase in the Cyber Kill Chain model is this attack likely to have been caught?
   1. Exploitation
   2. Action on Objectives
   3. Installation
   4. Command and Control

8. The security team notices that the user requested an email password reminder for this system at the end of last week. The email logs show that the email was read and deleted shortly after. The user is spoken to, and denies any knowledge of making that request.

Which of the following is the most likely vulnerability that the attacker has exploited?

1. A vulnerability in the remote desktop utility to gain access to the system
2. A vulnerability in the organization's email system to access and intercept the user's emails
3. A guessable password that's used to access emails
4. A physical vulnerability which allowed the user to access the user's laptop and access webmail using a saved password

9. The user is told to change the password that they use for their email to something that is less easily guessed. They are told to also change this password for any other systems they were using it for.

    Which of the following statements is true?

    1. The vulnerability has been closed but the incident is still ongoing
    2. The vulnerability has been closed and the incident is now over
    3. The vulnerability has not been closed so the incident is still ongoing
    4. The vulnerability has not been closed but the incident is now over

10. After some work to find the threat actor, the suspicion falls onto a former employee.

    Which of the following may have contributed to the attack?

    1. The use of two-factor authentication
    2. The use of standardized security questions (mother's maiden name and birth town) to reset email passwords
    3. The standard method of assigning usernames (`firstname.surname`)
    4. Default passwords for new users set up as their date of birth

Further reading

- Paul Pols from the Cyber Security Academy developed a Unified Kill Chain model which combined the Cyber Kill Chain with other frameworks (mainly MITRE ATT&CK). His report on this can be found at `https://www.csacademy.nl/images/scripties/2018/Paul-Pols---The-Unified-Kill-Chain.pdf`.

- Documentation for Metasploit can be found at `https://metasploit.help.rapid7.com/docs`.

- A presentation from BlackHat 2016 suggests a number of different models, including models for insider threats. This can be found at `https://www.blackhat.com/docs/us-16/materials/us-16-Malone-Using-An-Expanded-Cyber-Kill-Chain-Model-To-Increase-Attack-Resiliency.pdf`.

13
Incident-Handling Activities

In this final chapter, we look to combine the learning from all the previous chapters in discussing incident handling activities. Specifically, we will look at how the techniques we have previously investigated fit within the *National Institute of Standards and Technology Special Publication 800-61 Revision 2 (NIST.SP800-61 r2*; Computer Security Incident Handling Guide); and *Special Publication 800-86 (NIST.SP800-86*; *Guide to Integrating Forensic Techniques into Incident Response*) guidelines.

The guidelines identify which activities are required throughout the life cycle of an attack. This means that while the Cyber Kill Chain is focused on the timeline of an attack, NIST focuses on the timeline of a defense. NIST also provides guidance on evidence collection and running investigations, which bring us full circle to *Section 1*!

The ability to communicate using a common framework is related to these guidelines; a concept also covered in covered in the first section of the book.

The following topics will be covered in this chapter:

- VERIS
- The phases of incident handling
- Conducting an investigation

VERIS

The **Vocabulary for Event Recording and Incident Sharing (VERIS)** provides a common language for describing security incidents. The metrics allow for a structured and repeatable approach to describing and categorizing incidents.

210-255 exam requirement 5.5 is to apply the VERIS schema to a given incident. In this section, we will look at some of the key terms. We will then practice these and give further analysis in the questions and worked answers:

> *Implementing Cisco Cybersecurity Operations (210-255) topic list:*

> *5.5 Apply the VERIS schema categories to a given incident*

The VERIS schema is divided into four elements (the four As), which help to segment categorization of an incident. A classification in each of the four elements is considered the minimum adequate description of an incident. Each of the four elements should therefore be considered independently.

Asset

Defining the compromised asset is the easiest of the four As. There are no sub-elements, so every property is relevant. Assets whose ownership, authenticity, or usefulness to the legitimate user is affected by the incident are described here.

The following screenshot shows some of the pieces of relevant information required about compromised assets, with some of the available options:

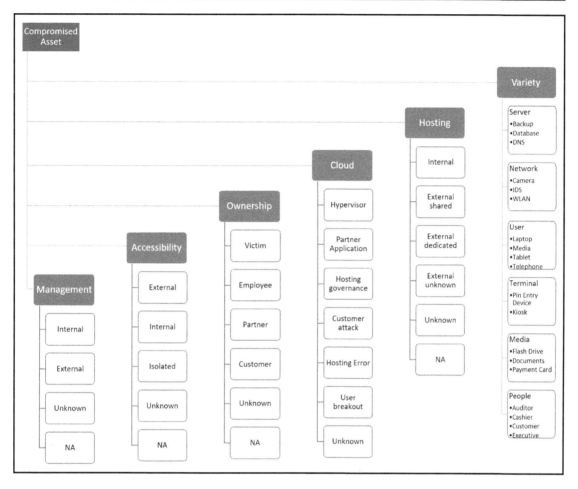

Information required about compromised assets and some of the available options

Under variety, the different asset types have been broadly separated into six categories. This can be used to assist searching, sorting, and filtering, but the category itself should not be selected in isolation; an incident should not affect simply media, but should be as specific as possible (for example, media—flash drive). While it is not expected that operators will know the entire enumerated list, the six categories under variety should be known. For each sub-item, the category is denoted by a single character (S, N, U, T, M, or P). The assets listed here help other security analysts quickly determine which incidents or vulnerabilities may at some point be relevant to their own organizations. Some incidents affect multiple assets. If this is the case, these can be entered individually.

Actors

Threat actors are the entities (people, groups, organizations, and states) that cause or contribute to an incident. There can be more than one actor involved in the incident, and their actions do not need to be intentional. If involvement is only contributory (it did not directly cause the incident), the actor is not included. Otherwise, the list of actors involved may become so big as to mask the real threat. An example of this might be the software engineer who produces a product in good faith, but ends up vulnerable to an exploit that is then successfully breached by another actor. The threat is the second actor, not the software engineer.

Actors are labeled relative to their relationship with the affected organization: internal, partner, or external. Linked to their relationship with the affected organization is the implied trust or privilege that each category might have. It is here that the real value of these categories is realized.

An internal threat actor (for example, a disgruntled employee) is assumed to have some privilege (for example, physical access to the computer system) that an external actor would not. A partner organization shares a business relationship with the organization, and can be assumed to have some privilege or trust level between that of the internal and external actors. For example, a partner organization might have physical access to the building for deliveries, but wouldn't be expected to have a log-in for the corporate network.

The aim of VERIS is to use common language to help identify, compare, and manage risk. It is for this reason that while the labels appear to categorize based on relationship, the important distinction is based on privilege and trust level. A former employee is therefore classified as external as they shouldn't have that physical access to the computer system anymore. The opposite of this is a contractor, who would be classed as internal due to their day-to-day legitimate access.

Within each sub-element, a number of properties can be used to enhance analysis and search terms can be used. These are shown in the following screenshot:

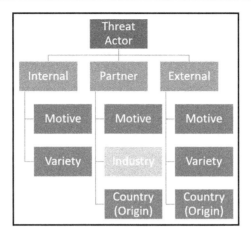

The Threat Actor sub-elements and their properties

Each property, barring the notes field (available for every VERIS element, which is free text), can be enumerated (picked from a fixed set of options), which helps the searchability of the data. All the boxes in dark blue allow multiple selections to be made; the industry property only allows single selection, or free text, and is generally drawn from the NAIC list of industries (available at `https://www.census.gov/cgi-bin/sssd/naics/naicsrch`).

Actions

Threat actions describe the activity that caused or contributed to the incident. There are seven primary categories: malware, hacking, social, misuse, physical, error, and environmental. The following quick reference classifier outlines the key differences between them:

Category	Defining Features
Malware	Software
Hacking	Illegitimate and Intentional
Social	Targets/manipulates human elements in the system
Misuse	Unauthorised and intentional
Physical	Requires proximity, or threat of proximity to the asset
Error	Unintentional action
Environmental	Changes to the infrastructure or physical environment surrounding the asset

he threat actions sub-elements

Again, there are properties that can be added to these actions to aid grouping and searchability. These are shown in the following diagram:

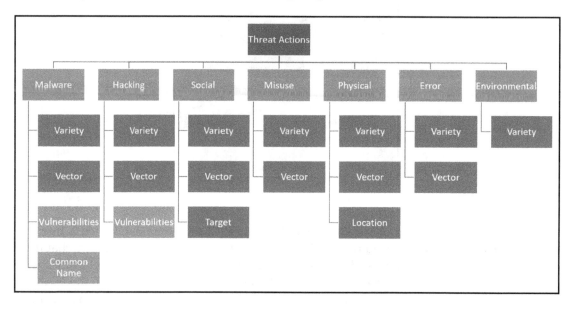

The threat action sub-elements and their properties

Some incidents contain multiple threat actions. If this is the case, each action is graded independently. The VERIS framework can scale to as many categories as is considered appropriate for each incident, but consideration must be given to whether adding too many threat actions will add value or add noise to the report.

Attributes

The effect of the incident on the organization is listed against the same threat triad as in the CVSS Impact metrics (confidentiality, integrity, and availability). Where the severity might be reached using CVSS, VERIS allows for more detail to be given, grouped using the enumerated classes given in the following diagram:

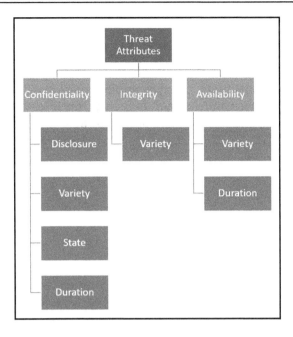

The Compromised Attribute categories and their properties

The information that is considered and added to the report using VERIS should inform the CVSS score, and vice versa. VERIS data should provide sufficient information to explain the reasoning behind the CVSS score given.

The phases of incident handling

The NIST incident handling process looks at the other (non-technical) activities that must be taken during an incident. You will notice that these are aligned, though not perfectly, with the NIST Incident Response Life Cycle. In this section, we will apply the NIST incident handling process to an event, defining activities as they relate to each phase in the incident handling process. This will cover topics 5.2 and 5.3a-f of the 210-255 specification:

Implementing Cisco Cybersecurity Operations (210-255) Topic List:

5.2 Apply the NIST.SP800-61 r2 incident handling process to an event

5.3 Define these activities as they relate to incident handling
5.3.a Identification
5.3.b Scoping
5.3.c Containment

5.3.d Remediation
5.3.e Lesson-based hardening
5.3.f Reporting

We will look at the phases separately, using examples where possible that will best differentiate between one phase and another. In reality, this is less clear cut, but the exam questions will be written in such a way that you will be able to clearly identify the phase from the event activity.

Identification

Identification occurs in both the preparation and detection phases of the Incident Response Life Cycle.

Identification during incident handling involves slightly different tasks to during incident response. Identification is not focused so much on technical elements of the organization's planning (for example, looking for emerging threats). Instead, identification here is about monitoring the effectiveness of existing security measures, and ensuring that the organization is being both compliant and proactive.

Identification during detection is again much more focused on communicating effectively with the correct stakeholders: regulatory bodies, customers, and law enforcement. While this will require knowledge of the technical situation, it is more important that people are not misled. Identification of the threat, likely consequences, and the correct entities to keep informed are vital to the organization's response, even if these activities do not directly combat the threat.

Scoping

Scoping leads on from identification, as it informs the degree of publicity that will be received, the number of people who will need to be informed, and potentially the amounts of compensation that will need to be provided.

Scoping to determine which networks, systems, or applications are affected, as well as how fast and how far the incident might spread, is important to prioritize the organization's actions. In an ideal world, the impact of the incident should be limited to a few systems and people as possible, but this will still require people to be told, in particular for customers and workers to potentially have accounts protected or frozen.

Containment

Knowing the scope of the incident, containing the incident is the next step. Is the business able to maintain the bulk of their services? If not, how limited will the service be and how will this impact the customers? What if no service will be available to customers at all?

Depending on the business, these priorities will differ. An electricity provider can probably not take the entire electricity grid offline without considerable regulatory and customer unhappiness, but the hosting service for an intranet site might not have so much impact.

With ever-increasing connectivity, the organization must also consider how to keep the incident in-house; could it spread to other entities (customers, partner organizations, the other devices in the office block)? If it could, how will they be warned off?

Remediation

Where the CSIRT will be taking steps to recover and fix devices affected by the incident, the organization will also need to consider how to make good the damage for all the other stakeholders. Customers might need to have their accounts reset, and/or their data recovered. In some cases, particularly where customers' data has been lost or compromised, compensation will need to be considered. This might also be required for unforeseen consequences caused by the issue.

In 2018, TSB Bank was affected by issues due to a changeover of IT systems. People were unable to pay their bills or make their daily purchases. This all needed to be remediated.

If there is potential that the incident may have exposed other entities (for example, partners), informing them will be vital to ensuring they are able to maintain their own practices. Imagine if a company providing security as a service were to go offline; every organization that they were protecting may now have to enter their own responses, potentially aided by the provider's own CSIRT.

Lesson-based hardening

Once the incident has been resolved, the organization must ensure that it does not occur again. The CSIRT will be looking at the technical hardening that is required, and this will be supported by the organization in general (particularly financially). However, there are other areas where lessons might need to be learned. For example, the ability of the company to rapidly open communications channels with other stakeholders might need to be improved; does a hotline for reporting incidents need to be established? Does the organization need a larger CSIRT? Is the organization over-reliant on some entity or another?

Reporting

Reporting will be a requirement for every incident. Under certain circumstances, the organization will have to report the details of the incident to law enforcement, the national CSIRT, vendors, and other entities.

Additionally, reporting the incident (for example, using the VERIS structure) helps all other organizations learn from the incident. Regardless of whether two businesses are rivals in business, information security is a shared responsibility for all legitimate entities.

Conducting an investigation

In this section, we will look at guidelines contained in *NIST.SP800-86*. This will develop on the techniques and principles that were described in `Chapter 3`, *Computer Forensics and Evidence Handling*, placing the theory in the context of the industry guidance. This will cover topic 5.4a-d, thus completing the Cisco 210-255 specification:

> *Implementing Cisco Cybersecurity Operations (210-255) Topic List:*
>
> *5.4 Describe these concepts as they are documented in NIST.SP800-86*
> *5.4.a Evidence collection order*
> *5.4.b Data integrity*
> *5.4.c Data preservation*
> *5.4.d Volatile data collection*

In this section, it will be worth cross-referencing with `Chapter 3`, *Computer Forensics and Evidence Handling*, so that the guidance is viewed in concert with the overall theory.

Evidential collection order

Collecting evidence is easier at some times than at others. Remember from `Chapter 3`, *Computer Forensics and Evidence Handling*, that collection does not simply mean picking it up; forensic techniques must be followed: logs including what it was, who collected it, from where, and using which method must be created and maintained as a minimum. Collection can be complicated by the volume of evidence present, or because the evidence is time-sensitive.

NIST.SP800-86 does not dictate the order of evidence collection, but recommends that consideration is given to the evidence's volatility, its likely value, and the amount of effort required to collect it.

Volatile data should be collected before non-volatile data; if both are needed, the non-volatile data can be collected later. If you imagine investigating a hit-and-run accident in the rain, it would be important to collect samples that might get washed away, rather than the damaged wall that will likely be there when the rain stops/when the other samples are safely collected.

Evidence that is known to have high likely value should be collected before low-value data. This is obviously an assessment; a small piece of evidence might be pivotal, but the *likely* value is what will guide priority. A random discarded piece of rubbish at the crime scene would be less likely to be of high value than the paint flecks from the car mounting the kerb.

If evidence requires so much effort to collect that it would impact on collecting other evidence, this should be dropped down the priority list. In the hit-and-run investigation, trying to find the last piece of broken headlight that fell down the drain might be less critical than getting the CCTV footage from the area.

The following diagram shows a 3D plot of volatility against ease of collection against likely value, rated on an arbitrary 10-point scale. The highest value items that are easiest to collect and have the highest volatility are colored darkest purple, and should be collected first:

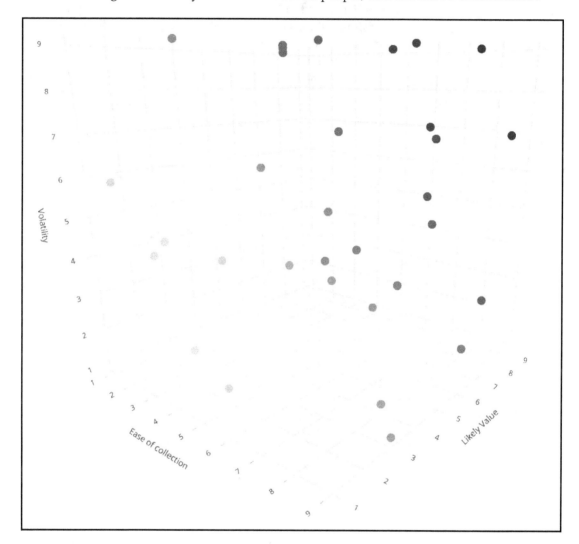

The balance between volatility, ease of collection, and likely value that guides evidence collection order

The priority given to each of those three factors, and even a specified order of collection, should be included in an organization's training, techniques, and procedures.

Data integrity and preservation

Data integrity and data preservation are fundamental to the value of electronic evidence. The data must be preserved well, so as to protect it from damage. Maintaining data integrity means that the data should mean the same from point of collection through to the point of use.

To help with both, data should be collected through standardized and recorded processes and procedures to ensure that all the evidence is equally representative of the true status of the systems at the point of collection.

Trust in the integrity of the evidence can be increased by comparison to the original. If direct, bit-by-bit comparison is possible, this is the highest possible standard. If this is not possible or practical, proxies such as using hashes, or maintaining logs and chains of custody can be used instead.

As we discussed in Chapter 10, *Data Normalization and Exploitation*, sometimes it is more efficient to use centralized logs, and even more so if the data is normalized to reduce redundancy. To aid the maintenance of data meaning, the original, transformed, normalized, and analyzed logs should all be kept. Alternatively, a copy of the original data can be kept alongside a record of all the actions taken. If the results can be reproduced (for example, by the defense team or independent verifiers), this will increase the trust in the evidence.

Volatile data collection

There are several areas where electronic data can be volatile. The most obvious is that RAM is cleared when the system is powered down.

The following table shows the order of volatile data collection suggested by *NIST.SP800-86*, and why the data is considered volatile:

Data Item	Priority	Source of data	Source of Volatility
Network Connections	1	Netstat	Adjacent network devices may be taken offline, or new devices put online. LLDP updates (if used) may also be interrupted
Login Sessions	2	Unix: e.g. w Windows: e.g. query user (see Network and Server Profiling for more)	Particularly for remote connections (e.g. VNC or SSH/Telnet), the adversary will want to terminate the connection as soon as possible
Contents of Memory	3	Unix: /dev/mem > *filename* Windows: Third party utilities	On power down, or overwritten by another process on release (e.g. by the very tools needed to conduct the subsequent collections)
Running Processes	4	Unix: ps Windows: Task Manager	Processes, once stopped, will be pruned from the list (and will release the memory as above)
Open Files	5	Unix: lsof Windows: Third party utilities	Files, once closed, will be pruned from the list, and any changes could be discarded
Network Configuration	6	Unix: ifconfig Windows: ipconfig	DHCP, if used, can expire and the configuration changed.
Operating System Time	7	Unix: date Windows: nlsinfo or date or time commands	Time zone information and current system time could change if reconnected to a NTP source

Volatile data sources and the priority for their preservation

Automation of these tasks will help an investigator to collect the data in a timely way, hopefully with the loss of as little data as possible.

Summary

Communicating threats is vital for the defense of organizations from cybersecurity threats. This communication assists in every stage of the incident handling chain, which will involve multiple organizations and stakeholders. The VERIS framework provides a common language for describing security incidents, split into four elements: actor, action, asset, and attributes. These elements (and their sub-elements) guide operators through the process, with multi-selectable options to aid their classification.

A common vocabulary, used consistently, allows organizations to share information, and research the threat environment and threat history. This allows them to work proactively, benefiting from the lessons learned by others.

In Chapter 7, *Roles and Responsibilities During an Incident*, we looked at the Incident Response Life Cycle. In this chapter, we looked at the phases of incident handling, which is where the non-technical elements of incident response come together. We noted how incident handling is aligned with incident response, but also brings in many more agencies and organizations. Incident handling being aligned depends on high quality, standardized communication to allow all organizations to work together with the common aim of keeping customers secure.

In the final section of this chapter, we have looked at how to conduct an investigation; aligned with Chapter 3, *Computer Forensics and Evidence Handling*, we have looked at prioritization of evidence collection, basics methods, and particularly how non-volatile data should be handled to preserve integrity and consistency.

Questions

1. Which of the following is true about volatile data?
    1. The operating system time is not volatile because it is synchronized with other network devices using NTP.
    2. Network connections are volatile because the attacker's device is likely to be removed from the network on detection.
    3. Paging files are volatile because they are cleared when the process is ended.
    4. Network configuration is not volatile because addresses are burnt in or statically assigned.
2. The CSIRT needs to send some of the failed hard drives to be destroyed. They choose to use a courier, but a road traffic accident leads to the hard drive containing the data being lost in transit
   Which of the following is the best characterization of this new incident?
    1. Asset: M - Disk Drive | Actor: Partner | Action: Error, Physical accidents
    2. Asset: M - Disk Drive | Actor: Partner | Action: Error, Loss
    3. Asset: M - Disk Drive | Actor: External | Action: Physical, Theft
    4. Asset: M - Disk Drive | Actor: External | Action: Error, Disposal Error

The following four questions relate to the following scenario. Further information is given in the individual questions if required.
An employee reports that their vehicle was stolen over the weekend, and their corporate laptop was among the items that was in their car:

3. What is the best characterization of the affected attributes in this incident?
   1. Attribute: Confidentiality, Availability
   2. Attribute: Confidentiality, Integrity
   3. Attribute: Confidentiality only
   4. Attribute: Integrity, Availability

4. The security team notices that the device connected via the VPN yesterday (after the vehicle is meant to have been stolen). A number of emails were accessed. The employee says that their diary might also have been in the car. The user's passwords were written on the back page, but fortunately the diary is otherwise brand new.

   Which of the following additions to the attributes section would be expected?

   1. Confidentiality: .DataDisclosure: Yes/.Data.Variety: Personal and Credentials
   2. Confidentiality: .DataDisclosure: Yes/.Data.Variety: Personal and Internal
   3. Confidentiality: .DataDisclosure: Yes/.Data.Variety: Internal and Secrets
   4. Confidentiality: .DataDisclosure: Yes/.Data.Variety: Credentials and Internal

5. The security team has changed the employee's passwords, and are able to remotely wipe the laptop next time it connects to the internet. Once this happens, what phase will the incident handling team be in?
   1. Containment
   2. Remediation
   3. Hardening
   4. Reporting

6. Some time later, the police have contacted the team to inform them that an individual has been arrested and charged with vehicle theft. The company laptop has been recovered. What is the likely value of the laptop to the organization?
   1. There is no evidential value remaining on the laptop.
   2. There may still be forensic evidence to trace the threat actor.

3. Any volatile evidence will be gone, but old files are still available.
4. Evidence on the hard disk might reveal any of the thief's use while offline.

The following four questions relate to the following scenario. Further information is given in the individual questions if required.

An organization's CSIRT is assembled after reports that a dump of customer data has appeared online. The CSIRT examines the logs, and it appears that a former employee accessed a number of non-public records and subsequently sent large encrypted files out of the company after they had been given notice of termination last week.
The customer data appears to include usernames and partially masked passwords, as well as truncated credit card numbers:

7. What actor details would be reported under VERIS?
    1. Actor: External: .Motive: NA/.Variety: Former employee
    2. Actor: External: .Motive: Grudge/.Variety: Former employee
    3. Actor: Internal: .Motive: NA/.Variety: End-User
    4. Actor: Internal: .Motive: Grudge/.Variety: End-User

8. Which attribute(s) have been affected in this incident?
    1. Confidentiality only
    2. Confidentiality and Availability
    3. Integrity and Availability
    4. Integrity only

9. Which of the following remedial actions should be considered by the organization?
    1. Informing card issuers to block credit card numbers
    2. Ensuring that user accounts are disabled immediately on termination of employment
    3. Ensuring that any encrypted files can be decrypted and inspected before exiting the system
    4. Communication with customers, advising them to change passwords

10. Which of the following items would be the highest priority for evidence collection?
    1. Running processes
    2. Network traffic logs
    3. Encrypted files from the TCP stream
    4. Contents of memory

Further reading

- More detailed guidance on VERIS can be found at: http://veriscommunity.net/
- The full NIST.SP800-61 r2 document can be accessed at: https://nvlpubs.nist.gov/nistpubs/specialpublications/nist.sp.800-61r2.pdf
- The full NIST.SP800-86 document can be accessed at: https://nvlpubs.nist.gov/nistpubs/Legacy/SP/nistspecialpublication800-86.pdf

Section 6: Mock Exams

The 210-255 certification requires knowledge in each of the domains we have covered, but working in a cyber security operation role will require that all the elements are brought together, considered critically, enacted, and communicated. The first step, though, is to pass the certification.

This section contains two mock examinations consisting of 50-60 questions. Before doing these mock examinations, you should endeavor to do the questions at the end of each chapter first. These will help you to assess readiness.

A mock exam should take approximately 90 minutes, but you will get the most benefit from spending around double this time analyzing your results and testing yourself on related questions. For example, if a question in the mock exam is a definition of *integrity* regarding CVSS v3.0, you should ensure you could answer definition-style questions about all other CVSS v3.0 terms that you have learned.

Cisco exams do not allow you to go back and review answers. You should also attempt to do this for these mock exams, as questions are designed to become progressively more complex, and some of the latter questions may give you clues to earlier answers.

The following chapters are included in this section:

- Chapter 14, *Mock Exam 1*
- Chapter 15, *Mock Exam 2*

14
Mock Exam 1

1. Which function in the Linux shell allows for collection of regex groups?
   1. `pcregrep`
   2. `ls`
   3. `grep`
   4. `man grep`

2. Under which framework are auditable backups mandated?
   1. SOX
   2. HIPAA
   3. PCI DSS
   4. FOI

3. Why is DNS an important service for cybersecurity operators to monitor?
   1. It is commonly used by threat actors.
   2. It is commonly used in many legitimate applications.
   3. It is commonly used by threat actors because it is also used in common legitimate applications.
   4. It can be used to identify a targeted system.

4. An administrator suspects that a vulnerability exists on one of the host computers. It is communicating with the command and control host using HTTP messages. The hosts are all running Windows and Mozilla Firefox. Which user-agent string might be suspicious?

    1. Mozilla/5.0 (Windows NT 5.1; rv:7.0.1) Gecko/20100101 Firefox/7.0.1
    2. Mozilla/5.0 (Windows NT 10.0; WOW64; rv:50.0) Gecko/20100101 Firefox/50.0
    3. Mozilla/5.0 (Windows NT 6.1; Win64; x64; rv:25.0) Gecko/20100101 Firefox/29.0
    4. Mozilla/5.0 (X11; x86_64; rv:21.0) Gecko/20100101 Firefox/21.0

5. Which of the following is a description of deterministic analysis?

    1. Analysis based on potential vulnerabilities
    2. Analysis based on likely causes
    3. Analysis based on log files only
    4. Analysis resulting in conclusive results

6. Which of the following is true about tcpdump compared with Wireshark?

    1. tcpdump uses relative timestamps, where as Wireshark's packet list pane uses UTC time.
    2. tcpdump uses UTC time, where Wireshark's packet list pane uses relative timestamps.
    3. Wireshark's packet details pane displays only layers 3-7, where as tcpdump can show all details in Hex and ASCII using the (-X) option.
    4. Wireshark is able to open PCAP files made in tcpdump, where tcpdump is not able to open PCAP files made in Wireshark.

7. Which of the following correlation rules should be investigated first?

    1. A rule with priority 3 in a policy with priority 2
    2. A rule with default priority in a policy with priority 5
    3. A rule with priority 1 in a policy with priority 4
    4. A rule with priority 2 in a policy with priority 1

8. Which of the following correctly lists the four elements under the VERIS schema?

    1. Actors, Actions, Assets, Attributes
    2. Action, Blame, Countermeasures, Device
    3. Threat, Target, Technique, Tactics
    4. Preparation, Detection, Containment, Post-Incident

9. Which of the following is the most likely reason that a threat actor might try to capture corporate email addresses using the reconnaissance phase of the Cyber Kill Chain?

    1. To determine the format for emails within the organization in order to generate whale phishing targets from the publicly accessible directors list

    2. To make contact with potential insider threats

    3. To reveal the email hosting provider used by the corporation

    4. To determine the location of a SMTP or POP server

10. Which of the following is a general principle for a standard data format?

    1. As generic as possible

    2. As tailored to local settings as possible

    3. As readable as possible

    4. As few formatting marks as possible

11. Which method of allocating virtual memory allocates full pages to applications, which is faster but sometimes results in higher memory usage?

    1. HeapAlloc

    2. LocalAlloc

    3. CoTaskMemAlloc

    4. Virtual Alloc

12. Which of the following statements is true?

    1. At the network layer, the address is maintained from the sending computer to the destination computer

    2. At the transport layer, the address is changed at every device

    3. At the application layer, the address is the application's physical ID

    4. At the physical layer, the address is the logical address of the next hop device

13. A vulnerability allows an attacker to insert fraudulent invoices into the list that is sent to a company's finance department to be processed. Which score might this vulnerability be given?

    1. Privileges Required: High

    2. Availability: High

    3. Confidentiality: Low

    4. User Interaction: Required

14. Which of the following are impact metrics?
    1. Attack Vector | Availability | Privileges Required
    2. Attack Vector | Attack Complexity | Privileges Required
    3. Confidentiality | Integrity | Availability
    4. Attack Complexity | User Interaction | Scope

15. Which of the following might occur in the weaponization phase of the Cyber Kill Chain?
    1. Potential vulnerabilities are identified.
    2. Exploits are sent to users.
    3. Exploits are linked to observed vulnerabilities in the system.
    4. Privileges are escalated.

16. Which of the following pieces of data should be kept with a hard drive removed for evidential purposes? (Select all that apply):
    1. Name of the investigator
    2. Date of collection
    3. Tools used for hard drive removal
    4. Suspect Name

17. Which of the following statements on integrity of evidence during data normalization is untrue?
    1. Some data is removed during the normalization process.
    2. The format of data is changed during the normalization process.
    3. Only a copy of the original data should be changed during the normalization process.
    4. Changing the data does not affect integrity if the process is documented.

18. Which of the following is not one of the 18 identifiable features according to HIPAA?
    1. Last name and initial
    2. Cell phone number
    3. Year of birth
    4. Email address

19. Which of the following is an example of probabilistic analysis?
    1. An HTTP communication with a known command and control server is identified as a potential threat.
    2. Analysis of a suspicious piece of software in a sandbox shows the same behaviors as a piece of known malware.

3. A flow involving a connection via the corporate VPN is labeled as safe.

4. A flow involving a Tor exit node is identified as a potential threat.

20. Looking at the following screenshot, what is suspicious about the NetFlow records?

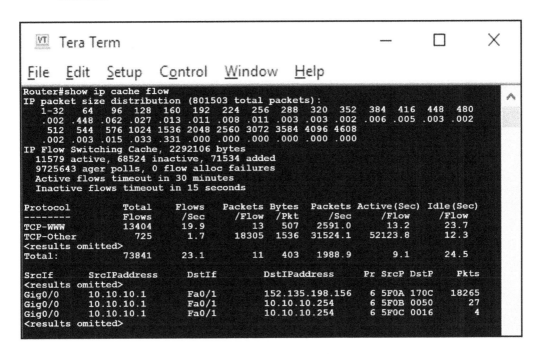

1. An external is port scanning the internal server.

2. An internal host is sending large amounts of data out of the network.

3. An internal host has established a very long session with another internal host.

4. Several similar external addresses have established sessions with internal hosts.

21. Which character on the Linux command line allows the results of one function to be passed to another?

1. The pipe character (|)

2. The greater than sign (>)

3. The caret sign (^)

4. The ampersand character (&)

22. Which attributes would be scored under VERIS if an encrypted USB pen drive was stolen?

    1. All attributes have to be given a score under VERIS.
    2. Confidentiality is affected as for all lost items.
    3. Availability is affected as the device is not available for use by the legitimate user.
    4. Confidentiality and Availability are both affected, so both should be scored.

23. Which of the following statements is true?

    1. The layer 2 address is assigned by the system administrator.
    2. The layer 3 address cannot be changed.
    3. The layer 3 address is hierarchical.
    4. The layer 2 address is assigned by the IANA.

24. Which of the following entities must comply with SOX?

    1. Any company that processes Visa Electron card payments
    2. A privately held corporation in America
    3. A Canadian charity with US branch offices
    4. A European company that has over 300 US shareholders

25. Which of the following is true about a telnet session?

    1. NetFlow would record two flows.
    2. Telnet would show flows to port 22.
    3. Telnet will encrypt the flow.
    4. Telnet does not require a password.

26. A user in finance follows a link sent to them from HACME bank, their company's business banking supplier. The user accessed it through Mozilla Firefox on Windows 10. Which log is suspicious?

    1. GET HACME.com/login.php HTTP/1.1 in the proxy log
    2. Records to [hacme.com]:443 in NetFlow, where [hacme.com] is the correct IP address for the bank's web server
    3. user-agent Mozilla/5.0 (Windows NT 10.0; Win64; x64; rv:66.0) Gecko/20100101 Firefox/66.0 in the proxy log
    4. Records to [hacme.com]:80 in NetFlow, where [hacme.com] is the correct IP address for the bank's web server

27. Which of the following VERIS entries would describe loss of data caused by a wildfire affecting a data center?

    1. Asset: P - Maintenance | Action: Physical: .Variety: Unknown
    2. Actor: External | Action: Physical: .Variety: Tampering

3. Asset: U - Other | Action: Environmental

4. Actor: External | Action: Environmental

28. Which is the best description of a logical copy of a disk?

   1. Best evidence

   2. A copy of every sector on a disk

   3. A copy of the files on a disk

   4. Unaltered disk image

29. A network administrator is investigating 10 user service desk tickets saying they are unable to connect to the wireless network. The network has not been compromised. Which of the following might be the cause of this?

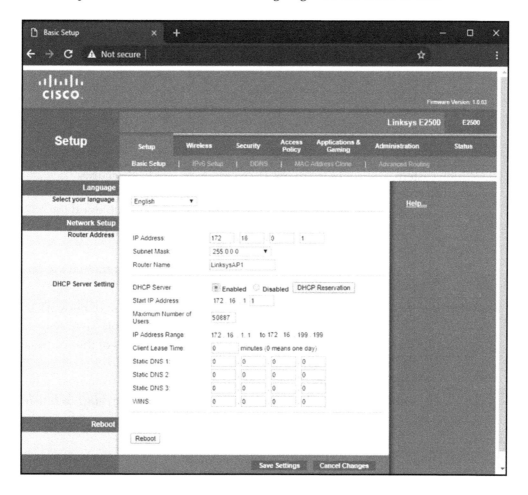

1. DHCP pool depletion caused by too many users
2. DHCP pool depletion caused by excessively long lease time
3. MAC address filtering on the access point
4. Disruption of the network between the Access Point and the DHCP server

30. Which of the following is a reason to attempt threat actor attribution?
    1. To deter future attacks
    2. To prevent poor publicity
    3. To help detect future attacks
    4. To allow the SOC to demonstrate its abilities

31. The following data is extracted from a data stream. Which application layer protocol is most likely?
    Source: `10.10.10.10.52357`
    Destination: `10.10.10.128.443`
    1. DNS
    2. SSL
    3. SSH
    4. DHCP

32. Which system components are not in the scope of PCI DSS security requirements?
    1. Technologies that store, process, or transmit cardholder data
    2. Applications that share data with applications in the CDE
    3. Systems in the same subnet or VLAN as the CDE
    4. Systems on the transmission path for cardholder data that are on public infrastructure (for example, the internet)

33. What feature of the IP 5-tuple makes it suitable for correlation of network events?
    1. The 5-tuple identifies the application layer protocols involved.
    2. The 5-tuple identifies the specific physical address of the source and destination.
    3. The 5-tuple is unchanged throughout the journey from host to host.
    4. The 5-tuple includes details of the route taken from start to finish.

34. Which organization draws data from a number of sources in order to provide insights into future actions or trends?
    1. Coordination centers
    2. Analysis centers
    3. Managed security service providers
    4. Distributed Internal CSIRTs

35. Which actions are carried out in the detection and analysis phase of an incident response?
    1. Profiling networks and servers to establish new baselines for activity
    2. Updating IPS/IDS/Firewalls
    3. Placing infected hosts in quarantine
    4. Verification of suspected incident

36. Which of the following is not a reason to use retrospective analysis?
    1. Detecting polymorphic malware through behavioral analysis is slow.
    2. Long dwell times between breach and detection.
    3. Not all threats have existing signatures.
    4. To detect future threat.

37. Which of the 4 As relates to the impact of the incident on the affected organization?
    1. Assets
    2. Actors
    3. Attributes
    4. Actions

38. Which command could be issued in Command Prompt on a user device to determine who was logged into it?
    1. `last | grep "logged in"`
    2. `query user`
    3. `w`
    4. `whoami`

39. A legitimate file enters the system, but the IDS incorrectly flags it as malicious. What does the administrator have to do?
    1. Nothing. The IDS has taken no action, so the file reached its intended target.
    2. Find, contain, and remove the malicious file. The IDS was correct, but has taken no preventative action.
    3. Advise the intended user, and remove the file from quarantine.
    4. Run a virus scan.

40. Where would you find a log of non-critical system messages?
    1. `~/log`
    2. `/var/log/messages`
    3. `/etc/log/info`
    4. `/bin/info`

41. In which phase of the Cyber Kill Chain might an exploited device signal the attacker using a bespoke HTTP message?
    1. Exploration
    2. Communication
    3. Actions on objectives
    4. Command and control

42. What is the defining characteristic of an attack that has completed the installation phase in the Cyber Kill Chain?
    1. An attacker has *hands-on-keyboard* access.
    2. An attacker has persistent access.
    3. An attacker has achieved their objective.
    4. An attacker has executed the exploit.

43. Which of the following regex statements could be used to match the terms beginning in *SS* (for example, SSH and SSL) but not SSD?
    1. (SSH | SSL)
    2. [SSHL^D]
    3. SS[^D]
    4. SS(H|L)

44. Which of these questions might be asked to test the planning for containment, eradication, and recovery within the organization?

     1. What precursors of the incident, if any, might the organization detect
     2. What could be done to prevent similar incidents
     3. To which people would the team report the incident
     4. Which sources of evidence, if any, should be acquired

45. In which phase of the Cyber Kill Chain might an attacker attempt to take services offline?

     1. Reconnaissance
     2. Exploitation
     3. Actions on objectives
     4. Command and control

46. What is the most significant benefit of using a SIEM over the systems individually?

     1. Cybersecurity operators need only review a single log
     2. Understanding of the context of each entry
     3. Alerts all come from a single source
     4. Automated normalization

47. How does NetFlow use the IP 5-tuple?

     1. As a primary key
     2. To determine whether a new connection is being established
     3. To identify the appropriate flow
     4. To apply the ACL

48. What Cisco technology can be used to reveal layer-7 information?

     1. CDP
     2. LLDP
     3. NetFlow
     4. NBAR

49. Which of the following questions does not relate to the lesson-based hardening phase in incident handling?

     1. How could communication with the public be improved?
     2. How should employees be trained differently?
     3. What changes need to be made to the security audit and compliance policies?
     4. Have all the customer effects from the incident been reset?

50. How does NTP help log collation?
    1. By maintaining a unified time across all the devices in the network
    2. By maintaining a unified time format across all the devices in the network
    3. By providing time with a greater precision than would otherwise be available
    4. By coordinating when each service submits its logs to the collator

15
Mock Exam 2

1. Which of the following are exploitability metrics?
   1. Attack Vector | Availability | Privileges Required
   2. Attack Vector | Attack Complexity | Privileges Required
   3. Confidentiality | Integrity | Availability
   4. Attack Complexity | User Interaction | Scope

2. Which transport layer protocol is the most likely to be used for the destination: `192.168.1.254:snmp`?
   1. DNS
   2. TCP
   3. HTTP
   4. UDP

3. Which of the following will be matched by the regex statement, `[PacktPub]{8}`?
   1. packtpub
   2. Packt Pub
   3. PACKTPUB
   4. backtack

4. What element of a network profile describes how much data is successfully transmitted over the network per second?
   1. Total throughput
   2. Session duration
   3. Critical asset utilization
   4. Running tasks

5. Which of the following is a reason to conduct probabilistic analysis?
    1. Innovative threats
    2. Inconsistent timestamps on logs
    3. Incomplete logs
    4. Integrity concerns on processed logs

6. How can an operator extract an application that's been downloaded from a website using Wireshark?
    1. **File | Export Objects | HTTP....**
    2. **File | Export Objects | UDP....**
    3. **File | Export Objects | Application/octet-stream.**
    4. Applications can only be downloaded from a TCP stream.

7. Which of the following is true of trends in the analysis for cybersecurity?
    1. Increasing processing power means analysts are ahead of attackers.
    2. Increased information sharing means deterministic analysis is becoming accessible for smaller companies.
    3. Machine learning techniques are increasingly being used to support probabilistic analysis.
    4. Increasingly sophisticated attacks are pushing deterministic analysis into popularity.

8. A user in finance follows a link that's sent to them from HACME bank, their company's business banking supplier. The user accessed the website through Mozilla Firefox on Windows 10. Which log is suspicious?
    1. GET HACME.com/login.php HTTP/1.1 in the proxy log
    2. user-agent Mozilla/5.0 (Windows NT 10.0; Win64; x64; rv:66.0) Gecko/20100101 Firefox/66.0 in the Proxy Log
    3. GET %D2%A2ACME.com/login.php HTTP/1.1 in the Proxy Log
    4. Records to [hacme.com]:443 in NetFlow, where [hacme.com] is the correct IP address for the bank's web server

9. Which of the following teams may act as a *response team of last resort*, leading the response for organizations that may not have their own response team?
    1. Coordination centers
    2. Analysis centers
    3. Managed security service providers
    4. National CSIRT

10. A signature-based antivirus software is an example of what type of analysis?

    1. Deterministic analysis

    2. Probabilistic analysis

    3. Narrative analysis

    4. Predictive analysis

11. What is the purpose of ARP?

    1. To map IP addresses to MAC addresses

    2. To map IP addresses to port numbers on a switch

    3. To map sockets to port numbers on a switch

    4. To map sockets to MAC addresses

12. Which of the following might occur in the reconnaissance phase of the Cyber Kill Chain?

    1. Unsolicited emails are sent, telling users to click a link.

    2. Unsolicited telephone calls are made, telling users to allow a remote desktop connection.

    3. Unsolicited professional social media requests are made, asking for information about an upcoming job opportunity.

    4. Unsolicited merchandise, including USB pen drives.

13. Which of the following is not a category of a safeguard under HIPAA?

    1. Administrative safeguards

    2. Preemptive safeguards

    3. Technical safeguards

    4. Physical safeguards

14. Which of the following is a property of the NTFS filesystem?

    1. Maximum file size of 4 GB

    2. Maximum directory depth of 60 levels

    3. Support for encryption

    4. Full journaling (metadata and file data) support

15. Which of the following is a feature of sandbox detection?

    1. Sandbox detection allows the API calls to be recorded.

    2. Sandbox detection can negate some of the complexities associated with polymorphic malware.

    3. Sandbox detection is faster than signature-based detection.

    4. Sandbox detection uses file features extracted from the file itself to classify unknown files using machine learning.

16. Which of the following might occur in the exploitation phase of the Cyber Kill Chain?
    1. The attack code is launched.
    2. The attack code is downloaded to an infected host.
    3. The attack code is constructed based on the observed vulnerabilities.
    4. The infected host's beacon back to the command and control server.

17. Who will coordinate the incident response activity if there is a single, distributed CSIRT in a large organization?
    1. Coordination center
    2. Organizational senior management
    3. IT support
    4. Information assurance

18. What can an organization use to manually configure alert priorities?
    1. Correlation rules in the Firepower Management Console
    2. Traps for syslog messages
    3. Severity scores in the IDS
    4. Metasploit

19. Who is ultimately responsible for reviewing and accounting for deficiencies under SOX?
    1. IT service managers
    2. Executive board members
    3. External auditors
    4. Internal verifiers

20. An email attachment enters the system and is characterized as malware. Which of the following is true?
    1. If the attachment was malicious, this is a true negative.
    2. If the attachment was legitimate, this is a true positive.
    3. If the attachment was legitimate, this is a false positive.
    4. If the attachment was malicious, this is a false negative.

21. The network's security software went offline two days ago. An investigator suspects that malware has found its way onto a user's computer in this time. Which of the following would be considered corroborative evidence?
    1. Antivirus scan logs that detected no threats
    2. Network data showing a spike in traffic from that computer over the last two days
    3. Activity logs showing that the computer has not been used in a week
    4. Multiple files on the computer being deleted over a number of months

22. Which of the following is a benefit of removing partial and transitive dependencies during normalization?
    1. Removing anomalies
    2. Reducing duplication
    3. Structuring metadata
    4. Collating information

23. An IPv6 packet has a length field value of 0. What might this mean?
    1. The packet header has been corrupted.
    2. The packet has no payload.
    3. The packet has a total length greater than 65,535 bytes.
    4. The packet is being used to establish a session.

24. Which of the following items is sensitive authentication data?
    1. Cardholder name
    2. Service code
    3. Magnetic-strip information
    4. Cardholder address

25. Which of the following is the highest priority item for collection according to *NIST.SP800-86*?
    1. Network connections
    2. Running processes
    3. Contents of memory
    4. Open files

26. Which option allows case sensitivity to be enforced with `grep`?

    1. `-i`
    2. `-o`
    3. `grep` is case-sensitive by default
    4. `-C`

27 Which of the following precautions reduce the threat to data during an investigation? (Select all that apply.)

    1. Antistatic wristbands used during physical handling
    2. Performing analysis on the original drive
    3. Storage in specialist storage facilities
    4. Encrypting the data

28. Which of the following statements about the following screenshot are true? (Select two.)

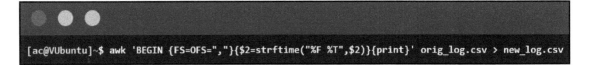

    1. Creating a new file creates duplication and, therefore, may create update anomalies.
    2. A new file should be created with the | command.
    3. Creating a new file with the > command maintains the integrity of the original.
    4. A new file should be created with the `mv` command.

29. Which of the following HTTP responses might indicate that the web server is currently experiencing a denial of service attack?

    1. HTTP/1.1 408 Gateway Timeout
    2. HTTP/1.1 503 Service Unavailable
    3. HTTP/1.1 301 Moved Permanently
    4. HTTP/1.1 400 Bad Request

30. A network administrator issues the following command. What are they trying to do?

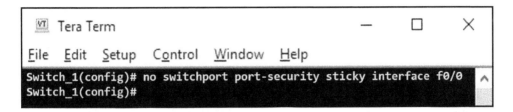

1. Shut down this unused port
2. Prevent an unauthorized host using this unused port
3. Prevent an unauthorized host from unplugging the legitimate device and using the port in its place
4. Reset the saved MAC addresses associated with the port

31. In which phase of the Cyber Kill Chain does lateral movement and privilege escalation occur?
    1. Exploitation
    2. Installation
    3. Command and control
    4. Actions on objectives

32. How can an investigator collect information about the network connections on a device running Windows?
    1. The CLI command, w
    2. The CLI command, netstat
    3. The CLI command, ifconfig
    4. The CLI command, ipconfig

33. The following screenshot shows part of a NetFlow output for an organization using PAT. What can be said about the position of the NetFlow collection device relative to the network?

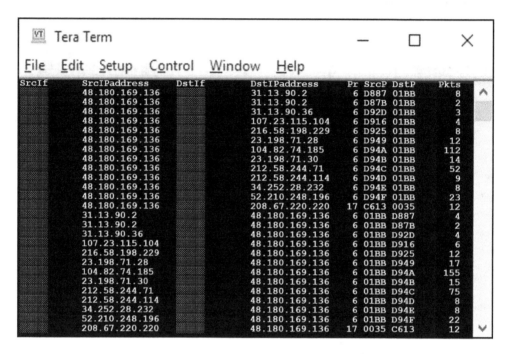

1. The data is being collected before translation has been applied on the outbound interface and before translation has been applied on the inbound interface.

2. The data is being collected before translation has been applied on the outbound interface and after translation has been applied on the inbound interface.

3. The data is being collected after translation has been applied on the outbound interface and before translation has been applied on the inbound interface.

4. The data is being collected after translation has been applied on the outbound interface and after translation has been applied on the inbound interface.

34. A system has 10 publicly routable addresses, a publicly accessible web server, and a /8 private (internal) addressing scheme. Which of the following should be considered?
    1. Applying a dynamic NAT to utilize the full publicly routable address pool
    2. Applying a PAT to allow more hosts to connect to the Internet simultaneously
    3. Applying a static NAT from one of the public addresses to the web server, pooling the other addresses for other users
    4. Using a static IP address allocation to apply control over every host's IP address

35. What would be listed under Actor in a VERIS report concerning a "script kiddie" who found some code on a "dark web" site and was seeing what it would do?
    1. Actor: External: .Motive: Fun/.Variety: Unaffiliated
    2. Actor: External: .Motive: NA/.Variety: Unaffiliated
    3. Actor: External: .Motive: Unknown/.Variety: Unaffiliated
    4. Actor: External: .Motive: Grudge/.Variety: Force Majeure (chance)

36. Which of the following is a reason to establish asset attribution?
    1. To prove that the item is in its original form
    2. To assert copyrights
    3. To prevent theft
    4. To allow the item to be shared

37. At what point should the public affairs and media relations team be notified?
    1. As soon as an incident has been verified.
    2. As directed by senior management.
    3. When the incident has been identified.
    4. The Public Affairs and Media Relations team will contact the CSIRT if a comment is required.

38. In which phase of the Cyber Kill Chain might an attacker exfiltrate data from the system?
    1. Reconnaissance
    2. Actions on Objectives
    3. Exploitation
    4. Delivery

39. A vulnerability allows a remote attacker to pretend to be an employee and access internal documents. Which metric is likely to be affected the most?
    1. Confidentiality
    2. Privileges Required
    3. Scope
    4. Availability

40. For which phase of the Cyber Kill Chain is the use of honey pots an effective defensive tool?
    1. Actions on Objectives
    2. Delivery
    3. Command and Control
    4. Exploitation

41. An incident has arisen after a series of successful phishing emails were sent. Which would be the correct VERIS action?
    1. Social
    2. Misuse
    3. Error
    4. Malware

42. Which piece of the data is required at a minimum to qualify as CHD under PCI DSS?
    1. CVV2
    2. PAN
    3. Expiry date
    4. PIN

43. Which command allows the results of one function to be output to a file?
    1. The pipe character (|)
    2. The greater than sign (>)
    3. The caret sign (^)
    4. The ampersand character (&)

44. Which protocol allows an administrator to determine the IP addresses of routers between two hosts?
    1. ICMP
    2. IPv6
    3. IPv4
    4. TCP

45. Which of the following lines from Unix permissions indicates that a file can be executed by anyone within the same group as the owner?
    1. `0764`
    2. `-rw-rw-rw-`
    3. `0710`
    4. `-rwxrw-r--`

46. Which of the following is not a barrier to retrospective analysis?
    1. Historic log file truncation
    2. Incorrect/inconsistent date stamps
    3. Log file collation and normalization
    4. Rolling log files

47. Which of the following questions does not relate to the remediation phase in incident handling?
    1. What are the communication timelines for the resumption of services to customers?
    2. What is the effect of reverting to a previously backed up version of the data?
    3. Will compensation be required?
    4. How can customer relations be improved?

48. An administrator suspects that a vulnerability exists on one of the host computers. It is communicating with the Command and Control host using HTTP messages. The hosts are all running macOS and Safari. Why is the following user-agent string suspicious?
    User-agent string: Mozilla/4.0 (compatible; MSIE 5.16; Mac_PowerPC)
    1. The user-agent string is too short.
    2. The user-agent string appears to be Mozilla, which is associated with Firefox.
    3. The user-agent string appears to be running Internet Explorer, which is not installed on the hosts.
    4. The user-agent string appears to support Mozilla/4.0 instead of Mozilla/6.0.

49. Which of the following entities would not be considered in the identification phase of incident handling under NIST.SP800-61 r2?
    1. Partner organizations
    2. Regulators
    3. Threat actors
    4. Customers

50. What command can be issued in the Terminal on macOS to display the list of tasks currently running on a device?
    1. Activity monitor
    2. tasklist
    3. ps -e
    4. last

Assessments

The answers that are provided for each of the end-of-chapter questions are designed to expand your understanding of the subject matter. The rationale presents knowledge that is just beyond the 210-255 exam scope, because it is this knowledge that a prospective cybersecurity operator should be striving for.

Some of the rationale and specific examples are not covered directly in this book; there are elements where judgment calls need to be applied, and this will come with practice. The 210-255 exam may well provide examples that aren't in this or any other book; this is the idea – to keep the value of the certification, the questions are held secretly within a tight circle. The idea behind the questions here – and in the mock and the actual 210-255 exam – is to test understanding rather than memorization. Sometimes, an answer will reveal itself by eliminating the options that are definitely irrelevant.

The questions, together with the rationale provided here, should be used to identify where there are weaknesses in your understanding. This can be improved by exploring the *Further reading* section of each chapter.

Chapter 1: Classifying Threats

1. **(1)**
   The **attack vector** relates to the physical and logical pathway and distance from which an attack can be launched. The further away a potential attacker can be from the vulnerability, the more potential attackers there are, and the more dangerous the vulnerability is.
   Attack complexity is described in *question 2*.

2. **(2)**
   A high **attack complexity** describes a situation where there are many conditions beyond the attacker's control that are required to successfully exploit a vulnerability. The lower the attack complexity, the more dangerous the threat.
   Privileges Required refers to the level of privileges an attacker must possess before successfully exploiting the vulnerability. Obtaining these privileges is within the attacker's scope.
   Attack prerequisites does not refer to a CVSS v3.0 metric.
   Attack vector is described in *question 1*.

3. **(2)**

    Confidentiality relates to the ability to access unauthorized content. If the victim has not accepted the call, they haven't authorized the attacker to listen to the microphone content. An example of this would be similar to the FaceTime vulnerability from 2019. (Availability is described in *question 6*.) The victim's microphone would still be available to the victim during the attack, but the attacker is able to listen too. (Integrity is described in *question 4*.) The attacker is unable to change any data from the microphone, so integrity has not been compromised. (Scope is described in *question 5*.) The vulnerable component is the app that controls the calls. The same app controls access to the microphone, and so the scope is unchanged.

4. **(2)**

    Integrity relates to the ability of an attacker to create, edit, or delete files that they are not authorized to. It is assumed that they don't have the authority to change this file under normal conditions.

    (Availability is described in *question 6*.) This attack does not deny other (legitimate) users from accessing the file.

    (Attack Vector is described in *question 1*.) The attack is conducted on the network. While it might seem like this should be ranked as network, it is actually Adjacent, as the attacker's computer must be on the same network as the target.

    (Attack complexity is described in *question 2*.) There is no detail as to whether there are conditions beyond the attacker's control that must be met for the attack to be successful.

5. **(2)**

    An attack against a web server that compromises web browsers that connect to it. This would be an example of a scope change. The vulnerable component is the web server, where the affected component is the web browser. A **denial-of-service (DoS)** attack refers to denying the availability of a resource to legitimate users.

    (Editing the contents of a file on a networked computer is discussed in *question 4*.)

    Excel has access to the user's files, and so the scope hasn't changed. A parallel to this is specifically mentioned in the CVSS v3.0 specification document, and quoted in this chapter.

6. **(3)**

    CVSS:3.0/{Portion Removed}/C:N/I:N/A:H. The impact scores that are shown are in their summarized form. A threat that leaves the component offline could also be called a DoS attack, and relates to availability. There is no detail to suggest that confidentiality or integrity are affected, so these should both score **none**. Option 4, which has zero impact on any of confidentiality, integrity, and availability, is not a threat.

7. **(2)**

   CVSS:3.0/AV:N/AC:L/PR:N/UI:R/S:U/C:N/I:L/A:N. The CVSS scores that are shown are in their summarized form. The attack is conducted on a web server, so the attack vector is network. The attack complexity is low, the privileges required are none, the scope is unchanged, and the impact is the same for all four options. There isn't any detail in the description to judge these metrics in any way. The description does state that the URL must be clicked for the malicious code to execute, so the UI score must be **R**, required.

8. **(4)**

   A compressed (archive) file:

   The file extension is circled. As a `.zip` file, it is **a compressed (archive) file**. An image file would be, for example, a `.jpg` or `.png` extension. Portable document files are commonly seen as `.pdf`, and portable executable files include `.exe` and `.dll` files.

9. **(1)**

   Immediately quarantine and block access to the file:

This file has a score of 100, which means it is definitely a known malware file. The tier-1 analyst should **immediately quarantine and block access to the file**. A score of 75-90 is considered dangerous, and should be referred to tier 2. A score of 56-70 is still suspicious, but needs further expertise to analyze, and should be reported to tier 3. A score of 0 would be removed from quarantine.

10. **(3)**

    Ransomware:

The report says, with a confidence level of 100%, that the item is **ransomware**.

Chapter 2: Operating System Families

1. **(1)**

   HeapAlloc is used for dynamic allocation. When the application requests memory, the right amount of memory is allocated. (VirtualAlloc is described in *question 2*.) Swap is a Linux virtual memory system and is described in *question 3*. CoTaskMemAlloc is used when memory must be shared.

2. **(2)**

   VirtualAlloc utilizes reserved blocks of memory. This means that it is suitable for specialized usage where the memory required is known at the time of creating the process. HeapAlloc was described in *question 1*. LocalAlloc is a specialized version of HeapAlloc, which allows memory to be moved via reallocation. Pages are the files that store virtual memory.

3. **(1)** and **(2)**

   Linux can utilize **a swap partition** or **swap files** to provide extra memory on the hard disk drive or SSD to expand the system's physical memory. Swap file/swap partition capacity must be allocated before use, which means that there is no dynamic allocation. NVRAM is a type of persistent memory.

4. **(1)**

   Journalling is **a system that maintains a record of changes not yet committed to the filesystem**. This journal allows the system to know which files to check following an unexpected system shutdown (for example, power loss), rather than scanning the whole disk. Filesystem formats include ext4 and NTFS. A log of every action that's conducted would become very big, very fast. Logs would only keep track of important computer events.

5. **(1)**

   The /var/ folder contains data that changes during the normal operation of the Linux system. Log files are in the /var/log/ folder. A print spool is not a log, as it is only held until the point that the document finishes printing. This is held in /var/spool/, along with other spools, such as the mail spool.

6. **(2)**

   chmod is the Linux command-line command for changing the mode or permissions of a file. The first number relates to the owner's abilities, and 7 is for read, write, and execute. The second and third number relate to the owner's groups and global permissions, respectively. 3 is the designation for write and execute, 1 is the designation for execute only, and 0 is the designation for no permissions. The correct answer is therefore chmod 711 setup.sh.

7. **(1)**

NTFS collects **created** and **modified** data on every file. Last saved and last accessed dates are present in some files, but these are recorded in an alternative data stream.

8. **(2)**

The d denotes the file as a directory. Other clues to this are the color coding (purple/blue) and the file size of 4,096 bytes:

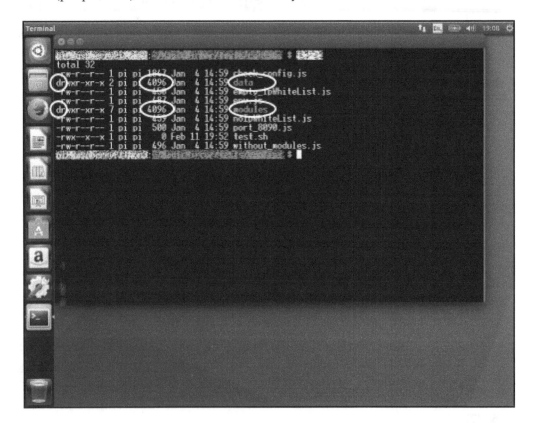

9. **(1)**

The output is a list (ls) of all the files within the directory, in long format (so the -l argument has been passed). The output doesn't show the . or .. directories, or any hidden files, so the -a argument hasn't been passed. To get this result, the ls -l command would be executed.

10. **(4)**

The test.sh has three x listings in its symbolic notation. The first marks the owner as being able to execute, the second states that the group can execute, and the third states that external users are also able to execute. Everybody is able to execute the test.sh file:

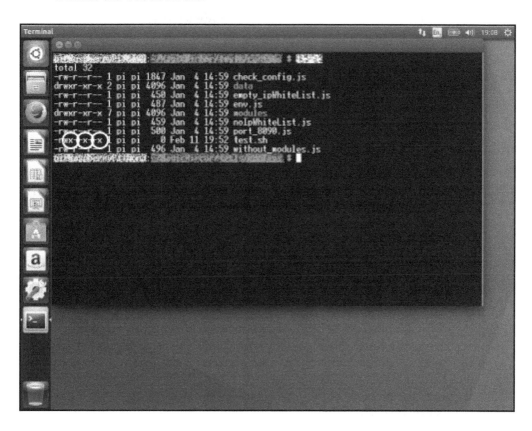

Chapter 3: Computer Forensics and Evidence Handling

1. **(2)**

   Corroborative evidence is best defined as **evidence that supports the conclusions made from a primary piece of evidence.** Evidence that stands alone and would be admissible in its current format in court would be **best** evidence. Evidence that contradicts the primary evidence is still direct evidence, and could – under certain circumstances – still be called **best** evidence.

   Evidence that requires explanation from expert testimony is called indirect or circumstantial evidence, and includes things such as DNA that require interpretation to draw conclusions.

2. **(3)**

   By copying the files to removable storage, the investigator has made **a logical copy, which will have a degraded value compared to the original drive.** The original drive would be considered **best** evidence, which could be submitted directly to court, regardless of whether direct attribution of the files to the identified client can be established.

   Copying the files doesn't necessarily contaminate the information, especially if the correct procedures are followed and the documentation is kept. Copying the files may mean that some date is missed (deleted files/metadata), however.

3. **(1)**

   The best available form of evidence in this case is to produce a **physical copy of the drive using block-by-block copying**. While this isn't as good as having the original drive, it does allow for further analysis of the free and unallocated space later. Having two logical copies doesn't change the fact that the logical copy isn't as good as the physical copy in terms of evidential quality.

   Using software such as Recuva to undelete files would still require these recovered files to be stored somewhere, possibly degrading a different sector of the disk. This could be a problem for evidential integrity. Additionally, the use of software such as Recuva would features including like timestamps and would put the investigator as the **author** or **last modified by** user.

   Installing spyware in order to collect further evidence is likely to breach the terms and conditions of the service agreement, and is also likely to be inadmissible in court since the investigator is not a law-enforcement professional.

4. **(4)**

Any activity, including **collection, movement,** and **access,** should be logged. This log should include what action was taken; who carried out the action or had access to it; and when the action was carried out.

Each piece of evidence should be separately serialized, and case notes should reference these items of evidence rather than the other way around. Before a piece of evidence is examined and analyzed, there is unlikely to be a case number, or even a good idea of who the case might focus on.

5. **(1)**

A physical, verified copy of the drive, including free and unallocated blocks, is considered a best alternative to the original drive because it includes hidden, deleted, and partially deleted files. A logical copy is the drive's visible files, and even if hidden files were included, it is still not a block-by-block copy, and therefore may be missing some file remnants in the unallocated space.

A physical verified copy (or image) of the device allows examination to be conducted that might otherwise damage the integrity of the original. This is why a physical copy is examined instead of the original device.

6. **(1)**

Comparing hashes is a quick method of verifying that two images are identical, and therefore that one has not been changed. This is not a perfect system, and there are collisions within the MD5 hashing system, but this is much faster than comparing both images block by block.

The MD5 hashing system was originally a cryptographic function, but encrypting a drive is not one of the aims of investigation. Moreover, encrypting the drive adds a level of complexity and increases the risk of evidence being lost or changed.

Hashing cannot be used to prove that the image has been created correctly. It will simply give a quick assessment. To truly prove that an image is correct, a full, block-by-block comparison would be needed.

7. **(4)**

Threat Actor attribution is about more than just **catching criminals**. The process also reveals the **Tactics, Techniques, and Procedures**, and punishments help to **deter future attacks**. It is thought that the anonymity associated with digital crime is part of the driving force, as criminals perceive the chances of getting caught as lower than in real life.

8. **(1)**

A physical disk copy allows for multiple tests to be carried out without risking damage to the original drive. The original should be retained and stored securely if possible since this remains the **best** evidence, although the physical disk copy is **as good as** the original in most cases.

Compression of the drive would require the contents to be modified; sometimes, important information is held in the unallocated space. This information is as important as the visible files for the court.

9. **(3)**

The **best** evidence would be **the original USB drive, which was the point of entry for malware onto the network**. This drive might contain additional information; for example, the DNA or fingerprints of the attacker. A physical copy is **as good as** the original in terms of the data held on the drive, but it doesn't contain the **non-digital** forensics that the original does.

A logical copy is not best evidence as it doesn't reflect the original state of the device. The network log would provide corroborative evidence, and is therefore not primary evidence.

10. **(4)**

Emailing incorporates time and date stamps, and identity information into the file transfer. Electronic file transfer exposes the file to risk as the file that's received is a copy of the file, rather than the original. The receiver also wouldn't have the hashes to verify that the file hadn't been changed in transit.

Uploading a file to a shared drive exposes the file to risk as it is easier for non-authorized persons to access the file.

Best practice would be to **physically transport the mass storage device containing the file, plus the MD5 hash,** for verification of image integrity.

Chapter 4: Identifying Rogue Data from a Dataset

More details on the grep command can be found at http://man7.org/linux/man-pages/man1/grep.1p.html.

More details on the cat command can be found at http://man7.org/linux/man-pages/man1/cat.1.html.

1. **(2)**

   The **10\.114\.115\.\d{0,3}** search string would match all of the addresses in the network. The /24 prefix means that the first three octets (10.114.115.) must be the same for every address in the network. The final octet can be any number that's up to three digits long (actually, only up to 255; this regex string doesn't specify the top limit).
   10.114.115.55 would only match the IP address stated, although it would also match longer strings as the lack of an escape character before the period sign means that this would match any character, not just the literal period sign.
   10\.114\.d{0.3}\.\d{0,3} would match the 10.114.0.0/16 network. The \D wildcard matches non-numeric characters.

2. **(2)**

   cron would match both the anacron and crontab descriptions. Using a set would only match for a single character from the set (either "C", "R", "O", "N", "c", "r", "o", or "n"), and the search term [cron]* would match every line, since the asterisk (*) character is acting as a zero or more multiplier rather than a wildcard.

3. **(1)**

   grep -i nastyfile\.exe ~/analyseme.txt would match the term nastyfile.exe from the ~/analyseme.txt file. The format of a grep command is grep [OPTIONS] PATTERN [FILE...], where the file is the file to be searched. Notice the escape sequence (\) required for the period sign. The escape sequence should always be before the character being escaped. (\e) would match ESC (ASCII 7) rather than e. The use of ~/ specifies that the file is in the home directory. The reference to ~analyseme.txt would have a full path of ~/~analyseme.txt (that is, it is looking for the tilde ~ character as part of the filename. In all of the grep commands listed, the -i option is used, which denotes that the regular expression is not case-sensitive.

4. **(3)**

   grep -i " (edit|replace) " ~/analyseme.txt would match either the
   word edit or the word replace. The carat (^) inside a set ([ ]) means a logical
   NOT, so this wouldn't match any of the letters in the set. The pipe, which is used
   as a logical OR, must be inside a set of parentheses, and not a set of brackets:

```
Feb  2 15:57:30 VVubuntu sudo:        ac : TTY=pts/4 ; PWD=/home/ac ; USER=root ; COMMAND=/bin/chmod +x alarm.sh
Feb  2 15:57:30 VVubuntu sudo: pam_unix(sudo:session): session opened for user root by (uid=0)
Feb  2 15:57:30 VVubuntu sudo: pam_unix(sudo:session): session closed for user root
Feb  2 15:58:41 VVubuntu sudo:        ac : TTY=pts/4 ; PWD=/home/ac ; USER=root ; COMMAND=/usr/bin/crontab -e
Feb  2 15:58:41 VVubuntu sudo: pam_unix(sudo:session): session opened for user root by (uid=0)
Feb  2 15:59:15 VVubuntu sudo: pam_unix(sudo:session): session closed for user root
Feb  2 16:00:50 VVubuntu pkexec: pam_unix(polkit-1:session): session opened for user root by (uid=1000)
Feb  2 16:00:50 VVubuntu pkexec: pam_systemd(polkit-1:session): Cannot create session: Already running in a session
Feb  2 16:00:50 VVubuntu pkexec[3241]: ac: Executing command [USER=root] [TTY=unknown] [CWD=/home/ac]
[COMMAND=/usr/lib/update-notifier/package-system-locked]
Feb  2 16:03:17 VVubuntu pkexec[3371]: ac: Executing command [USER=root] [TTY=unknown] [CWD=/home/ac]
[COMMAND=/usr/lib/update-notifier/package-system-locked]
Feb  2 16:07:01 VVubuntu CRON[3392]: pam_unix(cron:session): session opened for user root by (uid=0)
Feb  2 16:07:01 VVubuntu CRON[3392]: pam_unix(cron:session): session closed for user root
Feb  2 16:09:30 VVubuntu polkitd(authority=local): Registered Authentication Agent for unix-session:c2 (system bus
name :1.74 [/usr/lib/polkit-1-gnome/polkit-gnome-authentication-agent-1], object path
/org/gnome/PolicyKit1/AuthenticationAgent, locale en_GB.UTF-8)
Feb  2 16:10:16 VVubuntu pkexec: pam_unix(polkit-1:session): session opened for user root by (uid=1000)
Feb  2 16:10:16 VVubuntu pkexec: pam_systemd(polkit-1:session): Cannot create session: Already running in a session
Feb  2 16:12:01 VVubuntu CRON[4855]: pam_unix(cron:session): session opened for user root by (uid=0)
Feb  2 16:12:01 VVubuntu CRON[4855]: pam_unix(cron:session): session closed for user root
Feb  2 16:14:17 VVubuntu polkitd(authority=local): Unregistered Authentication Agent for unix-session:c2 (system bus
name :1.74, object path /org/gnome/PolicyKit1/AuthenticationAgent, locale en_GB.UTF-8) (disconnected from bus)
```

5. **(4)**

   grep sudo.*open would match all the lines with the words sudo and open,
   separated by as many other characters as required (the green section = a match;
   yellow highlights = other characters). The escaped period (\.) would mean that
   grepsudo\.*open would only match sudo.......open. The -o option only
   returns the matched string, and not the entire line as desired.

6. **(4)**

   pcregrep -o1 "(([0-9A-Za-z :]){15})sudo.*session opened" >
   newfile.txt would return the timestamps to the new file. The captured group
   is group 1 because it is the first opened parenthesis. Group 0 refers to the whole
   regex statement match. The pipe sign (|) is incorrect because the second
   statement is just a file name and doesn't have a function associated with it.

7. **(4)**

pcregrep -o1 "sudo.*COMMAND=(.*)]?" could be used to find the output commands. The period character denotes any characters. When it is escaped (\.), this only matches the literal period character. In some of the lines (pkexec), the command has a trailing close bracket (]), so this must be ignored by specifying it as optional (]?) outside of the parentheses (a desired match in blue; an undesired character in red):

```
[user@Vubuntu~]# cat log.txt | grep
07:05:59.551720 IP 192.168.16.20:ssh > 192.168.10.100:59657 : [ACK] SEQ=5
07:06:45.972341 IP 192.168.10.107:16354 > 192.168.78.8:http : [SYN] SEQ=0
07:06:58.065872 IP 192.168.78.8:http > 192.168.10.107:16354 : [SYN, ACK]
07:17:06.165521 IP 192.168.10.107:13549 > 192.168.22.13:ssh : [FIN] SEQ=1
07:17:07.064221 IP 192.168.10.107:16354 > 192.168.78.8:http : [ACK] SEQ=1
07:17:17.230351 IP 192.168.10.107:16354 > 192.168.78.8:http : GET / HTTP/
```

8. **(2)**

07:06:[0-5][0-9] would match any timestamp of 07:06:00 through to 07:06:59, which would match this time range. The * character is a quantifier, rather than a wildcard, so ^07:16:*$ will only match lines that start 07:16: and then have a continuous series of colon literals (:) until the end of the line. Sets in square brackets only refer to a single character, so you couldn't use [0-59] since this would only match the digits 0, 1, 2, 3, 4, 5, 9. When using the carat (^) and dollar ($) signs, the carat denotes the start of the line and the dollar denotes the end of the line.

9. **(2)**

The statement matches minutes and seconds, as well as hours and minutes (line 4), because the colons are not specified, instead using the non-alphanumeric wildcard. There is no problem with the IP:port combinations since the search string requires a non-alphanumeric character either side of 06. In IPv4, preceding 0 characters are dropped, so if the socket was 192.168.107.06:16354, this would appear as 192.168.107.6:16354, and this wouldn't match the search string. From the separators that are used, it is clear that the date timestamp doesn't include the date component; the separators for dates are either non-existent, whitespaces ( ), or dashes (-).

The use of the dollar sign is to denote the end of a line when it appears at the end of the search string. A carat sign precedes a search string that is matched at the start of a line.

The search string selects the whole string after the matched 07:06:XX sequence, but for clarity, I have highlighted only part of the line in green. Highlighted in yellow are the partial matches, with red denoting the characters that cause the match to fail.

10. **(2)**
(\d{1,3}\.\d{1,3}\.\d{1,3}\.\d{1,3}):ssh could be used to extract IP addresses for all devices supporting an incoming SSH connection. If the brackets are outside the character's SSH, it would extract `192.168.22.13:ssh`. If the brackets are used before the quantifier, this would extract the contents of the brackets separately (for example, "192.","168.", "22." or "13"). If the brackets include the literal period sign within them, without the "optional" identifier, this wouldn't have any matches, since it would be expecting something like `192.168.22.13.:ssh` (complete with a period sign before the colon to SSH).

Chapter 5: Warning Signs from Network Data

1. **(4)**
Layer 2 is the data link layer, which works between the network layer and the physical layer. The addresses at layer 2 are called physical, burnt-in, or MAC addresses; the addresses are (mostly) set at point of manufacture.
The network layer address is referred to as a logical address because the addressing system is hierarchical. The most common network layer protocol address scheme is the IP address.
The correct combination is therefore **Layer 2: MAC address | Layer 3: Logical Address.**

2. **(1)**
The **MAC address table** matches MAC addresses to the relevant exit interface on a switch. The interface list is a list of the interfaces that are present on the switch. The ARP table matches IP addresses to MAC addresses, and the routing table is used on routers to track how to get from one network to the next.

3. **(2)**
The **Cyclic Redundancy Check (CRC)** is used to check for **accidental damage to frames in transit**. There are some hash collisions that occur with the CRC as it is only a 4-byte hash (compared to MD5 with a 16-byte hash). These collisions mean that an intentional change could be made that still generates the same CRC check value. To check the order of segments arriving in TCP – and to rearrange them – the sequence number is used.

4. **(2)**

   In IPv6, the **Hop Limit** prevents packets persisting on the internet. With each router the packet passes through, the Hop Limit is decremented. When it reaches 0, the packet is dropped. The time-to-live field is in IPv4; extension headers process different handling options and methods; and sequence numbers are used by TCP.

5. **(2)**

   The **Domain Name Service** can use either TCP or UDP. DHCP is a UDP-only protocol on Port 67 and 68, HTTP is a TCP-only protocol on port 80, and POP3 is a TCP-only protocol on port 110.

6. **(2)**

   The source port of 51523 denotes that the segment is traveling from a client to the server. One such instance of this is **a request to start an SSH session**. This is corroborated by the well-known port 22. The registered port range is from 1024 to 49151. The server's certificate request would come from port 22, and it is a Telnet session that is sent in cleartext, not SSH.

7. **(3)**

   The request line HEAD /index.html HTML/1.1 will return the same status as GET /index.html HTML/1.1 because the status code and reason phrase are contained in the HTTP response header. The difference between HEAD and GET is that the request HEAD doesn't receive the body of the response in response. The POST method exists and is spelled correctly so it wouldn't return a 501 error; the GET method may not always be successful for either client or server side errors; the method Post is incorrectly spelled, and so it wouldn't be completed successfully – this would return a 501 error.

8. **(2)**

   ICMP has been used to reach `packtpub.com` successfully. ICMP is the protocol that powers both `ping` and `tracert`. POP3 is involved in sending emails, DHCP is involved with configuring host network settings, and SNMP is involved in network monitoring.

9. **(3)**

   The tec directory doesn't exist on the server of www.packtpub.com, which is causing a 404 (resource not found) error. The `packtpub.com` server must have been resolved in order for it to respond at all, and there is an SSL version of the site for the same reason; if the directory was behind a paywall, the response would be a 401 (unauthorized) error.

10. **(2)**

The a character in `packtpub` is actually the character ą – notice the dot below? It was obscured by the underline in the link, and was not noticeable in the address bar. Using a **domain name** that **includes a rogue character that appears to be normal but is incorrect** is a common way to send victims to a rogue site. Genuine looking emails and links (particularly of banks or common sites) can be used in phishing attacks. The DNS server is definitely online because the `ping` was successful; the `packtpub.com` server is online because it is sending responses (even if it's 404); the IP address for the host is correctly configured because it is able to access the DNS server and web server.

Chapter 6: Network Security Data Analysis

1. **(1) and (4)**

A PCAP file can be opened in Wireshark using the **File | Open** menu option. Wireshark can read in an ASCII hex dump and write the data described into a temporary libpcap capture file for display and analysis. This is useful for packet capture technologies that are unable to output in another of Wireshark's accepted file formats.

The libpcap filetype is a menu option for saving Wireshark captures, but in opening files, Wireshark will attempt to interpret files internally, so it isn't necessary to specify the libpcap format.

Dragging and dropping the PCAP file into Wireshark will also open up a PCAP file.

2. **(1)**

The port number is a 2-byte field, and therefore is 4 hexadecimal characters in length. 0080 is the hexadecimal representation of the number 128. **0050 is the port value in Hex for HTTP**. The packet bytes pane also has an ASCII representation. As a 2-byte field, the ASCII representation would be two characters. The character at ASCII 80 is the letter "P", so this field would appear as -P (not ---P). 80 in ASCII would be the value 0x3830 or 0d14384.

3. **(1)**

An `.exe` file is classified as **application/octet-stream** in Wireshark. This is the IANA Media Type designated in RFC 2045 and RFC 2046. The file extension (`.exe`) is used in some media type designations (for example, `.gif`) but not all. The portable executable "pe" is a designation in many firewalls, but not in the IANA standard list. The list doesn't include "executable" as a registry.

4. **(3)**

   ImagePath = \SystemRoot\System32\drivers\BasicDisplay.sys is the correct path for this registry entry. System services should be in the `\SystemRoot\System32` folder. The `Program Files` folder normally relates to user-installed programs. The period (.) character before a folder name is used in Linux to create a hidden folder. The `\System32\` and `\.System32\` folders are not the same location.

5. **(1)**

   HTTP Request header: CONNECT index.html HTTP/1.0 would require more investigation. The version is 1.0, which is unusual, and the request method is also non-standard.

6. **(2)**

   This is a False Negative. A False Positive would be when legitimate data is classified as malware. There are a number of reasons why a False Negative might arise in signature-based antivirus software, including polymorphic malware and zero-day attacks. Not enough information has been given for us to know what has caused this, though.

7. **(1)**

   IP addresses are hierarchical, so the large classes were generally bought up by countries and ISPs. These classes and address ranges are registered with IANA, which helps us find out who owns what address. IP addresses are retained from source to destination host, except for NAT and PAT, where MAC addresses change per hop. This allows the original host to be identified by IP address. The fact that **IP addresses can be assigned dynamically using DHCP** doesn't contribute to determining the country of origin for a packet.

8. **(1)**

   The flows show **large amounts of data being sent out of the network**. All the suspicious flows have a source inside the network and a destination outside the network over the internet. The number of packets is quite low, but the average packet is 2 MB, which means that many of them are likely to be jumbo packets.

9. **(4)**

   Across all three internal (host) networks, **multiple internal addresses are communicating with the same external address** (85.251.128.77). There is insufficient information to know what country the destination originates from, but it is clear that the address is outside the network from the position of the NetFlow collector and the network diagram.

10. **(1)**

    The port that's used is associated with HTTP, but the transport layer protocol is UDP. HTTP is generally associated with TCP port 80; UDP port 80 is also associated with HTTP, although TCP is generally used for web browsing over HTTP. Packets of this size being transmitted over UDP suggest that data is being indiscriminately harvested. SSL is associated with TCP port 443, and telnet is associated with port 23.

Chapter 7: Roles and Responsibilities During an Incident

1. **(2)**

    The mission specified by NIST is the organization's mission. **The organization's mission will dictate which actions cannot be taken**; that is, the boundaries within which the CSIRT can operate. The IT team mission is important, but the incident response capability is owned by the organization as a whole, rather than the IT department specifically. The CSIRT mission will guide the team's priorities, but it is the organization's priorities that inform the CSIRT's actions, not the other way around.

2. **(1)**

    The NIST guidelines specify that metrics are required **to measure the effectiveness of the plan**. The incident response plan will be designed for a number of different eventualities, from benign to severe. Risk is assessed as part of the preparation phase, and will be accepted when it passes through senior management approval. There are many difficulties in quantifying the value of the CSIRT. The value of the CSIRT is acknowledged in the agency and capabilities agreed in the plan.

3. **(2)**

    The preparation stage is where you have the opportunity to **train the CSIRT on the systems and technologies in use**. Collecting and documenting evidence requires there to be evidence of an incident. Therefore, it occurs in all phases except the preparation stage. Fixing damaged host machines and recovering data from backups could be considered routine tasks, but these are more accurately placed in the recovery phase.

4. **(1)**

   The **internal CSIRT** contains staff who are directly employed by the affected organization. The analysis center may be internal to the organization, but can (and more often is) be an external agency. A vendor CSIRT contains staff from the manufacturer or developer of given hardware and software. Incident Response Providers is the Cisco term for Managed Security Service Providers. These are outsourced teams who are employed by a third-party provider.

5. **(1)**

   The incident response plan is signed off by **Senior Management**, and they are responsible for the implementation of the incident response plan. The other three teams are stakeholders, and may contribute staff to the incident response, but command responsibilities lie with senior management.

6. **(3)**

   Restoring host computers, either from backups or from the original installation media, is part of the **Containment, Eradication, and Recovery** phase. The incident has not ended until "normal service is resumed", so this task must occur before post-incident analysis.

7. **(2)**

   Cisco providing emergency updates for older routers is an example of vendor CSIRT activity. When Cisco is responding to a DoS attack on `cisco.com`, it is operating as an internal CSIRT. When it is providing information about new trends, it is acting as an analysis center. When it is providing security as a paid-for service, it is acting as an MSSP.

8. **(2)**

   The incident has been verified. Containment should now begin. The incident is the revelation of users' login details, and containment of this can now occur. The fraud element is a separate incident, and a parallel detection and analysis phase should be run to discover and rectify (if possible) past fraudulent transactions. The other activities would be done in the Containment, Eradication, and Recovery phase.

9. **(3)**

   All of these actions will help reduce the impact of an information leak and prevent future fraud. However, they don't change the vulnerability – the fact that the listed users' accounts are compromised. The action you would take to contain this incident is to **suspend all the listed users' accounts**.

10. **(1)**

The question, **how did the fraudster acquire the information?**, is important for determining the extent of the attack. The containment phase cannot be completed until the CSIRT is assured that no further information will leak, and that the gap that allowed the information to be revealed has been rectified. This might be a keylogger or a rogue employee, but whatever the leak, it needs to be plugged. The other options refer to a separate incident of fraud. These are individual actions that stem from the information leak.

Chapter 8: Network and Server Profiling

1. **(1)**

A change in company workforce planning to create two shifts a day instead of a regular 9-5 working day would be the most likely scenario where an organization would create a whole new network profile. Depending on how much overlap there was between shifts, this working day would likely redistribute traffic on the network through the day, although it will also mean that resources were active for longer (for example, less **downtime** for servers). Changes for daylight-saving time are likely to affect the whole organization, and would therefore just shift the normal pattern of life an hour forward or back. Members of staff going on parental leave, and a move to BYOD in a single branch, are unlikely to impact on the organization's traffic as a whole unless the individual or branch is particularly important or large compared to the rest of the organization.

2. **(3)**

Additional traffic out of the network, outside of work hours, could be an indicator of a vulnerability in the network, particularly if the data flows are mainly out of the network.

An increase in total throughput could have a number of explanations, including uplift in staff or workload. This is particularly relevant as it is both internal and external data.

A decrease in internal throughput might be caused by an increase in network congestion and therefore more dropped packets. However, if it is the traffic (that is, attempted transmissions) rather than throughput (that is, successful transmissions), it is unlikely that this is caused by data leaving the network. The best indication of an incident is a deviation from the normal pattern of life. Not enough information has been provided for us to know whether network congestion at a specific time is normal or not.

3. **(1)**

   LLDP is a multi-vendor-supported protocol for devices so that they can identify themselves. Cisco products can also use the **Cisco Discovery Protocol** (CDP). Port security refers to MAC address filtering on Cisco products, and port forwarding redirects traffic to a defined destination port on a specific host. This is particularly useful if there is dynamic NAT or NAT overload (PAT) in operation.

4. **(2)**

   Profiling the critical asset address space ensures that important devices such as routers and servers, are able to receive the right addresses and access the network correctly. A crucial attack that might occur is a **Man-In-The-Middle attack**. If a malicious device were to claim the address of the default gateway, they would be able to intercept outgoing messages. This kind of attack would be disrupted by removing the default gateway address from the DHCP pool and/or checking for address duplication on the network.

   The IPv6 transition can be managed by using dual stacking – implementing both IPv6 and IPv4 addressing simultaneously.

   NetFlow and/or packet captures would be used to look at network utilization, and possible data exfiltration.

5. **(2)**

   The `nmap -sT` command will attempt to connect to each port on the target in turn. This can be conducted from inside or outside the network.

   The CLI `netstat` command must be conducted from the host itself, with the `-a` option displaying the listening ports and the connected ports (by default, `netstat` only shows connected ports and not those in a listening state).

   The `show control-plane host open-ports` command does the same as `netstat` on Cisco IOS devices.

6. **(3)**

   Users should be given the minimum access rights required to perform their job. Restricting a user's access rights can be counterproductive if they are unable to perform their roles. People will just learn to circumvent the security systems. At the same time, users shouldn't be given maximum rights if they don't require this. This policy would allow a breach of a single user's account to expose 100% of the system's functionality.

   Users should be grouped in order to profile what they should be accessing, but the risk of confidentiality breaches is only limited if action is taken based on that profiling.

7. **(3)**

   To answer this question, we should also consider some of the other information in the NetFlow artifact. Not only are the sessions short, they are from a single source to a single destination host, but varying in the port number. It is likely that **port scanning is in progress**. The source is trying to determine whether the port is open and whether a service is being run from it, which it does by establishing and then dropping a session with each port.

   If the network was suffering from high congestion, the window size might be reduced to the extent that segments are dropped, and sessions reset. A more likely symptom of this would be that all the NetFlow sessions were impacted. The short sessions are associated with the same IP source and destination, suggesting that it isn't a DHCP lease issue.

   There is no information that suggest that the server is malfunctioning.

8. **(2)**

   The extended, high volume session on the unknown port is a concern. The session wasn't open in the previous scanning period, and the high volume suggests that significant amounts of data are leaving and entering the network. The HTTP service normally runs on port 80, and this is similar in volume and number to previous scans.

   The low number of sessions being established could be for a number of reasons, and would have to be compared to previous scans.

9. **(2)**

   The `whoami` command can be used on Linux hosts. The Remote Desktop Services Manager is used on Windows hosts which are running a Remote Desktop Connection. The `query user` command can be used from the command line on Windows hosts as well. The Access Management Console is a Citrix tool.

10. **(1)**

    Using a VPN to create a secure connection for the developer would be a suitable idea. A VPN would ensure that the end-to-end connection is encrypted, and the developer would be within the "trusted" space wherever they were located.

    The external IP address is likely to be used only for the duration of the conference as a maximum, so whitelisting the IP address would open up a risk from any other user accessing from that site. While this risk is low, whitelisting this IP address would expose the organization unnecessarily.

    Allowing internet-based collaboration tools may enable greater remote use, but this carries other risks, such as confidentiality. Preventing remote access has the opposite effect, possibly meaning that other business functions (for example, the remote help desk) are hindered.

Chapter 9: Compliance Frameworks

1. **(1)**

   Using the out-of-the-box settings for the firewall runs counter to requirement 2. To comply with the *do not use vendor-supplied defaults for system passwords and other security parameters* requirement, custom passwords and settings should be used. Installing a firewall is covered in requirement 1, while applying patches and updates is covered in requirement 6.

2. **(2)**

   The threat landscape is constantly changing, so it is important to **maintain and evolve security awareness across the organization**. Maintaining training programs is important, but these must also evolve to account for the changing threat landscape.

   Imposing strict access controls is not defined well enough to be applicable here. Access control should be appropriate; controls that are too strict might limit accountability and transparency that's required by SOX. Third-party software that's PCI DSS-compliant must still be hosted on a system that is compliant.

3. **(3)**

   Masking, encrypting, and truncating cardholder data are techniques that can limit the exposure of cardholder data. Before these techniques are considered, the requirement to store the data should be evaluated. If the cardholder data doesn't need to be stored, this would reduce any risk to zero. **Storing only the data that's required** is therefore the best method for preventing the exposure of cardholder data.

4. **(3)**

   HIPAA specifies that a full name or surname and initial, count as identifiable information. **Mr. Doe**, while differentiating this individual from Miss or Mrs. Doe, doesn't contain any reference to first name, and therefore is not judged as identifiable according to HIPAA.

5. **(1)**

   Audit controls that record and evaluate access to systems are listed in all three frameworks (PCI DSS Requirement 10, HIPAA Technical Safeguard 2, and SOX Audit Guidance Note 3). Encryption is mentioned in PCI DSS, but specifically notes that encryption doesn't take a PCI DSS environment out of scope. Data expiration is not mentioned in any of the standards. Backups are a requirement of SOX, but not specifically listed in either PCI DSS or HIPAA, except to extend the scope of the framework to backups, as well as live systems.

6. **(3)**

    SOX may still apply if the company has registered debt securities with the US Securities Exchange Commission. Public US ownership is only one of the criteria that puts a company in scope for SOX, so it isn't clear that SOX doesn't apply at this time. Operating in the US is not a criteria for SOX; SOX is about ownership and share issues.

7. **(1)**

    Both the systems are in scope for HIPAA because they store identifiable health data. The app is able to share health data with providers and specifically link this data to the individual customer. Regardless of whether or not the phone number is supplied, this ability would fit under the feature *any other unique identifying number, characteristic, or code*. Terms and conditions of service do not exempt systems or companies from regulation and compliance frameworks.

8. **(4)**

    The system must be regularly monitored, as this is a specific requirement of PCI DSS (requirement 11). PCI DSS requirements, as well as the threat landscape, evolve over time, and compliance is only valid for that specific snapshot in time. It is good practice to regularly monitor the system; continuous monitoring may be beyond the means of many companies.

9. **(4)**

    The company could comply with the "Restrict physical access" requirement under PCI DSS by moving all the devices in the open-plan environment to a different subnet to the CDE and ensuring that no data is shared between the two systems. If these devices were in a different network segment, and no data was shared between these devices and the CDE, these devices would be out of scope.

    This site office may well only include business development people or coders working on representative (non-real) data; it is unclear whether the office would actually handle card holder data or e-PHI.

    Locking away a server doesn't necessarily ensure compliance with workstation and device security safeguards, as there may be other devices that are not locked away (for example, user workstations) that still have access to the data (for example, over the network).

10. **(2)**

The company still needs to comply with HIPAA because it processes payments in relation to healthcare provision to individuals. This is specifically in the definition of PHI. The fact that payments are processed means that the company isn't just relaying information to its customers. The company is connected to some covered entities (pharmacies), but this is only relevant if the covered entity is providing information to the company, and not the other way around.

Historical data would still need to be stored in compliance with HIPAA, but this is not the only area where the company would need to be compliant.

Chapter 10: Data Normalization and Exploitation

1. **(3)**

strftime(%F %T, 1232467200) would format the time and date stamp as 2009-01-20 16:00:00. 1232467200 is the Unix time code for this time and date, but conversions are not required for the 210-255 exam. Notice how this is the same for all four options.

%F is the formatting option that's used for dates in the RFC 8601 format, and presents time in UTC, which is equivalent to the GMT (+00.00) time zone. Using the %c option presents the date in the format that's used in the local system. %T is used to present 24-hour time in seconds.

2. **(2)**

The awk command can be used to read through a serial file line by line, separating fields. The default is to use whitespace between fields, but this can be changed, for example, to comma-separated values or other delimiters.

The grep CLI command can be used to search through data using regular expressions. pcregrep can do this and also use grouping. The split command can be used to create separate files by number of lines or by number of bytes.

3. **(2)**

   One of the aims of normalization is **minimizing duplication of data**. While redundancy is useful in many other areas (for example, redundant hardware, connectivity, bandwidth, and so on), redundancy of data is often undesirable as it introduces the risk of consistency errors.

   Ideally, log file space requirements should be minimized through all cybersecurity operations. One of the criticisms or costs of normalization is that drawing in data from, or writing to, multiple tables or calculating fields *on the fly* introduces a higher processing overhead.

4. **(4)**

   Atomic data is a rule that's applied at the first normal form (and therefore applies to all subsequent normal forms). It requires that **each field may only contain a single value**; that is, there are no fields with a list of values.

   The contents of each field doesn't need to be unique; this is only required of the key field, or the composite key fields in combination. The requirement for each field title and each record to be unique are separate requirements of the first normal form.

5. **(1)**

   The **Cisco ASA** checks to see if there is an existing connection for the source and destination hosts for that specific traffic. If there is an existing connection, the Cisco ASA bypasses the ACL checks and performs application inspection checks. Cisco AMP relates more closely to packet inspection for threat detection, NetFlow is more closely related to the volume of data transfer, and firewalls perform the ACL checks.

6. **(1)**

   The completed command would be **awk '{$2=strftime("%c %T",$2)} {print}'** **orig.log > new.log**. The first item is the command (`awk`), while the section enclosed in single quote marks are the actions to be carried out. First, the second field is changed to reflect human-readable time using `strftime`, and then the result of this is output using `print`. The final statement is to provide the input and output file names.

7. **(3)**

   Using the `%c` conversion specification uses the local time settings to apply the conversion. **The local time settings on the other operator's computer doesn't match**; they are likely in the wrong time zone, or in a different format.

   The logs were both using Unix time, which starts from 1 January, 1970. This can be seen from the scale of the numbers, which wouldn't make sense for `GetSystemTimeAsFileTime` on Windows. Because they are both using Unix time, the time zone is not applied.

8. **(2)**

The HTTP GET message is shown in line 10. The file would have been downloaded in reply to this message (likely the entries starting in lines 16-20). The details of the 5-tuple are as follows:

Source IP: `219.83.193.158`

Source Port: `80`

Destination IP: `81.173.237.255`

Destination Port: 59918

Protocol: TCP

9. **(2)**

The inside local IP address was **10.10.10.40**. This is translated into the public-facing socket `81.173.237.255:59918` using port address translation (NAT overload). The outside IP address was `219.83.193.158` and refers to the destination. We don't know whether further translation happens at the far end (although this is very likely).

10. **(4)**

Cisco's **AMP** includes Network File Trajectory, along with other retrospective analysis tools out of the box.

While AMP, Splunk, and QRadar do have SIEM capabilities (to a greater or lesser extent), retrospective analysis is only available (without customization) on Cisco's AMP.

Chapter 11: Drawing Conclusions from the Data

1. **(2)**

HTTP is not a secure method of bulk data transfer. Data transferred over HTTP is sent in plaintext. HTTPS is a better and more secure protocol, and there are also more efficient methods of bulk data transfer (for example, FTP).

DNS and HTTP are fundamental to many network applications and therefore are likely to be enabled on corporate networks. This gives data relating to an incident a greater likelihood of successfully entering or leaving the network. This data will also be masked by the large volume of legitimate traffic.

DNS allows attackers to create code that doesn't directly reference the destination IP address. They can use a domain name or URL, which can then be registered closer to the time of deployment.

2. **(3)**

 Utilizing a public internet location (for example, public Wi-Fi or internet cafés) doesn't do much to hide the attacker's general location. The resolution of location data based on IP address is generally poor (limited to state and possibly city). Unless the attacker uses an internet café in a different city, this is unlikely to hide their location.

 Utilizing the Tor network or a VPN allows the attacker to appear to be somewhere else. The exit points from these services tend to be fairly well-known, but they are still likely to be flagged as threats, even if the attacker's location is difficult to pinpoint.

 Utilizing a spoofed IP address allows the attacker to appear to be somewhere else. In fact, it allows the attacker to appear to be *somebody* else – potentially a legitimate user.

3. **(4)**

 In deterministic analysis, conclusions can only be drawn from the hard data that's available. This is different from probabilistic analysis, since probabilistic analysis can also take into account data that isn't available. This might be because the data wasn't collected, or because the incident hasn't actually happened and the analysis is only being done in theory. The absence of evidence is not direct evidence of absence in either probabilistic or deterministic analysis. This is because the evidence may not have been collected. Absence of evidence could be used to corroborate a theory, however.

4. **(1)**

 Probabilistic analysis yields results that aren't definitive, whereas in deterministic analysis, **results are specific and factual.** In deterministic analysis, a lack of evidence means that the numbers of positive results (those flagged as incidents) are lower than in probabilistic analysis. This means that the numbers of False Negatives is also higher.

5. **(4)**

 There is a trend toward probabilistic analysis as the rate of malware evolution increases. While it is true that storage space is becoming more plentiful (and cheaper), the number of required data points to make a deterministic judgment is increasing too; multiple (and exponentially increasing) versions of malware are emerging constantly, along with symptoms that overlap with each other and with legitimate usage. It is much harder to conclusively pinpoint the root cause of many issues than it was only 5-10 years ago.

 Probabilistic analysis is possible for threats that have been seen previously and for those that haven't yet affected the system. The downside to this is that they often yield multiple results rather than the single, specific result, which is typical of deterministic analysis.

6. **(3)**

   If the priority 3 rule triggers, the event priority would be 3 as the rule priority takes precedence. Correlation policies and rules can have priorities independent of each other. The most severe (highest priority) is 1, while the least severe (lowest priority) is 5. Events are tagged based on the priority of the rule. If no priority is defined on the rule, it will derive the priority from the policy.

7. **(4)**

   The security team doesn't need to find the cause of the problem in order to fix it. Although the logs are incomplete, there is a chance that the limited logs that have been captured may facilitate deterministic analysis. The security team can still look for the sandbox-checking behavior, as well as possibly a log for one of the IP addresses. It isn't necessarily the case that these IP addresses conclusively mean that the attacks are linked. If the symptoms are different (for example, no sandbox check), these could be different exploits/attacks originating from similar sources. Tor nodes can be used by multiple entities for a variety of reasons; there is nothing to say that two different attacks may have originated from the same Tor node.

   Regardless of the cause of the problem, the security team must fix the problem. They will have to do a probabilistic analysis and patch for all the possible causes.

8. **(2)**

   The security team could **use FireSIGHT to create a correlation rule specifying SSL Certificate Subject Organization (O) DontTrustMe.Inc**. The multi-domain certificate makes it difficult to specify individual domains or subdomains, or to inspect the traffic.

   Blocking HTTPS/SSL (port 443) traffic would have a significant impact on legitimate traffic.

9. **(4)**

   The URL from the HTTPS header in the beacon message could be used to help find the threat actor. The fact that the organization is DontTrustMe.Inc doesn't mean that the domain name will be donttrustme.com or its subdomains. Corporate registrations of DontTrustMe.Inc might reveal information about this organization, but this doesn't necessarily mean that they control the server – just that they are named on the SSL certificate.

   The information that can be specifically linked to this attack is the URL in the beacon message.

10. **(4)**

The organization should **create a single rule where the filetype is a portable executable file and not a .dll file**. The rules allow for the use of logical operators (and/or/is/is not) so that legitimate users can be excluded.

Creating more than one rule or whitelist exemption increases the complexity of managing and updating the rule; they can be grouped into a correlation policy, but each rule still needs to be updated individually if the intelligence changes. Keeping the existing rule would create high volumes of False Positive alerts.

Chapter 12: The Cyber Kill Chain Model

1. **(2)**

Port scanning is often deployed during the reconnaissance phase. Searching Metasploit is commonly linked with the weaponization phase; phishing is normally linked with delivery; and installing a key logger is linked with the installation phase. Each of these can be used for finding out more about the organization or target, but are more commonly associated with other phases.

2. **(3)**

Attackers often focus energy on researching an organization's public-facing services (for example, websites) because **a flaw in the website might expose a server, which would be in the organization's trusted domain**. The website may be at a static IP address, but this is likely to be a public routable address, rather than an internal address. The website may reveal addresses, but this is likely to already be in the public domain. Most cyber attacks occur over a logical network rather than involving a physical penetration; the risks involved with being physically on premises is often too great.

The organization's hierarchy and high-value targets are also likely to be in the public domain, with professional social networking sites being a much richer source of information on the personalities of targets.

3. **(3)**

Nessus provides an **automatic mapping of exploits to scanned vulnerabilities**. It provides a single tool for both reconnaissance and weaponization since it conducts the scan along with matching suitable exploits.

The Nessus 2.2.11 engine and previous versions were open source, but Nessus has been proprietary since Nessus 3. PCI compliance-checking may reveal potential areas where the system doesn't comply with PCI, but this may be non-compliance short of a vulnerability.

Nessus has the ability to do dictionary password attacks through a third-party tool, rather than as an integral feature.

4. **(3)**

   When **a user clicks on a link in an email that downloads a rootkit**, this is an action in the delivery phase. The rootkit will only be downloaded to the host device during this action. It isn't clear that this will be run.

   Running a script that opens a backdoor, guessing a password, or accessing the working memory of another process provides the attacker with temporary access to the system, and is therefore in the exploitation phase.

5. **(2)**

   The **installation** phase is where the attack establishes persistence. This means that even if the original vulnerability were patched, the attacker may still have access to the system (an "inside man"). Persistent access to the system may well be the attacker's aim, but action on objective normally entails a material impact on the confidentiality, integrity, or availability of one or more resources.

   Persistence and defense evasion are phases in the ATT&CK model from MITRE.

6. **(1)**

   Weaponization is the phase in the Cyber Kill Chain model where an attacker tries to match a vulnerability with a feature that's been observed on the target system.

   Execution is a command activity that occurs during operations according to the US Army Operations Process, and also a phase in the ATT&CK model that relates to the running of code on attacker-controlled devices.

   The delivery and exploitation phases occur after a vulnerability has already been identified.

7. **(4)**

   Privilege elevation is a typical action in the **Command and Control** phase. To complete this phase, the attacker must maneuver themselves into a position with hands-on-keyboard access to a device and user group with sufficient privileges to conduct the actions on objectives. The exploitation and installation phases must have been completed to give the attacker persistent access to the system.

8. **(3)**

The most likely vulnerability is **a guessable password that's used to access emails**. The attacker with access to emails can then intercept password reminders or password reset emails to gain access to other systems. Social engineering is becoming increasingly common, compared to technical vulnerabilities. The fact that an individual (low-level) user has been targeted suggests that the email system or the remote desktop utility doesn't have a vulnerability. If there was, you would expect the attacker to have given themselves more privileges on entry.

Stored passwords on a browser can cause issues for a user if their devices are unencrypted, lost, or stolen. If this had happened, this would likely have been reported when the security team spoke with the user.

9. **(1)**

The vulnerability has been closed, but the incident is still ongoing. The initial vulnerability gave the attacker access to the user's emails. This has now been closed. However, the attacker achieved persistence by opening up another route into the system (through the remote desktop) during the installation phase. The incident will continue until that has also been closed off and the passwords for that system have been updated.

10. **(3)**

The standard method of assigning usernames (firstname.surname) may have contributed to the attack. The former employer would have known this, and would therefore only need to know the password.

There is no information to suggest that the attacker used the security questions to reset the user's email account, especially since the user didn't report that the password had been changed. If two-factor authentication had been used, it would have been less likely that the attacker would have been able to establish and maintain access to the user's emails.

Chapter 13: Incident-Handling Activities

1. **(2)**

   Network connections are volatile because the attacker's device is likely to be removed from the network on detection. Volatile data is characterized by data that can be changed or removed by factors outside of the investigator's control (for example, time or actions by other entities).

   The operating system time is volatile because it can be synchronized using NTP. If there was a discrepancy between system time and the NTP time, this discrepancy would be invisible to the investigator once it was re-synchronized. Paging files are not cleared when the process is ended; they simply go to unallocated. They are cleared when a new process requires that paging file and writes data to it.

   Network configuration can also be volatile. This is particularly true if DHCP is used.

   The CSIRT needs to send some of the failed hard drives to be destroyed. They choose to use a courier, but a road traffic accident leads to the hard drive containing the data being lost in transit.

2. **(2)**

   The **Asset: M - Disk Drive | Actor: Partner | Action: Error, Loss** characterization is the best characterization of this incident. There is no evidence that the hard drive was stolen (intentionally by an external body), nor that physical damage was caused to the asset. The action must relate back to the asset; the accident involved the courier, and not the hard drive.

   The disk drive didn't arrive at the disposal company, so this is not a disposal error.

3. **(1)**

   Confidentiality also encompasses the notion of loss of possession, and is included on all lost assets. **Availability** is also affected because the employee no longer has access to that asset for as long as it takes to be replaced.

   There is nothing to suggest that integrity has been affected.

4. **(4)**

   This new data means that the incident can be updated with **Confidentiality: .DataDisclosure: Yes/.Data.Variety: Credentials and Internal**. There is no indication in the scenario that trade secrets were exposed, nor any personally identifiable data.

5. **(2)**

   The incident handling team would move into the **remediation** phase. The effects of laptop theft would have been contained by the remote wipe, and changing the passwords will contain the effects of the diary loss. The remediation phase will not be complete until the employee has a replacement laptop (to fix the availability issue). Some hardening (for example, re-education about credential storage) and reporting may have already occurred, but the organizational-level changes will not be completed until after remediation.

6. **(1)**

   There is no evidential value remaining on the laptop. The forensic evidence that links the threat actor to the incident will have already been found for the police authorities to arrest and charge this individual. Any volatile evidence will be gone and any files are likely to have been destroyed via the remote wipe.

7. **(2)**

   The correct actor designation would be **Actor: External: .Motive: .Grudge/.Variety: Former employee**. If an employee resigns or is let go before the incident, the correct designation should be **External | Former employee**. The NA motive is only used when the action is considered unintentional.

8. **(1)**

   The impact of this incident was felt on **confidentiality only.** The integrity of the data within the organization hasn't been affected; the customer data dump is a copy, and no evidence is presented to say that it has been tampered with. The availability of the data is not affected for legitimate users.

9. **(4)**

   Communication with customers and advising them to change passwords would be an appropriate remedial action. Blocking credit card numbers shouldn't be required, as the credit-card numbers were incomplete and no authorization information (PINs, CVV, and so on) was included. Communication with customers to advise them to look out for fraudulent transactions would be enough to mitigate the risk from the card details. Ensuring that user accounts get disabled promptly, and that encrypted files can be inspected, are examples of lesson-based hardening activities.

10. **(2)**

    The **Network Traffic Logs** are the priority for evidence collection. The running processes and the contents of the memory are likely to be irrelevant due to their volatility and the time that has passed since the data actually left the system. The encrypted files from the TCP stream are no good to the investigators unless they can decrypt them. There is no evidence to suggest that they have the private key for this.

Chapter 14 – Mock Exam 1

1. **1.** pcregrep.
2. **1.** SOX.
3. **3.** It is commonly used by threat actors because it is also used in common legitimate applications.
4. **4.** Mozilla/5.0 (X11; x86_64; rv:21.0) Gecko/20100101 Firefox/21.0.
5. **4.** Analysis resulting in conclusive results.
6. **2.** tcpdump uses UTC time, where Wireshark's packet list pane uses relative timestamps.
7. **3.** A rule with priority 1 in a policy with priority 4.
8. **1.** Actors, Actions, Assets, Attributes.
9. **1.** To determine the format for emails within the organization in order to generate whale phishing targets from the publicly accessible directors list.
10. **1.** As generic as possible.
11. **4.** Virtual Alloc.
12. **1.** At the network layer, the address is maintained from the sending computer to the destination computer.
13. **4.** User Interaction: Required.
14. **3.** Confidentiality | Integrity | Availability.
15. **3.** Exploits are linked to observed vulnerabilities in the system.
16. **1.** Name of the investigator, and 2. Date of collection.
17. **4.** Changing the data doesn't affect integrity if the process is documented.
18. **3.** Year of Birth.
19. **4.** A flow involving a Tor exit node is identified as a potential threat.
20. **2.** An internal host is sending large amounts of data out of the network.
21. **1.** The pipe character (|).
22. **4.** Confidentiality and availability are both affected, so both should be scored.
23. **3.** The layer 3 address is hierarchical.
24. **4.** A European company that has over 300 US shareholders.
25. **1.** NetFlow would record 2 flows.
26. **4.** Records to [hacme.com]:80 in NetFlow, where [hacme.com] is the correct IP address for the bank's web server.
27. **4.** Actor: External | Action: Environmental.
28. **3.** A copy of the files on a disk.
29. **2.** DHCP pool depletion caused by excessively long lease time.

30. **1.** To deter future attacks.
31. **2.** SSL.
32. **4.** Systems on the transmission path for card holder data which are on a public infrastructure (for example, the internet).
33. **3.** The 5-tuple is unchanged throughout the journey from host to host.
34. **2.** Analysis centers.
35. **4.** Verification of suspected incident.
36. **4.** To detect future threat.
37. **3.** Attributes.
38. **2.** query user.
39. **1.** Nothing. The IDS has taken no action, so the file reached its intended target.
40. **2.** /var/log/messages.
41. **4.** Command and Control.
42. **2.** An attacker has persistent access.
43. **3.** SS[^D].
44. **4.** Which sources of evidence, if any, should be acquired.
45. **3.** Actions on objectives.
46. **2.** Understanding of the context of each entry.
47. **3.** To identify the appropriate flow.
48. **4.** NBAR.
49. **4.** Have all the customer effects from the incident been reset?
50. **1.** By maintaining a unified time across all the devices in the network.

Chapter 15 – Mock Exam 2

1. **2.** Attack Vector | Attack Complexity | Privileges Required.
2. **4.** UDP.
3. **4.** backtack.
4. **1.** Total throughput.
5. **1.** Innovative threats.
6. **1.** File | Export Objects | HTTP....
7. **3.** Machine learning techniques are increasingly being used to support probabilistic analysis.
8. **3.** GET %D2%A2ACME.com/login.php HTTP/1.1 in the Proxy Log.
9. **4.** National CSIRT.

10. **1.** Deterministic analysis.

11. **1.** To map IP addresses to MAC addresses.

12. **3.** Unsolicited professional social media requests are made, asking for information about an upcoming job opportunity.

13. **2.** Pre-emptive safeguards.

14. **3.** Support for encryption.

15. **1.** Sandbox Detection allows the API calls to be recorded.

16. **1.** The attack code is launched.

17. **2.** Organizational senior management.

18. **1.** Correlation rules in the Firepower management console.

19. **2.** Executive board members.

20. **3.** If the attachment was legitimate, this is a False Positive.

21. **2.** Network data showing a spike in traffic from that computer over the last two days.

22. **2.** Reducing duplication.

23. **3.** The packet has a total length greater than 65,535 bytes.

24. **3.** Magnetic-strip information.

25. **1.** Network connections.

26. **3.** grep is case-sensitive by default.

27. **1.** Anti-static wristbands used during physical handling and 3. Storage in specialist storage facilities.

28. **1.** Creating a new file creates duplication and therefore may create update anomalies and 3. Creating a new file with the ">" command maintains the integrity of the original.

29. **2.** HTTP/1.1 503 Service Unavailable.

30. **4.** Reset the saved MAC addresses associated with the port.

31. **3.** Command and Control.

32. **2.** The netstat CLI command.

33. **3.** The data is being collected after translation has been applied on the outbound interface and before translation has been applied on the inbound interface.

34. **3.** Applying static NAT of one of the public addresses to the web server, pooling the other addresses for other users.

35. **1.** Actor: External: .Motive: Fun/.Variety: Unaffiliated.

36. **2.** To assert copyrights.

37. **2.** As directed by senior management.

38. **2.** Actions on objectives.

39. **1.** Confidentiality.
40. **1.** Actions on objectives.
41. **1.** Social.
42. **2.** PAN.
43. **2.** The greater than sign (>).
44. **1.** ICMP.
45. **3.** 0710.
46. **3.** Log file collation and normalization.
47. **4.** How can customer relations be improved?
48. **3.** The user-agent string appears to be running Internet Explorer, which isn't installed on the hosts.
49. **3.** Threat actors.
50. **3.** ps -e.

Other Books You May Enjoy

If you enjoyed this book, you may be interested in these other books by Packt:

CCNA Routing and Switching 200-125 Certification Guide
Lazaro (Laz) Diaz

ISBN: 978-1-78712-788-3

- Gain an in-depth understanding of networking using routers and switches
- Understand layer 2 technology and its various configurations and connections
- Configure default, static, and dynamic routing
- Design and implement subnetted IPv4 and IPv6 addressing schemes
- Troubleshoot issues and keep your network secure
- Study the importance of VLANs for security and optimizing the bandwidth

CCNA Security 210-260 Certification Guide
Glen D. Singh, Michael Vinod, Vijay Anandh

ISBN: 978-1-78712-887-3

- Grasp the fundamentals of network security
- Configure routing protocols to secure network devices
- Mitigate different styles of security attacks using Cisco devices
- Explore the different types of firewall technologies
- Discover the Cisco ASA functionality and gain insights into some advanced ASA configurations
- Implement IPS on a Cisco device and understand the concept of endpoint security

Leave a review - let other readers know what you think

Please share your thoughts on this book with others by leaving a review on the site that you bought it from. If you purchased the book from Amazon, please leave us an honest review on this book's Amazon page. This is vital so that other potential readers can see and use your unbiased opinion to make purchasing decisions, we can understand what our customers think about our products, and our authors can see your feedback on the title that they have worked with Packt to create. It will only take a few minutes of your time, but is valuable to other potential customers, our authors, and Packt. Thank you!

Index

remoteness 16
request header
　about 114
　HTTP version 115
　request method name 114
　Uniform Resource Identifier (URI) 115
　User-Agent (UA) 116
request method name
　about 114
　GET 114
　HEAD 115
　POST 115
response header 117, 119

S

sandbox detection 141
Sarbanes Oxley Act, 2002 (SOX)
　about 194
　access controls 195
　backups 195
　IT security policies 195
　logging 195
scope 29, 31
scope metric 30
second normal form (2NF) 206, 207
security information and event management (SIEM) 202
security rule 192
security technologies
　about 138
　network application control 143
　network indicators 139
　payload indicators 141
　reports 138
Server Message Block (SMB) 130
server
　applications, running 180
　listening ports 177, 178
　logged, in users/service accounts 178
　processes, running 180
　profiling 176
　tasks, running 180
Session Manager Subsystem (SMSS) 42
signature-based antivirus software 220
signature-based detection

about 141
　Metamorphic malware 141
　Oligomorphic malware 141
　Polymorphic malware 141
Simple Network Management Protocol (SNMP) 82
Source Address 103
source port 109, 110
Special Interest Group (SIG) 14
speed 172
start frame delimiter (SFD) 97
stateless address autoconfiguration (SLAAC) 176
strategies and goals 159
synchronize (SYN) 110

T

TCP header
　about 108
　acknowledgment numbers 110
　checksum 111
　destination port 109, 110
　flags 110
　header length 110
　sequence numbers 110
　source port 109, 110
　urgent pointer 111
　window 111
third normal form (3NF) 207
threat actor
　finding 218
threat
　about 10
　categorizing 9
　communicating 9
　False Negative 149
　False Positive 149
　True Negative 149
　True Positive 149
threats and victims
　host identification 211
　malicious file identification 211
　pinpointing 210
time element 105
Time-to-Live (TTL) 105
Total Length 105
Traffic Class 104

transport layer, segment
  about 107
  TCP header 108
  UDP header 112
True Negative 149
True Positive 149
tunneling 106
type field 104
Type of Service 104

U

UDP header
  about 112
  checksum 113
  destination port 112
  length field 113
  source port 112
Unified Extensible Firmware Interface (UEFI) 38,
  40, 41
Unified Threat Management (UTM) 143
Uniform Resource Identifier (URI) 115, 134
Uniform Resource Locator (URL) 134, 192
User-Agent (UA) 116

V

vendor teams 167
version 104
virtual private network (VPN) 218
VirusTotal 13
Vocabulary for Event Recording and Incident
  Sharing (VERIS)
  about 246
  actions 249, 250
  actors 248, 249
  asset 246, 247
  attributes 250

W

wildcard characters 80
Windows
  booting 42, 43
Wireshark
  about 128
  packet details, viewing 128, 130
  used, for extracting data 130

Y

Yara 13